T5-CVJ-839

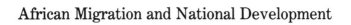

African Migration and National Development

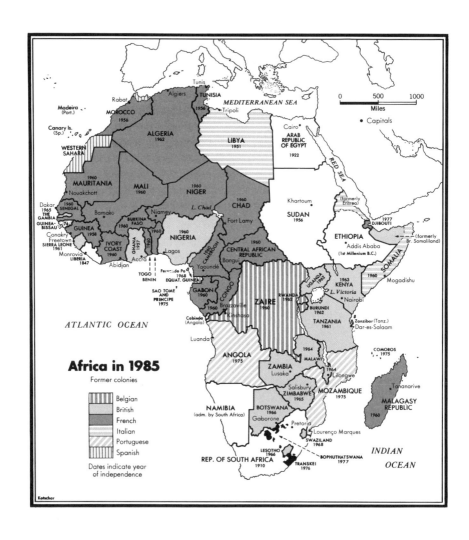

Africa in 1985

Former colonies

	Belgian
	British
	French
	Italian
	Portuguese
	Spanish

Dates indicate year
of independence

MEDITERRANEAN SEA

Madeira
(Port.)

Canary Is.
(Sp.)

Rabat
Algiers
Tunis
TUNISIA
1956
Tripoli

MOROCCO
1956

ALGERIA
1962

**WESTERN
SAHARA**

LIBYA
1951

Cairo
**ARAB
REPUBLIC
OF EGYPT**
1922

RED SEA

0   500   1000
Miles

• Capitals

1960
MAURITANIA
Nouakchott

MALI
1960

1960
NIGER

1960
CHAD

Khartoum

(formerly
Eritrea)

1977
DJIBOUTI

Dakar
1965
SENEGAL
**THE
GAMBIA**
**GUINEA-
BISSAU**
74

Bamako

**BURKINA
FASO**

Niamey

L. Chad

Fort Lamy

SUDAN
1956

ETHIOPIA
Addis Ababa
(1st Millenium B.C.)

(formerly
Br. Somaliland)

Conakry
GUINEA
1958
Freetown
SIERRA LEONE
1961
Monrovia
LIBERIA
1847

1960
**IVORY
COAST**
1960

1960
GHANA
1957

NIGERIA
1960

Lagos

Accra

**CENTRAL AFRICAN
REPUBLIC**
1960

Bangui

SOMALIA
1960
Mogadishu

Abidjan

TOGO
BENIN
1960
1960

Fernando Po
1968
EQUAT. GUINEA

CAMEROON
1960

Yaoundé

UGANDA
1962

KENYA
1963
Nairobi

1960

**SAO TOME
AND
PRINCIPE**
1975

GABON
1960

CONGO
1960
Brazzaville

Cabinda
(Angola)

ZAIRE
1960
Kinshasa

RWANDA
1962
BURUNDI
1962

L. Victoria

TANZANIA
1961

Zanzibar (Tanz.)
Dar-es-Salaam

ATLANTIC OCEAN

Luanda

ANGOLA
1975

1964
MALAWI

ZAMBIA
Lusaka

1964
Lilongwe

COMOROS
1975

Salisbury
ZIMBABWE
1965

MOZAMBIQUE
1975

Tananarive

**MALAGASY
REPUBLIC**
1960

NAMIBIA
(adm. by South Africa)

BOTSWANA
1966
Gaborone

Pretoria

Lourenço Marques

SWAZILAND
1968

*INDIAN
OCEAN*

LESOTHO
1966
REP. OF SOUTH AFRICA
1910

TRANSKEI
1976

BOPHUTHATSWANA
1977

Kotschar

AFRICAN MIGRATION
and
NATIONAL DEVELOPMENT

Beverly Lindsay, *Editor*

THE PENNSYLVANIA STATE UNIVERSITY PRESS
UNIVERSITY PARK AND LONDON

Map of Africa by Vincent Kotschar

Library of Congress Cataloging in Publication Data
Main entry under title:
African migration and national development.
Includes bibliographical references and index.
1. Migration, Internal—Africa, Sub-Saharan—Addresses, essays, lectures.
2. Africa, Sub-Saharan—Emigration and immigration—Addresses, essays, lectures.
3. Africa, Sub-Saharan—Economic policy—Addresses, essays, lectures.
I. Lindsay, Beverly.
HB2121.A3A37   1985   304.8′2′0967   85-6463
ISBN 0-271-00383-9

CONTENTS

PREFACE

The purpose of this book is to provide an analytical overview of the nexus among the economic, social, cultural, and political aspects of migration and national development in Subsaharan Africa. Particular attention is devoted to the role of "voluntary" labor or employment migration (for the purpose of wage employment) since job-seeking is a dominant reason for migration. Although less prevalent, commercial migration (for the purpose of business opportunity) is also discussed as a form of voluntary movement. Both forms have tremendous impact on national development. Because the subject is so large and the African continent so vast, our analytical discussion focuses on select aspects of migration and national development. Our aim is to be helpful both to scholars and students and also to policymakers and development planners. The book should raise as many questions as it answers. We bear in mind the statement of André Gunder Frank: "The mark of a . . . contribution, whether in the natural or the social sciences, is not that it reveals some eternal truth. It is, rather, that existing knowledge and analysis are put together in new ways, raising questions . . . which . . . push research and analysis into different areas."

The first three chapters provide conceptual frameworks and examine descriptive data that are applicable in vast regions of Africa. Chapter 3 also has special relevance to Nigeria and Ghana. The other chapters depict issues in Mali, Zambia, Lesotho, Senegal, and Kenya. The selection of countries was coupled with the identification of salient issues associated with migration and national development: the social conditions in village or rural areas, the health care services for migrants, the special problems of women migrants, and the brain drain resulting from some migration. Although "involuntary" migration (the refugee problem) is beyond the scope of this book, it is touched upon, especially in chapters 1, 2, 3, and 9.

Several criteria were established for selecting topics and authors. Development is defined and examined differently within the several social and behavioral sciences. Moreover, the relationships between migration and national development are manifested differently in the various African countries and geographical regions. The first criterion was to provide interdisciplinary perspectives, so we elicited the perspectives of sociologists, anthropologists, psychologists, educators, political scientists, and historians. Second, we sought scholars who had had African field experience, as a "hands-on" complement to their disciplinary orientations. A third objective was to present a reasonable sampling of the rich and varied African culture.

The idea for this book arose from discussions in the Black Studies Program of The Pennsylvania State University when Cyril E. Griffith was director of the program and the editor was a member of the faculty. The book began to take shape when Elliott P. Skinner and Robert J. Cummings gave invited lectures at Penn State on African migration and development. With their advice and that of Professor Griffith, I developed a table of contents and an appropriate team of contributors.

Several of the contributors are employed by the United States government; some have been the recipients of research grants provided by federal agencies. The views expressed herein are the writers' and do not necessarily reflect the policies of any governmental body or other organization.

A number of scholars and policymakers helped in the preparation of this book; some are acknowledged in particular chapters. While we cannot name all the friends and colleagues who gave us advice and support, we wish to express particular appreciation to the directors and faculty of the Black Studies Program at Penn State for their invaluable critiques and technical assistance. Three esteemed Africanists—Edmond J. Keller, Susan H. Mott, and Mabel M. Smyth—reviewed the manuscript for the Penn State Press and made constructive suggestions, as did the Press staff. As editor, I sincerely thank my coauthors for their contributions and critiques.

B.L.

CONTRIBUTORS

Robert J. Cummings is professor and director of the African Studies and Research Program at Howard University. His research and publications focus on economic history and social values in cross-cultural environments and the international community, based upon field research in East Africa.

Robert C. Johnson teaches education at Grambling State University. He has conducted research in Senegal and other West African countries on higher education and development. His work in Senegal has been supported through Ford Foundation grants.

Nellie B. Kanno is on the public health faculty at the University of Massachusetts, Amherst, and is a senior technical advisor for nutrition programs for the Agency for International Development. She has conducted research through Ford Foundation grants in Lesotho, Botswana, and Swaziland.

John Van D. Lewis is a rural development officer with the Agency for International Development. A former member of the graduate faculty in the African Studies and Research Program at Howard University, he has conducted extensive field research in economic anthropology in the West African Sahel.

Beverly Lindsay is a former senior researcher and manager at the National Institute of Education and consultant to the Agency for International Development. Her major areas of publication and research—

sociocultural and educational issues influencing Third World people—are based on field research in Africa, the Caribbean, and the People's Republic of China. She is the editor of *Comparative Perspectives of Third World Women: The Impact of Race, Sex, and Class.* Dr. Lindsay is special assistant to the vice president for Academic Services at Penn State.

Bennetta Jules-Rosette is professor of sociology at the University of California, San Diego. Her research focuses on urban migration, African religion, African art, cultural change, and women's roles. Dr. Jules-Rosette's field research has been conducted in Zambia, Zaire, and the Ivory Coast, sponsored by the National Science Foundation and the National Endowment for the Humanities. Her major books include *Symbols of Change, The New Religions of Africa, A Paradigm for Looking,* and *African Apostles.*

Elliott P. Skinner is Franz Boas Professor of Anthropology at Columbia University and a former fellow at the Woodrow Wilson International Center for Scholars of the Smithsonian Institution. His major books include *African Urban Life: The Transformation of Ouagadougou; Peoples and Cultures of Africa; The Mossi of Upper Volta;* and *Strangers in African Society* (coedited with William Shack).

Niara Sudarkasa is professor of anthropology and Afroamerican and African Studies at the University of Michigan. She is the author of *Where Women Work: A Study of Yoruba Women in the Marketplace and in the Home,* and is also associate vice president for University Affairs at her university.

1

MIGRATION AND NATIONAL DEVELOPMENT: AN INTRODUCTION[1]

BEVERLY LINDSAY

National development has been a major concern of African states since the dawn of independence. The statements of political leaders and of national five-year development plans and other major policy and planning documents call for national development through joint initiatives by the citizenry and the government. Individuals have their particular perceptions about the essence of national development and their roles in contributing to the process. National government bodies also suggest roles for citizens and elucidate problems and challenges which must be addressed to achieve national development. Some of the challenges and problems include the provision of adequate nutrition, health care, decent housing, basic education, employment options, and an infrastructure to bring such necessities to the populace.

Individuals often migrate within a country or internationally to pursue these necessities and to enhance their lifestyles. Concurrently, some of this migration is encouraged by governments, national business firms, and multinational organizations. From 1965 to 1975 approximately 6,900,000 people migrated within and between the countries of Ivory Coast, Senegal, Sierra Leone, Togo, Liberia, Gambia, Ghana, and Mali (Zachariah, 1980, 1:iii). These massive movements of people can, in some instances, stimulate national development. Quite often, however, they accentuate various problems associated with national development.

The basic purpose of this volume is to provide an analytical overview of the nexus among the several economic, social, cultural, and political aspects of migration and national development. To achieve this purpose, the objectives of the volume are to 1) examine conceptual frameworks depicting the relationships between various kinds of migration and national development; 2) analyze particular migration problems through select case studies from various countries and/or geographical regions; and 3) discuss policy considerations and recommendations for alleviating migration problems in order to enhance national development. This introductory chapter begins by articulating migration characteristics and trends and the factors causing the trends; examining conceptual frameworks of national development; and analyzing the role of development policies.

MIGRATION CHARACTERISTICS AND TRENDS

An examination of migration—what one geographer broadly defines as the physical movement of people from one area to another which results in residential change—necessitates the recognition of international and domestic migration characteristics and trends (Zelinsky, 1971). Much of the international migration is, in fact, intracontinental, wherein migrants move to neighboring countries. One area of intracontinental or regional movement involves migrant laborers from Botswana, Swaziland, and Lesotho to South Africa for employment in the mines. During the mid-1970s, approximately 21,000 migrants from Botswana, 10,000 from Swaziland, and 97,000 from Lesotho were in the Republic of South Africa. The 97,000 from Lesotho constituted approximately 50 percent of the nation's adult male labor force and 10 percent of that for the female labor force (United Nations, Department of International Economic and Social Affairs [UN, DIESA], 1980, 2:54). By 1985 the number of migrants from Lesotho is expected to increase to 180,000.

Some West African nations are also the recipients of labor migrants from neighboring countries. Until the mid-1970s, Ghana and the Ivory Coast were the target countries for migration of workers from Togo, Upper Volta (now Burkina Faso), and Mali (United Nations, Department of Economic and Social Affairs [UN, DESA], 1979; UN, DIESA, 1980, 2). At that time about 35 percent of the labor force in the Ivory Coast consisted of non-Ivorians. Some of the historical reasons for this migration are noted in Elliott P. Skinner's chapter 2, while contemporary reasons are discussed in both chapter 2 and John V. D. Lewis's chapter 4.

Migration within the central African region currently includes a considerable percentage of labor migrants to Zambia for work in the mines.

Within Zambia, there is also considerable migration from rural to urban areas; and some of the impact upon women is the focus of Bennetta Jules-Rosette's chapter 5.

In chapter 3, Niara Sudarkasa points out that commercial, in contrast to labor, migration also involves vast numbers of people in West Africa. From precolonial to contemporary periods, commercial migration has been important in this region. Particular ethnic groups—for example, the Yoruba, the Hausa, and the Dioula—have been primary commercial migrants.

While migrants move internationally and nationally for a variety of social, economic, and political reasons, as aptly discussed in chapters 2 and 3, several general trends appear to characterize the complex patterns of flow. Migrants often move from less developed to more developed countries or regions. This is quite evident with itinerant labor migrants from Southern African nations to the Republic of South Africa and from Togo and Mali, for example, to the Ivory Coast and Ghana. This migration may be temporary, semipermanent, or permanent depending on economic and political conditions in the home country. The various migration patterns are witnessed in moves from rural to urban areas or towns and from urban areas to villages or rural areas.

Refugees from oppressive political conditions, war, and famine, as well as undocumented labor migrants, comprise two additional categories that are discussed briefly in chapters 2 and 3. While these two categories are not central focuses of this volume, it is necessary to bear in mind their impact upon national development. The many issues associated with involuntary migration are witnessed by the incalculable number of refugees in various African nations. Estimates range from five to over seven million people. According to the United Nations High Commission for Refugees, there were, for example, about 665,000 refugees in the Sudan in 1983. Many are fleeing war and famine in Ethiopia (United Nations High Commissioner for Refugees, 1983). The unpredictable tenure of the refugees and their urgent immediate needs can seriously upset social and economic development plans and may threaten the labor market and various parts of the national infrastructure which are already under stress. At the same time, the original home country may be losing significant human resources that could contribute to domestic development. The problems associated with refugees continue to command emergency attention by African governments and international organizations such as UNESCO (United Nations Educational Scientific and Cultural Organization). A volume could be written on refugees.

Nevertheless, factors related to voluntary labor and/or commercial migration are a primary concern in this volume. Employment or entrepreneurial opportunities are examined as major reasons for migration. Moreover, it is quite difficult to obtain accurate information on undocumented African migrants, whether they are refugees or illegal laborers (UN, DIESA, 1980, 1:112, 187, 188; 2:67; UN, DESA, 1979). Given such factors, it would be quite difficult to analyze the issues of involuntary migration in a manner comparable to what this book undertakes for voluntary labor and commercial migration. But the refugee problem will loom large so long as the African nations vary in political stability. Political instability, moreover, is part of the universal legacy of colonialism.

Systemic and Individual Factors

Whether migration occurs in Southern, Western, Central, or Eastern Africa, it may be examined within the context of several conceptual tenets. Marenin (1980:695–98) points out that one basic view focuses on dual issues: the degree to which migration should be explained by systemic functions or by individual rationality. There is considerable historical evidence, as Skinner and Sudarkasa portray, which elucidates systemic or institutional factors causing migration. To pay taxes levied by Europeans, African farm residents often migrated to areas where they were paid in cash for their labor or where there were commercial opportunities. The development of mines in South Africa contributed to African migration. The location of industries, urban centers, and employment sites (some distance from traditional residential areas) are important factors in African migration. These factors become thoroughly entrenched in the social and economic systems of a country or a region, so they provide reasons for continual migration. There are also individual reasons for migration. Whether one moves to a town seeking employment for bride price, to assist rural relatives, for personal advancement, or to fulfill the desire to live in a different location may be viewed chiefly as individual reasons.

We must keep in mind the blending of systemic factors and individual reasons, since it is often difficult to discern differences between the two. A rural resident may make an individual decision to move to an urban area; yet it is the urban area which may provide industrial employment or commercial options through its place in the country's or region's economic system. In this instance an interactive effect is present. Individuals may migrate to an area, acquire skills, increase their income through employment and commercial opportunities, and then return to their original homes and use the skills acquired in different locations. Or individuals may send remittances to individual families in rural areas, as Nellie B. Kanno's chapter 6 depicts. These remittances are often used for necessities and in some instances (as in Kenya) for investments or innovations in local rural projects (UN, DIESA, 1980, 1:188–92). When individuals remit to rural areas, such contributions add directly to rural institutional development.

Moreover, systemic or institutional effects upon individuals may be noted when an individual or a family migrates to an urban area and is forced to restructure social interactions. Before migration, social interactions often occur within the context of the extended family. Urbanization may not permit this (Voss, 1973:32), so urban systems are influencing individual migrants, as chapter 6 illustrates.

Push and Pull Factors

The balance between individual and systemic factors may be examined within the context of what demographers often refer to as push and pull factors. Expanded population growth, limited employment options, rural poverty, limited arable land, and changing marital status may push migrants from their original homes (Fapohunda and Mott, 1979; Byerlee and Tommy, 1979). Robert J. Cummings's chapter 8 portrays how high growth rates of population push rural residents to towns and cities. Chapter 6 discusses how limited arable land and limited employment options push residents to new areas. These appear to be individual or family decisions; they are, however, often based upon the inability of social systems to respond adequately.

Employment opportunities, the lure of urban life, and the location of educational institutions, health facilities, and similar social services may pull migrants to other areas (Zelinsky, 1971; International Center for Research on Women, 1979:91–97). Such pull factors, along with commercial opportunities, are discussed in Robert C. Johnson's chapter 7 and in chapters 2 and 3. But the writers in this book move beyond the conceptual tenets of push and pull, first, by examining both macro and micro factors; second, by analyzing various conceptual frameworks of national development.

Chapters 2 and 3 delineate how migration may be examined with macro frameworks. General systemic conditions which push migrants from or pull migrants to areas are often examined with macro analyses in mind. Under this approach policymakers and social scientists might ask the following types of illustrative questions. To what extent might the introduction of strict residency requirements or stiff procedures for acquiring work and/or residency permits affect migration patterns? If major industries are shut down or there are overall economic downturns, what percentage of residents might be forced to return home or migrate to another region or country? What are the economic costs and benefits to the original country resulting from out and/or return migration? In short, macro analyses focus on the relationships among countries, institutional arrangements between or within countries, or economic or political conditions in major geographic regions. These last conditions are also focuses of chapters 2, 3, 7, and 8.

Micro analyses usually concentrate on specific migration patterns within a country or region *or* on individual reasons for migration. Chapter 4 focuses on factors at the micro level within Malian villages, while chapter 5 highlights individual examples.

These conceptual tenets help us to initially comprehend the nature of problems and challenges created by migration. *The World Population Situation in 1979* (United Nations, Department of International Economic and Social Affairs Population Studies [UN, DIESAPS], 1980:5) sheds some additional light on the nature of problems created by migration. This report states that "many governments are more concerned with problems of population distribution and migration within their countries than with the growth of the national population." Of 119 developing countries, 113 studied in a United Nations survey stated that migration causes problems in the imbalance of the labor supply in employment, housing, social services, and utilities (UN, DIESAPS, 1980:5, 104). This is not to overlook the problems of population growth which can be causes of migration; but the resulting problems of migration and population distribution are acute.

Another study (*Habitat: United Nations Conference on Human Settlements*, 1976:30) states that migration contributes to urban expansion, which—when unchecked—becomes urban sprawl with its ensuing problems. These problems usually cause considerable strain on various parts of the physical and social infrastructure such as poor health care services (a focus of chapter 6), restricted entrepreneurial opportunities (topics of chapters 3 and 5), or limited educational option (issues in chapters 7 and 8). Because national, provincial or state, and local officials are forced to address these acute urban problems, rural problems or projects are often relegated to a secondary status (Collier and Lal, 1980:48). Simultaneously, the rural exodus to urban areas contributes to rural underdevelopment and urban unemployment.

Migration for economic reasons often creates problems, despite individual and national desires to ameliorate personal and social conditions. What becomes quite important is to understand the interrelations among various dimensions of migration—economic, social, political, and cultural—since individual goals are frequently not attained (or are delayed) and problems are caused in urban and rural areas which hinder the development of African nations. Hence it is crucial to examine the various dimensions of migration in relation to national development (UN, DIESA, 1980, 1:118, 119).

CONCEPTUAL FRAMEWORKS FOR NATIONAL DEVELOPMENT

To comprehend the relationships between migration and national development, it is imperative to examine several alternative frameworks for national development. As African nations became politically independent, the governments, international funding organizations, policymakers, and scholars often concentrated on economic features of development (Rodney, 1972; Beckford, 1972; Harbison, 1973; Boserup, 1970). Many of the early development plans focused on economic growth and investment. Growth was most often measured in terms of the gross national product (GNP) or per capita incomes. Consequently, economic targets were identified to raise the nations' GNPs and per capita incomes. It was generally believed that concentration on economic growth would result in an increased standard of living for most, if not all, members of the society (Nigam, 1975; Berry, 1976).

Some writers contend that early development plans and related documents of the 1950s and 1960s generally focused on rapid industrialization to generate the employment and income that would stimulate urban and rural sectors. The "trickle-down" approach to development was perceived as a viable option in at least two ways. One was to concentrate on urban and industrial sectors whereby the economic benefits from these realms would trickle-down to other sectors (Sheffield, 1979); this approach was prevalent in Senegal and is discussed in chapter 7. The other way was to stimulate economic growth through investments by companies and individuals, with the expectation that benefits would trickle-down to other areas (Berry, 1976). Whether these or other perspectives of economic development were followed, it became evident that a primary focus on economic views as envisioned through a trickle-down approach was shortsighted. Economic development as envisioned through industrialization, higher GNPs, and investments often provided gross indexes of growth (*Towards A World Economy That Works*, 1980), yet considerable inequities became apparent among individuals within a nation and among various nations. Economic growth is an indispensable component of national development. The central issue, however, revolves around the extent to which economic power per se will eradicate or perpetuate inequalities (Berry, 1976). In chapter 2, for example, Skinner discusses how national and international labor migrants may help other countries or certain key areas within their own country develop economically, and often individuals obtain economic benefits. Yet there may be limited benefits to the country or place of origin.

Rodney (1972) argues that development is an overall social process which depends on the outcome of peoples' efforts to deal with their environments. There may, in fact, be limited economic options in the natural environment. Hence, the natural environment may push residents from their land, as is depicted in chapter 6 concerning Lesotho. Some economic benefits accrue to Lesotho and its residents, while many realms of development—for example, health care—are neglected. In essence, where is the delicate balance between economic growth and the enhancement of social, health, educational, and cultural features of the society?

Horowitz (1972) states that development involves a transformation of human relations within the economic and political spheres regardless of industrialization and urbanization. Moreover, he argues that development is an asynchronous process wherein the economic, political, and social sectors do not advance simultaneously. Since development is an asynchronous process, it is difficult to determine whether a nation is progressing or stagnating. We may recall the preceding subsection wherein it was pointed out that migrants may contribute to urban expansion *and* urban sprawl. Is development occurring? Or what types of transformations may be necessary to enhance overall social development? Questions such as these are addressed, for example, in chapters 7 and 8.

In a similar, yet more comprehensive perspective, Diene (the director of UNESCO in New York) raises comparable questions and issues regarding national development. National development is a total or macro process, he argues, wherein economic, social, and political factors are interacting simultaneously so that indigenous development occurs within each country. The concepts and processes of development should be determined by indigenous citizens. International assistance may be sought by developing countries. However, international cooperation involving a "give and take or exchange" between developing and developed countries should be the modes of interaction and communication, according to Diene, rather than dominance by one group over another.

During the past decade, development has been critically analyzed within the context of dependency theory and underdevelopment. Underdevelopment may be viewed as the product of the historical and contemporary exploitative relationships between nations or people within a nation (Cockcroft, et al., 1972). It is an explanation of the exploitative relationship derived from the perspective of those who are exploited and is based on the dependency relationship between developing nations and developed nations *and* within developing countries between the elite and the general populace (Cockcroft et al., 1972; Amin, 1972, 1974a; Rodney, 1972; Jorgensen, 1978; Hanna and Hanna, 1981). In the words of dependency theorists, the metropole or center developed at the expense of the satellite or periphery. The metropole and satellite are interrelated since they can be both nexus and locus of different degrees of socioeconomic activity. Witness the following quotation by Jorgensen (1978:4).

> The metropolis-satellite concept (however) does not reflect a *simple* two member relationship where one locus is metropolis and the other is satellite. Rather it deals with a *pyramidal* structure of political and economic power positions (nexus), and these power positions comprise a discernible ordering in space (locus). . . . Areas that concentrate less political and economic power are satellite to those that concentrate more. . . . The pyramidal structure [is that] wherein practically all nations, regions within nations, and urban areas are metropolises in some relations and satellites in others. . . . [Emphasis added]

Based upon his perspectives and those of colleagues who convened at a conference in Nigeria during 1978, Uchendu (1979:6, 9) states that dependency theory, is grounded upon the concept of global inequality which produces underdevelopment. Some essential principles of underdevelopment, according to summary conference material, are: 1) Underdevelopment results from dependence and exploitation. 2) Development and underdevelopment are dialectically linked. Development impoverishes underdevelopment and underdevelopment enriches development. 3) Underdevelopment is the product of a global, imperial history. 4) Underdevelopment is caused by piratically advanced capitalism, not by archaic social structures and traditional institutional arrangements.

In essence, the contributors agree upon some common features of dependency theory and underdevelopment. When international labor migration is viewed within the parameters of dependency theory, the result can be fruitful, as Skinner and Lewis demonstrate. Skinner also observes that individual desires or microanalytical factors can influence domestic migration patterns from rural to urban areas or from less developed to more developed regions within the country; yet such patterns are not always noted in dependency theory.

Similar to other conceptual frameworks are critiques of dependency theory and underdevelopment. Berry (1976) asserts that dependency theorists often fail to account for the various historical experiences among the peripheral nations. And in its essential character the economic and social stratification associated with dependency theory and underdevelopment is not just an economic or a social phenomenon. "The heart of stratification . . . is man's tendency to evaluate his fellows, and himself, as better or worse in terms of some cultural notion of good" (Berry, 1976:21).

Moving beyond Berry's assertions, Uchendu (1979:7, 8, 10) states that the rate of economic growth per se is not the central problem; rather, it is the various cultural, social, political, and technological factors which influence the growth. The many parameters of social and economic development should be integrally linked. Chapter 2 provides some insight here. For example, there is a dearth of high-level managerial personnel and limited technological capacity in most African nations, which fosters dependency relationships with the West. Yet there can be benefits of international labor migration through the exchange of professionals with technological and managerial skills. Chapter 8 discusses the necessity of transformations in relations between developing African countries and developed countries wherein technological, social, and economic development can occur, thereby lessening dependency relations which are perpetuated by migration.

Several writers have stated that an overemphasis on economic features of development is a myopic perspective, whether espoused as a dominant mode of national development by "traditional" economists or as a major critique by dependency theorists. An appreciation of the complex development process may provide the perspective to assist the African countries in moving toward national development. "An optimum scenario calls for a mutually reinforcing partnership between all the elements of the international development community: multilateral, bilateral, the private sectors, specialized groups . . . all playing their roles against a background of appropriate economic and social policies" (Clausen, 1981). As Doudou Diene of UNESCO has observed, genuine cooperation between developed and developing countries would result in authentic progress for the latter.[2]

National development is a process whereby the qualitative features (for example, health care, education, and family and social relations) and quantitative ones[3] (for example, employment, economic growth, and technological advancements) affecting individuals and the general society are blended in an optimum manner. Thus, each chapter in this book proceeds from this general working definition, seeking to highlight factors which need to be examined concurrently as African nations attempt to develop, while addressing the problems and challenges of migration.

POLICY CONSIDERATIONS FOR MIGRATION AND NATIONAL DEVELOPMENT

To address the nexus between migration and national development is to comprehend the role of development policies. Development policies provide the basic framework for identifying issues, comprehending interactions among components of the society, and formulating plans and programs to ameliorate social conditions. The formulation of plans and the implementation of programs, while often perceived as the most important components of development policy, cannot be achieved effectively without the two preceding phases.

Planning is a process to achieve the objectives and goals of national development through the efficient use of resources (*Habitat: United Nations Conference on Human Settlements*, 1976:20), whether physical, human, or institutional. The objectives and goals must be lucid to policymakers and the general populace. Rondinelli (1980) and Nigam (1975:4) maintain that the *commitment* by political leaders and policymakers is perhaps more important than the actual form of development policies. Otherwise, development plans and programs are doomed to failure. In chapter 8 Cummings discusses the failure of some contemporary leaders to sever their commitments to the colonial legacy. This may be the case, but commitment to authentic national development must be resolved by Africans.

Policies and plans for national development may be formulated within the parameters of some of the conceptual tenets of development already discussed here: economic and social development, dependency and under-development, and a complex integrated socioeconomic view of development which is attuned to micro and macro analyses. Tenets of this last conceptual framework should especially be integrated into policies and programs associated with key national characteristics, namely, social institutions, the physical or social infrastructure, or institutional infra-structures.

Social institutions are generally envisioned as the enduring formal and stable means for carrying out important functions which help assure stability and perpetuate the society. They are, in essence, the continuous significant relationships, practices, or organizations within a society. The infrastructures are viewed as the complex (often tangible or physical) network of features which bind the society together so that it functions. Transportation, communication, water supplies, sanitation, and utilities are a few basic examples. Closely linked to these are what some writers (Hughes, 1981; Todd and Shaw, 1980: 425) refer to as the social infrastructure, such as family relations, community groups or associations, and various social services such as schools or health centers. Infrastructures are the fundamental *operative* components of a society. Some United Nations documents (UN Background No. 20, late 1970s) use the term *institutional infrastructures;* these are recognized as the infrastructure and the linkages among its different parts. For example, health care services are part of the infrastructure; however, hospitals, clinics, and mobile health units are linkages within health care services. Perhaps a more stimulating or insightful perspective of institutional infrastructure is the nexus among components of the infrastructure such as health care services with overall economic, social, political, or cultural institutions. This last perspective offers the opportunity for some innovative policy formulation embodying a comprehensive and integrated approach to the complex dynamics of migration and national development.

Because policies provide a means of addressing migration problems so that national development can be enhanced, all the contributors address some aspect of development policy. A succinct discussion is warranted of the distinct and integrated features of policy development (and program implementation) to link migration and national development.

Policy development initially entails the identification of issues and the comprehension or conceptualization of interactions among various societal components. Various works (*Habitat: United Nations Conference on Human Settlements*, 1976:9, 10; UN, 1979:i–iii; Hennen, 1973:1) discuss conceptual economic perspectives. A consensus exists regarding the detrimental effects of limiting economic benefits to a minority of the populace. For instance, individuals who migrate to other countries, regions, or urban centers seeking economic benefits often benefit economically. And they are sometimes able to benefit from "advanced" infrastructures which resulted from accelerated economic growth in the area. In turn, the host society may benefit from migrants' contributions to economic growth. On the other hand, quite often migrants produce strains on various components of the infrastructure—health care, community associations, and education—so that policymakers must address acute problems in the infrastructure. By addressing these immediate problems which require expenditures, funds may not be available in rural or less developed locales. Government officials and policymakers may propose policies and plans for expenditures for the infrastructure in the original area of migration. In the long run, such reallocations might be reinvestments in human resources wherein the individuals and the society both benefit.

Chapters 2 and 7 provide some insight into the brain drain phenomenon from an international and national perspective. Individual and, often, societal economic benefits accrue to highly skilled and professional migrants and to the country of immigration. The international immigration of these highly skilled individuals contributes to a dearth of professional, managerial, and technological personnel and expertise, and stifles improvements within the infrastructures of the country of emigration. Thus, the dependency of developing African nations upon former colonizers or other more technologically advanced countries is witnessed. Skinner offers an alternative conceptual framework which may provide a basis for considering innovative developmental policies. According to him, international labor migration can serve as a basis for national development by enhancing the opportunity for exchanging professionals with insightful perspectives geared to national development needs for basic social institutions, economic growth and diversity, and improvements in the infrastructures.

Johnson examines the phenomenon of the internal brain drain wherein national migration patterns are analyzed for higher education students. Many students migrate to Dakar, the capital of Senegal; many indicate that they do not wish to reside in rural areas or small towns. Return migration, of course, could be beneficial to rural areas. Johnson suggests that policies and plans for decentralizing higher education institutions would provide an avenue for both students and the local community to benefit.

Johnson's views on policies regarding the decentralization of major institutions and the infrastructures are similar to those of Nigam (1975:25, 26) and Sheffield (1979:100, 101). National concerns with the unequal distribution of the population caused by migration (UN, DIESA, 1980:104, 105) could be addressed by decentralizing the institutional infrastructures. For example, Nigam examines several Kenyan planning documents which advocate the establishment of service areas for rural locales with populations ranging from 5,000 to 15,000. These service areas could become integral programs for rural development, thereby providing incentive for residents to remain in rural areas or towns. Incorporating policies and programs of decentralization into national development planning is being advocated since it is doubtful that local policies per se will provide sufficient means for addressing national and international migration.

Chapter 4 also provides some examples, although of a somewhat different nature, which emphasize that policymakers should be aware of how decentralized social institutions and infrastructures can influence migration and national development. Factors which influence village-level social institutions and their ability to affect young men's national or international migration are analyzed. Moreover, chapter 6 looks at the need for an examination of decentralized institutional infrastructures for health care. In short, both chapters examine social institutions and infrastructures in the rural sector and suggest policy considerations.

Chapters 3 and 5 focus on commercial and economic issues of migrants. They highlight the need for policy development between neighboring countries or regions and specifically for the urban milieu of individual states. The movement of commercial migrants among the West African nations, according to Sudarkasa, necessitates a linking of regional economic policies through bodies such as the Economic Community of West African States (ECOWAS) and the specific governmental policies of individual nations. Jules-Rosette discusses some policy alternatives that could produce changes in the urban infrastructures whereby women migrants might be integrated into plans for national development. For example, some community economic activities and individual endeavors are related to decentralized economic infrastructures in Lusaka.

Cummings postulates the need for transformations in major urban and rural structures so that institutions and organizations do not reflect policies of the colonial era. Such institutional structures and organizations are often ill-suited to address problems caused by migration. Indeed, he argues that some national institutions are basic causes of many problems accentuated by migration. At the local level, however, several decentralized institutional structures demonstrate the potential for alleviating problems caused by migration.

Fundamental transformations may be the ideal solution. Attempts to mitigate the most salient problems caused and accentuated by national and international migration are of foremost significance. Hence, we propose in this book pragmatic endeavors—which may contribute to an ideal solution—to address both immediate and long-range issues which retard national development. Development policies which clearly articulate linkages between migration and national development are an indispensable pragmatic ingredient. The policy and program planning involved should help transform the institutional infrastructures so that qualitative and quantitative improvements become evident in the lives of the citizenry and the nation.

NOTES

1. The views expressed in this chapter are mine. They do not reflect the views or policies of the National Institute of Education, the U.S. Department of Education, or any other federal or international organization with which I have been affiliated.

2. Dr. Diene made his observations in an address to a group of African educators at the United Nations, New York, on February 13, 1984.

3. A clear dichotomy between qualitative and quantitative features is not always discernible. For instance, the provision of health care services may be a qualitative feature, but it is certainly influenced by the number of health care workers, a quantitative feature.

REFERENCES

Amin, Samir. 1972. "Underdevelopment and Dependency in Black Africa: Their Historical Origin and Contemporary Form." *Journal of Modern African Studies* 10:503–24.

———. 1974a. *Neocolonialism in West Africa.* Translated from the French by Francis McDonagh. New York: Monthly Review Press.

Amin, Samir, ed. 1974b. *Modern Migrations in Western Africa.* Oxford: Oxford University Press.

Beckford, George. 1972. *Persistent Poverty: Underdevelopment in the Plantation Economies of the Third World.* London: Oxford University Press.

Berry, Sara S. 1976. *Inequality and Underdevelopment in Africa.* Boston: African Studies Center, Boston University.

Boserup, Ester. 1970. *Woman's Role in Economic Development.* London: George Allen and Unwin.

Byerlee, Derek, and Joseph L. Tommy. 1979. "Rural–Urban Migration, Development Policy and Planning." In Reuben K. Udo (ed.), *Education Source Book for Sub-Saharan Africa.* Nairobi, Kenya: Heinemann Educational Books.

Clausen, A.W. 1981. Preface to *Economic Development and the Private Sector.* Washington, D.C.: International Monetary Fund and the World Bank.

Cockcroft, James D., et al. 1972. *Dependence and Underdevelopment: Latin America's Political Economy.* New York: Doubleday Anchor.

Collier, Paul, and Deepak Lal. 1980. *Poverty and Growth in Kenya.* World Bank Working Paper No. 389. Washington, D.C.: World Bank.

Fapohunda, Olanrewaju J., and Frank L. Mott. 1979. "The Components of Population Growth in Africa." In Reuben K. Udo (ed.), *Education Source Book for Sub-Saharan Africa.* Nairobi, Kenya: Heinemann Educational Books.

Habitat News. 1981. Nairobi, Kenya: UN Centre for Human Settlements, vol. 3, no. 2 (August).

Habitat: United Nations Conference on Human Settlements. 1976. Vancouver (May 31 to June 11).

Hanna, William John, and Judith Lynne Hanna. 1981. *Urban Dynamics in Black Africa*. 2d ed. New York: Aldine Publishing Company.

Harbison, Frederick. 1973. *Human Resources as the Wealth of Nations*. New York: Oxford University Press.

Hennen, Benzing. 1973. "Economic Policy." In Joachim Voss (ed.), *Development Policy in Africa*. Bonn-Bad Godesberg, Germany: Research Institute of the Friedrich–Ebert–Stiftung, vol. 105.

Horowitz, Irving Louis. 1972. *Three Worlds of Development: The Theory and Practice of International Stratification*. New York: Oxford University Press.

Hughes, Helen. 1981. "Private Enterprise and Development—Comparative Country Experience." In *Economic Development and the Private Sector*. Washington, D.C.: International Monetary Fund and the World Bank (September).

International Center for Research on Women. 1979. *Women in Migration: A Third World Focus*. Washington, D.C.: Agency for International Development.

Jorgensen, Joseph C. 1978. "A Century of Political Economic Effects on American Indian Society, 1880–1980." *Journal of Ethnic Studies* 6 (Fall):1–82.

Killick, Tony. 1980. "Trends in Development Economics and Their Relevance to Africa." *Journal of Modern African Studies* 18, no. 3:367–86.

Mabogunje, Akin L. 1974–75. "Migrants and Innovation in African Societies: Definition of a Research Field." *African Urban Notes*. East Lansing: Michigan State University, serial B (Winter).

Marenin, Otwin. 1980. "A Review of *The Politics of Africa: Dependence and Development*." Edited by Timothy M. Shaw and Kenneth A. Heard. *Journal of Modern African Studies* 18, no. 4:695–98.

Nigam, Shyam B.L. 1975. *Employment and Income Distribution Approach in Development Plans of African Countries*. Addis Ababa: International Labour Office.

Rodney, Walter. 1972. *How Europe Underdeveloped Africa*. Dar es Salaam, Tanzania: Tanzania Publishing House.

Rondinelli, Dennis A. 1979. "A Review of *Development Planning: Lessons of Experience* by Albert Waterson." Baltimore: Johns Hopkins University Press.

Seidman, Ann. 1974. "Key Variables to Incorporate in a Model for Development: The African Case." *African Studies Review* 17:110–21.

Sheffield, James R. 1979. "Basic Education for the Rural Poor: The Tanzanian Case." *The Journal of Developing Areas* 14 (October): 99–110.

Todd, David M., and Christopher Shaw. 1980. "The Informal Sector and Zambia's Employment Crisis." *The Journal of Modern African Studies* 18, no. 3:411–15.

Towards A World Economy That Works. 1980. New York: United Nations, Department of Public Information.

Uchendu, Victor C. 1979. "Dependency and the Development Process: An Introduction." *Journal of Asian and African Studies* 14, nos. 1 and 2 (January and April):3–16.

United Nations Backgrounder. Late 1970s. No. 20. New York: United Nations, Division for Economic and Social Information.

United Nations. 1979. *Economic Growth and Human Resources*. New York: United Nations.

United Nations, Department of Economic and Social Affairs. 1979. *Trends and Characteristics of International Migration Since 1950*. New York: United Nations, Demographic Studies, No. 64.

United Nations, Department of International Economic and Social Affairs. 1980. *World Population Trends and Policies—1979 Monitoring Report*. New York: United Nations, vol. 1, Population Trends, Population Studies, No. 70; vol. 2, Population Policies, Population Studies, No. 70, 1980.

United Nations, Department of International Economic and Social Affairs Population Studies. 1980. *The World Population Situation in 1979*. New York: United Nations, No. 72.

United Nations High Commissioner for Refugees. 1983. *UNHCR Fact Sheet*, no. 8 (October): 1–2.

Voss, Joachim, ed. 1973. *Development Policy in Africa*. Bonn-Bad Godesburg, Germany: Research Institute of the Friedrich–Ebert–Stiftung, vol. 105.

Zachariah, K.C., et al. 1980. *Demographic Aspects of Migration in West Africa*. Washington, D.C.: World Bank, Staff Working Paper, vol. 1, no. 14; vol. 2, no. 415.

Zelinsky, Wilbur. 1971. "The Hypothesis of the Mobility Transition." *The Geographical Review* 61, no. 2:219–49.

2

LABOR MIGRATION AND NATIONAL DEVELOPMENT IN AFRICA

Elliott P. Skinner

The growing, if grudging, acceptance of the proposition that economic development in the poor nations will not take place without recognizing, and changing, the inequalities to which these nations have been subjected, places the relationship of labor migration to national development in Africa in its proper global and historical perspective. In precolonial Africa small kin groups left parent stocks to explore and to occupy more fertile lands; cattle herders moved about or traveled in transhumance cycles to find better pastures; warrior groups left one polity and went off to conquer and rule neighboring populations; and merchants and traders traveled extensively within and between the more complex West African societies, establishing special "stranger" wards or *zongos* in many of the larger towns. However, all of these movements were largely based upon, or stimulated by, local conditions in Africa.

Modern labor migration in Africa, on the other hand, came about as a direct result of the expansion of the West, and the fitful but progressive incorporation of Africa in the emergent global capitalist economy. The largely involuntary migration of millions of Africans to the New World, from the fifteenth century onwards, not only made the "new-found-lands" productive for their European masters but fueled the growth of a European-based, globe-encircling capitalist system. Then, as Europeans conquered and colonized almost all of Africa, the local people were forced to migrate to perform labor in the developing mining, plantation, transportation, urban, and, later, industrial complexes geared largely to a highly developed but foreign economic system. Paradoxically, while this process largely "underdeveloped" Africa, and developed Europe, it also stimulated the growth of a nationalism which eventually challenged and largely eliminated European colonial rule. The decolonization of Africa, however, did not end the economic dependence of the emergent nation states on a still largely European-controlled global economic system. Independent Africans are now part of a much expanded and more universal labor migratory system still geared largely to European interests. Moreover, the trauma of decolonization, with its attendant military coups, pogroms, and famines (as contrasted to natural droughts), has made refugees of millions of African men, women, and children. So great are the problems facing contemporary African societies that many of their leaders are convinced that only the promulgation of a New International Economic Order, with radical changes in the global economic system (and not the pious hopes that came out of the Can-cún conference), can bring about the development of their continent. They are aware that their ideas are viewed as unrealistic by many, but they point to the global economic crisis as forcing the major economic powers to rethink their strategies.

The crucial role of modern labor migration in the transformation of African societies has been recognized by most social scientists. In his foreword to Samir Amin's volume devoted to *Modern Migrations In West Africa*, Daryll Forde declared that

> The large-scale modern migrations of workers in West Africa are . . . one element in a still wider transformation of the economic, political, and community life of the peoples of West Africa—a transformation which has been stimulated from without and which has also led to their increasing involvement with external economic cultural forces. The new opportunities and demands, together with the stresses and incompatibilities to which the far-reaching technical, economic and political changes have given rise, extend into every field, presenting urgent problems of internal and external policy, of administration and of education with which the governments of the countries of West Africa are having to grapple. (Amin, 1974:xi)

What Forde said about West Africa holds true for all parts of the continent, for there has not been a single traditional African society that has not been influenced by the effects of labor migration.

While there is general consensus that labor migration did contribute greatly to the transformation of Africa, there is still a great deal of debate as to whether it has contributed to the "development" of that continent, or to its "underdevelopment." Amin boldly asserted that labor migration was generally bad for the Africans in that the system imposed costs both on employers and on the economy of Africa as a whole. The economic loss suffered by the African communities included an adverse effect on traditional agriculture and land; loss of productivity and possibilities of acquiring skill and experience resulting from high labor turnover; a great wastage of manpower involved in the constant trekking back and forth between villages and towns; and the economic consequences of the social disruption caused by the system (1974:48–49). Viewing labor migration in Africa from the standpoint of dependency theory, Amin hypothesized that

> Emigration impoverishes the region from which the migrants come; it also prevents the socioeconomic structure from undergoing radical, progressive change; also, to defend themselves, to survive, these societies react by reinforcing those aspects of their traditional structure, which enable them to survive this impoverishment. But at the same time, this impoverishment reinforces the push-effect on certain elements of the population, reproducing the conditions of emigration. The form that this development then takes is that of a degenerated, agrarian capitalism corrupted and poor. (1974:104)

Amin concluded that migration results in a substantial loss of GNP for those societies that furnish large numbers of migrants, and that since the labor recipient countries are locked into a dependent condition with exogenous economies, almost all the African countries suffer from "underdevelopment" (1974:102–3).

Looking at labor migration in Africa from a liberal economist's perspective, and citing data from West Africa, Elliot J. Berg contended that the labor migrant system represented an "efficient" adaptation of Africans to the economic environment in West Africa. Historically, it permitted that region to enjoy more rapid economic growth than would otherwise have been possible since it benefited both the labor-exporting villages and the recipient areas. He insisted that since labor migration permitted a better allocation of resources than would be possible under any other form of labor utilization, it was not likely to disappear until fundamental changes occurred in African economies (Kuper, 1965:161).

If one considered this debate from a global or *macroeconomic* perspective, then Amin's position is undoubtedly correct. The economic behavior of the Africans is dictated by forces beyond their control, and often beyond their knowledge. Nevertheless, on a practical level as well as on a theoretical level, the fact remains that the decision of many contemporary Africans to migrate for work is made with *microeconomic* concerns in mind. These people are therefore prone to see labor migration as linked to their own progress and not necessarily to the development of their nation-states. Therefore, despite the difficult situation of African economies in the world system, the burgeoning towns with their squatter settlements all attest to the belief of rural Africans (and their urban peers) that their personal livelihood would be enhanced if they moved about the continent, and even outside of it, seeking work. Some African leaders have even tried to halt migration to the cities to foster the production of badly needed foodstuff in the rural areas. Invariably they fail, and the flow of labor migrants within their own countries or across their countries' borders continues, and is creating local, national, inter-African, and now intercontinental or global problems.

HISTORICAL ASPECTS OF CONTEMPORARY AFRICAN LABOR MIGRATION

A number of factors must be considered if the impact of labor migration on specific African societies and upon the later emergent nation-states is to be fully understood. First, not all African societies reacted in the same manner to European demands for labor. Second, labor migration was only one of a number of forces also causing changes in these societies, and cannot properly be isolated from them. Third, labor migration, although introduced by the Europeans, became so institutionalized in a number of African societies that it lost the need of active European force or support for its continuation. Fourth, labor migration of both Africans and non-Africans is now very much a factor in the attempt of African nation-states to develop. And, last, the migration of Africans to foreign states, both inside and outside the continent, has economic, political, social, and cultural implications for the global community.

The early European explorers, travellers, traders, and missionaries to Africa needed help during their travels. They found few Africans willing to hire themselves out as guides and porters, and had to rely upon African rulers to provide the labor they needed. When the Europeans finally conquered Africa, the stage was set for the recruitment of labor and the beginning of modern labor migrations.

The South African Boer Voortrekkers employed some Kgatla and Malete as farm hands as early as 1844, but treated them so badly that the latter migrated into Bechuanaland (Botswana) between 1850 and 1870 (Schapera, 1947:25). The resulting shortage of labor was so great that in 1899 the administration introduced a hut tax among the Nyuswa to force Africans to migrate in order to get cash. According to Mbatha, "the effect of the hut tax was that every kraal-head was forced to send all or some of his sons to work for cash wages under Europeans on farms in the towns" (1960:103). The discovery of diamonds and gold in the Transvaal increased the need for labor, and when the number of Africans forced into the mines by hut taxes proved insufficient, the mine owners attempted to get help from outside of Africa. They brought Chinese into South Africa, but these were found threatening to white miners. The lot of providing the necessary labor fell to the Africans.

Like the British in South Africa, colonial governments in many parts of the continent experimented with outside labor in order to meet their needs. The French introduced Annamites and Cubans into Congo Brazzaville, and even attempted to introduce Chinese laborers. These efforts failed, as did the attempts of the Belgians to use labor imported from Cuba and Barbados (Buell, 1928, 1:1043; 2:258, 321, 502, 507). Finally all the colonial governments took measures to get Africans to work on local projects or to migrate to areas where they were needed. By 1895, large numbers of Thonga from Mozambique went to work in the Transvaal mines, driven there by harsh military rule, high taxes, and agreements between the Portuguese government and the mining companies (Harris, 1959:59). The Africans of neighboring Southern Rhodesia (Zimbabwe), Nyasaland (Malawi), and Northern Rhodesia (Zambia) were subjected to high taxes, and they, too, left their villages and migrated to work for wages (Buell, 1928, 1:228, 240–51, 252). Missionaries complained that many Africans from Northern Rhodesia were "forced to leave their homes and walk hundreds of miles to . . . the Belgian Congo in order to earn their tax money on the mines or elsewhere" (Buell, 1928, 1:241). This annual exodus of tax-paying males was so great that it was said to unravel the whole fabric of African life, since many villages were almost denuded of adult males so necessary for food production.

When in 1898 the Africans in Kenya resisted attempts to force them to migrate long distances to work on lands seized for European farms, Lord Delamere, voicing Kenya settler opinion, declared: "We have got to come to legalised methods and force the native to work; and I hope that we may rely on the Government to meet the case . . ." (Buell, 1928, 1:330). Taxes were raised, and since few of these Africans could find work on the reserves to gain money for taxes, they were forced to migrate to work for Europeans. Those Africans who could not find paid employment squatted on European farms and share-cropped for the white farmers. The colonial governments in nearby Tanganyika and Uganda were also petitioned by the settlers to provide labor for their farms. In Uganda "the administrative officials exerted 'pressure' upon the natives so that they would work on plantations" (Buell, 1928, 1:507, 627–28).

The labor policy in King Leopold's Congo was especially brutal. The government "obliged the natives to perform certain 'prestations' for the benefit of the State or of private employers" (Buell, 1928, 2:429). Many Africans who were forced to labor under harsh conditions to collect rubber, cut timber, or work on railroads, died in great numbers. The government defended its cooperation with private economic interests by alleging that during the transition from "a primitive to an industrial society, 'there must be a period in which the territorial authority continues a more or less direct intervention, at least in the region where circumstances justify it'" (Buell, 1928, 2:550–51). The labor policy of the French in their Congo and neighboring territories was almost as bad as that of Leopold. The draconian measures that they took to get labor so shocked André Gide that his report and those of other visitors to the region created a scandal that shamed the otherwise callous officials at the Ministry of Colonies (Gide, 1929).

The migratory labor policies of the colonial governments had differential effects in West Africa. Because of a long precolonial period of commercial relations with Europeans, Africans in Nigeria were fairly well disposed to migrate to European enterprises for work. Yet even here, they resisted complete absorption into the wage economy and had to be forced to work on many projects. "Political" labor was recruited and sent to build many of the railroads (Buell, 1928, 2:658). Similarly, the British in the Gold Coast were initially able to get workers for their mines, but after a while the Africans so resisted mine work that the mine owners considered importing East Indians. The situation was eased when the introduction of taxation in the Northern Territories induced young men to migrate to the mines. Nevertheless, the mining department reported that the "boys" in that area were reluctant to leave their region and the chiefs did not want them to go. Moreover, they disliked underground work and felt no need for the money that they could allegedly earn (Buell, 1928, 1:825). The officials of the Chamber of Mines needed these laborers very badly, but, in contrast to the whites in South, Central, and East Africa, they did not wish the government to use force to get workers. They only counseled the district officers to stop the traditional rulers from telling their young men that they did not have to go to the mines (Buell, 1928, 1:827–28).

The colonial governments in some parts of French West Africa used the same brutal measures as their counterparts in French Equatorial Africa to get African labor. These included forced labor, various types of prestations, and the imposition of hut taxes designed to get labor for private enterprises as well as for the administration. Tauxier, a French administrator, reported that after the conquest of the Mossi of Upper Volta (Burkina Faso) in 1896, the French imposed increasingly heavy taxes on the local people. The Mossi initially reacted by selling their animals to pay their taxes, something they disliked doing. To make matters worse, they were forced to exchange 15,000 cowries for a five franc piece when the usual price for the coin was 10,000 cowries (Tauxier, 1912:538; Mangin, 1929:722).

In desperation many Mossi started to migrate for work in order to obtain French money. The problem was that the French needed more labor for their plantations and railroads than that provided by the Mossi who sought work to earn money for taxes. Therefore they imposed a forced labor regime, and many Mossi laborers were drafted to work in both the public sector and in private commercial enterprises in the Sudan and Ivory Coast. In 1922 the Upper Volta was made to send 6,000 workers to work on the Thies-Kayes railway in the Sudan (Mali), replaceable every six months. Likewise, it furnished 2,000 laborers to build railroads in the Ivory Coast. In addition, each year the governor of Upper Volta permitted private companies to recruit 1,000 workers from the regions of Ouagadougou and Bobo Dioulasso to work in the Ivory Coast (Ledange, 1922:133–36).

Albert Londres, who visited the Upper Volta in the late 1920s, reported that Mossi country was known to the Europeans as a "reservoir" of manpower: three million Negroes. Everyone went there to get these laborers as one would go to a well for water (Londres, 1929:126). So important was Mossi labor to the Ivory Coast that when the Upper Volta was abolished as a territory in 1932 for its insolvency, Mossi country was attached to the northern Ivory Coast. Only in 1937, and after the economic depression had slackened, did some official recognize that "a grave injustice had been done to the Mossi people simply to further the interests of a small and selfish group of coastal planters and foresters" (Thompson and Adloff, 1958:174). The impressment of Mossi laborers for private companies was thereafter prohibited, but forced labor for public works and military conscription was continued.

The Americo-Liberian government in Liberia conscripted thousands of laborers for work in the Cameroons and also granted Germany the right to do so. The government further required its native and district commissioners to use traditional rulers as labor recruiters for such private rubber plantations as Firestone. The resulting abuses were so great that the government itself was charged with practicing slavery in order to get laborers to migrate for work, and the entire matter went before the League of Nations.

What this rather dismal record shows is that the early colonial regimes in almost every part of Africa resorted to all sorts of subterfuges to obtain the necessary labor either for the public sector or for the private enterprises of their own citizens. In this period of rapid capital accumulation, the Africans and the continent of Africa were brutally exploited. However, after World War I a number of factors—economic change, social protests, and, later on, pressure from the International Labor Office—led many of the colonial regimes or governments in Africa to abolish the more coercive aspects of forced labor. In fact, even before World War I, the British in Southern Africa extended governmental control over the recruitment of African labor and in some cases exacted penalties against both recruiters and chiefs who obtained labor fraudulently. In 1908 the Belgian government also ended the worst aspects of forced labor in the Congo when it took that country from King Leopold II's hands. Nevertheless, that government continued to use its good offices to secure labor for both the private and public sectors of its colony. France, too, improved labor conditions in the Moyen Congo and its other territories, but it did not abolish forced labor migration and other prestations until after the Second World War. The Portuguese retained a system of obligatory labor in their colonies until the early 1960s, defending their action by suggesting that the Africans would not work unless forced to do so. The irony was that, despite the use of forced labor in Africa to help its economy, Portugal remained one of the more backward countries of Europe.

EARLY AFRICAN REACTION TO EUROPEAN DEMAND FOR LABOR

During the initial phase of labor recruitment and forced migrations, a number of African societies with certain structural features and specific historical experiences, readily responded to the demand for labor. Isaac Schapera reports that by the 1870s many men from Bechuanaland (Botswana) went to the Kimberley mines "of their own accord" because they were attracted "by reports of the goods (especially firearms) that could be earned there" (1947:26). Sir Harry Johnson was astonished by the Ganda's liking for European products such as gramophones and by their desire for cloth and almost every manufactured article. Johnson felt that those attitudes had a remarkable effect: "So strong was the desire for money with which to buy imported goods that many Ganda in the early years of British administration overcame their traditional aversion to ordinary labour, and rapidly became accustomed to paid employment, which was unknown in Buganda before 1895." (Richards, 1954:18). Similarly William Watson reported ". . . that before the British arrived, the Mambwe of Northern Rhodesia already had a range of goods obtained from outside their own subsistence economy, that they valued the goods brought from without." The result was that the Mambwe "were prepared for the introduction of a cash-economy, and for labour that would earn material rewards" (Watson, 1958:36–37).

Marvin Harris suggested that certain features of the Thonga social structure favored wage labor for men, who could thus alter their subordinate position within the traditional socioeconomic hierarchy.

> The goal of the Thonga youth was to become headman of his own village, to be surrounded by many wives and children, and to have abundant food and drink. Before the introduction of wage labour, ecological conditions imposed strict limits upon the number of males who might achieve this favoured status. Hence it is not surprising that wages were quickly accepted as welcome alternatives to the struggle to win status through the traditional mechanisms, and that even before the final pacification of the Thonga area in 1895 the English pound had already become the most prevalent form of brideprice. (Harris 1959:57)

On the other hand, the rulers of complex polities used many traditional institutions to profit from the Europeans' labor policies. For example, a number of Basuto (Lesotho) rulers manipulated their social and political institutions to accommodate the Europeans' need for labor migrants. These men controlled land which they were required by traditional law to grant to their subjects. However, many of them took advantage of the Europeans' presence to increase their land holdings at the expense of the commoners. The resulting shortage of land among many families forced the younger brothers to go "out to the mines to obtain a living" (Buell, 1928, 1:178). The Kgatla nobles in Bechuanaland reacted to the demand for labor by adopting the "policy of conscripting men from one or more of the able-bodied age-regiments in their tribes" for work with the Europeans (Schapera, 1947:29).

The existence of the corvée system in many African societies with complex political organization also facilitated the ease with which their men migrated to work for Europeans. In some ways labor migration was rationalized as a corvée for the Europeans, who were said to be the new chiefs (Skinner, 1960:157). On the other hand, the lack of corvée and other such structures among some African populations made them hostile to labor recruitment. The French never did succeed in obtaining many laborers from among the acephalous Lobi of the western Upper Volta. These people fought off tax collectors and labor recruiters as late as the Second World War. Likewise, the pastoral Masai apparently turned their backs on the Europeans and refused to take part in white economy, at least as migrant workers (Hailey, 1938:694).

MODERN VOLUNTARY LABOR MIGRATION

By World War II involuntary labor migration in most parts of Africa had been largely replaced by voluntary migration. Where at one time most Africans found labor migration irksome, they later came to accept it as necessary to meet their economic, social, political, and cultural needs. Throughout the continent, Africans responded to the new sociocultural conditions and to structural changes engendered by the presence and activities of the Europeans by voluntarily migrating to work centers. As we shall see, they found in these work centers not only the money they needed to acquire new necessities, but a new environment created by the syncretism of African and European cultural elements. In short, African labor migrants were now participating in a new way of life.

Because of the complexities of life in the mining, plantation, industrial, and urban centers into which Africans were now voluntarily migrating, the basic economic reason for this migration was often glossed over by many romantic social scientists. The maxim of French-speaking migrants that "Qui n'a pas été à Kumassi n'ira pas au paradis" (Who has not been to Kumasi [in Ghana] will not go to Heaven) was often interpreted as meaning that migration for young people represented adventure, bright lights, liquor, sex, and song. Jacques Macquet, for example, among others, declared that Africans migrate not so much because they wish economic gain but because they desire familial, social, and political emancipation from the conservatism of the society and because they desire to live out the myth which they have created about the European way of life (1956:6–8). Schapera tells us that for the Tswana:

> Going out to work for the first time is regarded by many youths as a form of adventure, and some admittedly go mainly in order to experience for themselves the attractions and excitement described by their more experienced elders. . . . Labour migration, moreover, has come to be widely regarded as a form of initiation

now that the old circumcision rites have been abandoned by the people. (1947:116–17)

A close examination of most studies of labor migration, however, clearly shows that the economic factor in migration is dominant. Schapera came to the conclusion that the "universal" cause of the migration of the Tswana to South Africa,

> . . . and certainly the most important of all, is economic necessity. . . . During the course of the past century, the people have learned to use new goods of many kinds, almost all of which are imported; they also pay taxes to the Administration and their own tribal authorities, and need money for various other purposes. In order to satisfy these new wants, they were obliged to find new sources of income. . . . Wage-labour has consequently become an indispensable source of income for the people generally, and since opportunities in the Territory are limited, the vast majority go to the Union, where there is a far greater demand for their services. (1947:136)

Audrey Richards found that "the economic motive was the one most frequently expressed by immigrants" leaving the former Belgian Congo to work in the cotton fields of Uganda (1954:67). (Richards and associates found that "out of two or three hundred men interviewed in Uganda, only one said that he wanted 'to see what Uganda was like'" [Richards, 1954:68]. Richards added that in discussing the reasons for migration, most men "spoke of sheer economic necessity or of a particularly unpleasant political or kinship obligation they wanted to avoid, rather than of desires to see European life, get a reputation for sophistication or similar motives . . ." [1954:68].)

Kirk-Greene found that the main reason why the "Hill-Tribes" of the Northern Adamawa traveled for hundreds of miles all over Nigeria and neighboring territories was "to acquire tax-money" (1956:369). Prothero also found that both population pressure and land hunger were the basic economic factors conducive to labor migration from the Sokoto Province of Nigeria. He declared: "The economic motive was shown to be outstanding in the reasons for migrating. . . . Ninety-two per cent may be said to have been seeking to supplement their incomes in various ways" (1957:253, 256). (Prothero denies that the people in the northwestern part of Nigeria sublimated their desire to indulge in warfare and slave-raiding during the dry season by going off to work. He emphasized that some of the young men looked on going away as an opportunity to prove themselves in the eyes of the community [1957:258].)

The Mossi of the Upper Volta migrated in large numbers to work in Ghana, the Ivory Coast, and parts of Dahomey and Mali, chiefly for economic reasons. When either the migrants or their relatives were asked why young men leave their homes, the answers were similar and extremely repetitious; "I am poor; I need money to pay taxes and to buy clothes," was the standard reply of young men. One declared: "I want a bicycle, clothes for myself, and clothes for my wife and relatives." The relative of an absent migrant replied to general questions about migration with the statement, "Men go off to find money"; about a specific man he said, "He went to get money to pay taxes." Behind these statements was the reality that agriculture no longer provided enough income to meet the traditional and modern needs of the Mossi people. Even if food production were to be increased—a questionable feat given the nature of the environment and agricultural cycle—it is not certain that the Mossi could obtain enough money to meet all of their needs.

The need to obtain money to pay the bride-price is a factor in the migration of Africans in a number of societies, though not in all of them. Harris reported that among the earliest Thonga migrating from Mozambique to the Transvaal mines were men seeking English pounds sterling for the bride-price (1959:57). Mbatha stated that as early as 1852, the Nyuswa of Botha's Hill in Natal, South Africa, in addition to migrating to earn money for taxes, were also going off to work "to find money to buy cattle in order to buy wives" (1960:105). Watson explains why money for the bride-price was an important factor in labor migration among the Mambwe:

> It is on young men that the pressure to migrate for work is greatest, for a young man needs a considerable sum for a marriage payment before he can marry. The essential item in the Mambwe marriage is an exchange of money and cattle, although a man also works in the garden of his parents-in-law. In the old days, cattle, goats, sheep, calico, hoes, axes, spears and arrows formed the marriage payment, but since the 1914–18 war cattle and money have taken the place of this wider range of goods. (1958:36–37)

The importance of labor migration as a source of money for Africans to buy new types of goods, or to obtain money to satisfy traditional as well as new sociocultural needs, underscores the changes that have taken place in their societies as a result of European conquest. The nature of the new needs themselves often reflected the way African institutions and values were changing or developing. Mbatha cites the case of a young Christian girl who felt that her family had not provided her with good clothes and had permitted her to go around half-naked in the hope that she would "revert to heathenism." However, this young girl was a "staunch Roman Catholic and decided to go to work to clothe herself so that she could go to church decently covered. She ran away to town where she found a job . . ." (1960:112–13). Gulliver reported that, among other things, migration for wage labor among the Ngoni and Ndebele was "involved in obtaining goods and services which are not obtainable in the tribal areas and with standards which are not those of the home community—bicycles and radios, a wide variety of clothing, cash for luxuries" in addition to an increased amount of traditional goods (1960:160). Watson listed among the reasons for the Mambwe's quest for wages the desire to obtain the clothes, food, and multitudinous manufactured articles which the missionaries introduced into their country: "Missionary teaching brought the Mambwe to despise 'naked savages,' and to look upon European clothes and other articles as essentials of progressiveness. The missionaries acted on the assumption that Mambwe life was barbarous; they made the people conscious of their own backwardness" (1958:39).

Kirk-Greene reported that young men of Northern Adamawa in Nigeria migrated to buy shirts and trousers, shoes, and even dark glasses (1956:377). Mossi migrants often returned home from abroad with the treasured bicycle and with trunks bulging with European manufactured products. In addition, they also brought back lounging chairs, beds, and bags of cement with which to plaster the mud-brick walls of their huts. Returning Mossi migrants have also been accused of attempting to use their currency resources to encourage elders to give them wives without having observed the traditional, long-term reciprocal relations. Of course no one would admit, although it was often alleged, that such attempts might be successful, but the very fact that people talked about them showed quite clearly that the migrants, at least, had changed their conception of marriage and were not above using the proceeds of their migration to change this institution.

There is little doubt that the domestic disputes and the desire to escape the control of relatives, lineages, and unwelcome aspects of rural life induced many Africans to migrate and seek a livelihood away from home. Some persons also see in migration the opportunity to escape sanctions for the violation of their societal norms. Schapera found that young Tswana who wished to escape either domestic or lineage control went away to work. Young men forbidden to marry the girls of their choice "will seldom hesitate to seek freedom by migrating to the Union [South Africa]" (Schapera, 1947:118). Girls who were tired of school ran off to Johannesburg.

In Zambia, Watson found that once Mambwe girls had visited the Copper Belt, "their whole attitude towards tribal life changed on their return" (1958:44–45). These girls not only refused to marry the men their families had chosen for them, but insisted on marrying their lovers. In addition, married women often put a great deal of pressure on their husbands to take them to the Copper Belt because they found the women's lot easier over there. Watson concluded that for the Mambwe, at least, "Apart from the direct economic and social pressures to go out to earn money, wage-labour offers an escape from unpleasant or intolerable social and economic situations at home" (1958:47).

A number of Mossi men from the area which I studied stole the affection of other men's wives and took them away. A few men who had committed crimes such as rape or theft, or who had been caught *in flagrante delicto* of adultery, also ran off to Ghana or the Ivory Coast. Since they seldom returned home, this cannot be considered true labor migration. Yet Mossi have always been free to seek a sure haven with their mother's patrilineage when they had difficulties with their lineages. Mossi women, rather than men, were the ones who frequently ran off to the neighboring territories, because of dissatisfaction either with their arranged marriage or with a difficult domestic situation. Women were even heard to warn the judge at court that if their husband did not reform, they were likely to run off with "any stranger on his way to Kumasi."

Schapera reported that among the Tswana, many freed serfs who remained attached by custom to their former masters ran off to work when irked by social discrimination against them. Richards also found that a fair number of migrants from Ruanda had left their homes to avoid unpaid feudal labor for their Tutsi rulers. Others migrated to avoid being punished or beaten by these chiefs; only when they heard that the chiefs were not beating anymore did they return home (Richards, 1954:70–71). The Mossi were the largest group of migrants from French colonies who ran off to British territories in order to escape forced labor and prestations from a sometimes rather harsh administration, or, as Church so euphemistically put it, in search of a "simpler administration" (1957:169).

CHANGING EFFECTS OF MIGRATION BETWEEN RURAL AND URBAN AREAS

While many Africans viewed labor migration as a means of personal liberation from tradition as well as a way of earning a livelihood, they also used the benefits of rural-urban labor migration to enhance their traditional and rural statuses. A widespread practice in most contemporary African societies is for the labor migrants who "made good" to return home in triumph, thereby enhancing their own prestige and that of their villages. The successful Igbo-speaking migrant, whether returning home with a foreign Ph.D. or with a Mercedes-Benz, is lifted high on the shoulders of the stay-at-homes. In order to validate his new status, however, he must contribute to the modernization of his village. His development project may be a school, a standpipe, or a clinic. In rural Nigeria one sees literally thousands of schools that were constructed by successful migrants, or by Home Town Improvement Associations, organized by migrants in far-off cities. The more successful the migrant, the more impressive his project. President Houphouet-Boigny of the Ivory Coast literally transformed his hometown, Yamoussoukro, into a showpiece with a first-class hotel and an airstrip capable of receiving jet aircraft. Maurice Yameogo of the Upper Volta attempted to do the same for his native Koudougou.

In addition to introducing modernizing projects in their villages, successful migrants also become the conduits through whom rural persons become part of a chain of an increasing number of migrants who "commute" between the rural and the urban areas. The earlier seasonal migrants usually spent a few seasons away from their villages before finally settling down at home or, less frequently, before staying permanently in town. Now, with better transportation and the growth of certain amenities in the rural areas, labor migrants move frequently between the country and the town. The object now is to take advantage of economic opportunities in the dual economies characteristic of many African countries. These migrants farm in the rural areas and perform nonfarm tasks in the towns. By so doing, they hedge their economic bets. By straddling the town and the country, the migrants also serve as a link between the areas. The question here again is whether, as Amin argues, these migrants exploit their villages in favor of the towns, or whether they exploit the towns in favor of the villages (1974:92–93). What again is not in question is that contemporary migrants make a greater contribution to the rural areas in the way of modern amenities than did the earlier migrants who did not commute. Moreover, it is clear that this commuting is preventing or delaying the all-too-common process by which the ways of city people diverge from those of rural ones.

POLITICAL CONSEQUENCES AND CAUSES OF MIGRATION

While solidarity between labor migrants and their rural kin can promote economic and political integration in African nation-states, the converse can also be true. It was noted that during the colonial and immediate postcolonial periods the tendency for labor migrants from the same rural ethnic group or region to be endogamous and to live segregated lives in their own worlds or *zongos* resulted in division and plurality in the emerging societies. When, as in Nigeria, the migrants from the South were viewed as sociological strangers who aided the structural interest of the British by playing an intercalary role between the rulers and the ruled, they were the repeated victims of pogroms, one of which led to a civil war and the near dissolution of the state. Similar labor migrant solidarity in Ghana, the Ivory Coast, Mali, Niger, Uganda, Zaire, and other African states had equally nefarious effects on the internal development of these states and threatened to disrupt their relations with their neighbors. In Ghana the Yoruba, Hausa, and Mossi labor migrants were not only viewed as sociological strangers whose presence was inimical to the security of Ghana, but when they "interfered" in the "internal" politics of their "hosts" and were expelled, their home governments almost broke diplomatic relations with Accra.

In an ironic and cruel twist of fate, Ghanaian labor migrants were later not only expelled from the Ivory Coast and Nigeria, but many of them also lost their lives in the process. Early in March 1981 police in the Ivory Coast swooped down on illegal labor migrants (some of whom they suspected of being criminals) and locked some sixty persons "in a small cell in the police barracks on the outskirts of Abidjan. Forty-six of them, all Ghanaians, died when police refused to hear their cries for air and water." The Ivorians later explained that "the men died because their cell was too small and insufficiently ventilated" and that President Houphouet-Boigny had ordered an investigation. Yet when President Limann of Ghana sent an emissary to the Ivory Coast, President Houphouet-Boigny refused to see the envoy, referring him to a subordinate instead. This slight so infuriated the Ghanaians that the students sacked the Ivorian embassy in Accra and expelled its occupants; President Limann announced several days of mourning; the Ghanaians boycotted a meeting of the Union of African Parliaments which met in Abidjan; and Ghana protested to the Economic Commission of the West African States (ECOWAS) against "inhuman treatment of her citizens in neighboring countries." Criticizing its government for the affair in Abidjan, *The Pioneer,* a daily paper in Accra, Ghana, charged that the nation's people were being turned into "wanderers and vagabonds" and that the "inability of Ghana's economy to offer jobs to the people, the lack of effective economic planning and of consumer goods are the causes of the exodus" (Foreign Broadcast Information Service, 10–14 March 1981). It took the intervention of the presidents and diplomats of the surrounding states to resolve peacefully the conflict between Ghana and the Ivory Coast.

The problem of labor migrants from Ghana, in this case linked to Nigeria's concern for its own national development, is still creating severe conflict between the West African states. Enriched by the OPEC-induced oil shortage since 1973, Nigeria welcomed close to two million labor migrants, who took advantage of work opportunities in the building trades, nursing, farming, herding, and even street peddling, to migrate to the rural areas, oilfields, and urban centers of Nigeria. Everyone was aware that most of these workers had no work permits and for that reason were in contravention of the ECOWAS codes regulating the flow of people between member countries. Because these workers were needed, nothing was said or done about their presence in Nigeria. But when late in 1982 the oil glut occurred and Nigeria found itself short of revenue to continue its development, including the building of a new capital at Abuja, the illegal labor migrants, especially the Ghanaians, became the scapegoats. President Shehu Shagari accused the illegal immigrants of ruining his country's economy and draining his nation's wealth. He allegedly notified the governments of the neighboring states that he wished their citizens to leave, but when no resolute steps were taken, he decided to expel the migrants. He gave the foreign workers two weeks to leave the country, and when the deadline came, two million of these persons, including more than one-half million Ghanaians, flocked to the borders. These repatriates allegedly increased Ghana's population by some ten percent almost overnight, depleting that country's already short stocks of food supplies and forcing it to plead for emergency aid. However, there was another aspect to this expulsion. There were unconfirmed reports that Shagari feared that as sociological "strangers" (Shack and Skinner, 1979), and therefore as persons having no deep interest in Nigeria's political future, these migrants might attempt to participate in his country's coming election and would create confusion by selling their illegal votes to the highest bidder (Newsweek, 14 February 1983:32–34). In both conflicts between Ghanaian labor migrants and the people of the Ivory Coast and of Nigeria, the migrants viewed their own (micro) interests as more important than the national (or macro) interests of their hosts.

Other postindependence conflicts within and between African nation-states also contributed to a new type of migration throughout the continent—namely, that of refugees. The first of these refugees were probably those politicians whose parties had lost the electoral battle for power just prior to the independence of their states in the early 1960s. Quite a number of these persons received sanctuary in Nkrumah's Ghana. Then, as ethnic conflict led to veritable pogroms in such countries as Ruanda and Burundi, refugees fled to neighboring regions. The attempts at So-mali anschluss in the Horn of Africa led to conflict between that state and its Ethiopian and Kenyan neighbors and the flight of thousands of refugees. Civil war in the Southern Sudan, Nigeria, and Chad created additional thousands of refugees. Finally, the exodus of thousands more from Angola, Guinea-Bissau, Eritrea, Mozambique, Rhodesia/Zimbabwe, Southwest Africa/Namibia, and South Africa not only provided recruits for the various National Liberation Armies but additional refugees to swell the tide. To aggravate the situation, droughts and famines not only plagued these refugees, but created additional thousands in the Sahel and other regions so stricken. Those African states that provided sanctuary for the refugees did their best in the tradition of "African hospitality." Some of these states even provided education and jobs for their involuntary guests. Yet so poor were these host societies that by 1981 the United Nations High Commission for Refugees estimated that "more than 6.3 million refugees—half of the world's total—are struggling for survival across the continent of Africa. The tragic victims of war, famine, the remnants of colonialism, despotic rule or apartheid, they *are* the forgotten refugees of our times. Until now the world has failed to heed their desperate pleas for help" (*New York Times*, 13 December 1981).

AFRICAN MIGRATION AND THE GLOBAL ECONOMY

Aside from what has been termed "the Western world's traditional prejudices," Africa's underdeveloped condition (except for mineral production) and its marginal role in the global political economy are the factors that account for the neglect of its refugee problem. Yet, on the other hand, Africa and African labor migrants are being integrated into the global economic system more rapidly than ever. The issue here is still whether this relationship benefits individual African states, or African individuals, or the outside world. For example, every year literally thousands of highly skilled Africans leave their countries to settle in America or Europe, or do not return home after being educated abroad. There are now more Togolese doctors practicing in France than in doctor-short Togo. Given the cost to Togo of rearing and training the now-absent doctors, these professional labor migrants are judged selfish by many of their compatriots. They are accused of seeking greater personal salaries than their countries can afford, and also of making a greater contribution to the health of French society than to their own suffering people. In response, the expatriate Togolese doctors assert that their training would be wasted in their undeveloped society. Moreover, they claim that the officials in Togo because of jealousy would never accord them either the honor or salaries they automatically receive in France. Obviously the truth is somewhere in the middle. The more difficult problem, and one which has still not been resolved, is how to make it possible for Togolese doctors who are needed in their country to return and practice there.

There are now also thousands of unskilled Africans doing menial work in France, from sweeping the streets of Paris to working as laborers in the factories. In a case that attracted international attention, the Communist mayors of the Paris suburbs of Saint Maur and Vitry-sur-Seine were charged with discriminating against Malian laborers and demolishing their shanties (*The Guardian*, 1 March 1981:11). It was not so much that the French feared competition from the Africans but that they did not want them as neighbors. Surprised and alarmed, one Malian was quoted as stating: "We love France. She is good for us. We are good workers. We never strike. Why then do the people destroy our houses?" (*L'Express*, 7 March 1981:72–75). These labor migrants, like the Togolese doctors, feel that they are fairly well paid, compared to their relatives at home. Just before important Muslim holy days they descend from their Paris-Dakar-Bamako jets laden with presents for their families. These presents often include transistor radios and even small water pumps to irrigate their arid plots along the banks of the local rivers. After the festivities are over, many migrants return to Paris; those who stay at home are often replaced abroad by their younger relatives.

The only distinction between the African laborers in Paris and the Togolese doctors there is that while the former are viewed as exploited Third World proletarians who perform tasks now scorned by French workers, the Togolese doctors are considered the exploiters of their own people. And although these doctors are ashamed of their brothers who labor in Paris, and do not fraternize with them, the two groups share the common goal of seeking their own micro economic interests. They are also members of different migrant labor social classes which are gaining worldwide membership. The Togolese doctors are no different from their Indian, Phillipino, West Indian, and European counterparts who are seeking better employment opportunities outside their homelands. The African laborers are no different from the Portuguese, Italians, Greeks, and Turks who leave southern Europe to work in the factories and hotels of northern Europe. They are not too different from those West Indians who sweep the streets of London, run its underground, and perform the menial work in its hospitals.

An important theoretical as well as practical point which the above data suggest is that the development of African nations, like the functioning of many contemporary European economies, will increasingly be the task of international labor migrants servicing a more highly integrated global economy. The main contrast between Africa and Europe or America is that while the latter do not need migrants for development but only to service their consumer economies, Africa needs highly skilled international labor migrants for its industrial development. The class of persons who will aid in the development of the African nations is represented in the Peace Corps, the U.S. Agency for International Development, the French Volunteers for Progress, the French Agency for Cooperation, the European Economic Community Funds for Economic Development, the World Bank and UN agencies, and the peripatetic staffs of the multinational corporations. Of course, few of these persons would wish to view themselves as labor migrants—a status they would limit to laborers. Nor would many Third World ideologues (ignoring the "labor theory of value") view these more skilled members of the labor fraternity as labor migrants. Yet these skilled workers must be viewed in that light. The lead article on Africa in the *New York Times International Economic Survey for 1978* was entitled: "An African Dilemma: Using Foreign Experts." The article states:

> The contradiction pervades the consciousness of much of black Africa and underscores what is probably the greatest dilemma facing the Continent's emerging nations: how to utilize vitally needed foreign skills and foreign capital without pawning their national souls and stirring discontent among Africans resentful of the privileges accorded expatriates.
>
> In the case of Mozambique, on Africa's east coast, pressing needs outweigh any consideration of future consequences. The country has committed itself enthusiastically to a program of universal education—an enormously ambitious project considering that in 500 years of Portuguese rule only 2 percent of the people ever went to school.
>
> Volunteers are building schools. But where will the teachers come from? "We need our own mechanics, doctors, nurses—everything," the planner said. "But to get these we need someone else's teachers."
>
> The Government is offering generous inducements to Portuguese-speaking foreign teachers—not only high salaries and housing but also the right to accumulate as much as two-thirds of these salaries in precious foreign reserves for deposit abroad. Like many African nations, Mozambique, while pursuing egalitarian ideals, is recruiting with the promise of privilege.

Truly, the development of Africa poses a dilemma, but as in many human endeavors, dilemmas usually indicate that one is in the presence of a dialectic whose resolution is often truly surprising since it is unexpected. Let me suggest that it might well be that these foreign experts working in often unviable African nation-states may be the harbingers of that Pan-African unity without which African states cannot really develop. Coming as they do as "strangers" from the global level, these technicians are often free of those parochial loyalties and prejudices which, along with foreign imperialism, have prevented economic cooperation among African states. As expatriates, they may be inclined to pursue the logic of development across state boundaries. They may also be prone to view development problems in macro terms—a perspective perhaps more in harmony with the growing reality of Africa's position in the global economic system. These foreigners may well view Africa more in terms of viable economic regions than might the citizens of individual African states.

One might well argue that the international labor migrants, like those additional thousands of Frenchmen who now live and work in francophone Africa, are only the tools of Western imperialism and are therefore irrelevant to African development. This possibility does not, however, halt the emergence of a more integrated global economy. This fact in itself might well sharpen the contradiction between the haves and the have-nots, thereby amplifying the call for a New International Economic Order. The resistance of European powers to this demand for a restructuring of the global economy could well mean an Africa-wide reaction against them, thereby establishing the basis for African economic cooperation, development, and perhaps unity.

REFERENCES

Amin, Samir, ed. 1974. *Modern Migrations in Western Africa.* Foreword by Daryll Forde. Oxford: Oxford University Press.
Berg, Elliot J. 1965. "The Economics of the Migrant Labor System," In Hilda Kuper (ed.), *Urbanization and Migration in West Africa.* Berkeley and Los Angeles: University of California Press.
Buell, Raymond L. 1928. *The Native Problem in Africa.* 2 vols. New York: Macmillan.
Church, R.J. Harrison. 1957. *West Africa.* London: Longmans.
Dussage-Ingrand. 1974. "L'Émigration Sarakollaise du Guidimaka vers la France."

Pp. 239–57 in Samir Amin (ed.), *Modern Migrations in Western Africa*. Oxford: Oxford University Press.

Foreign Broadcasts Information Service. 1981. Department of State, Washington D.C. March 10–24.

Gide, André P. 1929. *Travels in the Congo*. New York: A.A. Knopf.

Guardian, The. 1981. "A Racism Not All Red." March 1:11.

Gulliver, P.H. 1960. "Incentives in Labor Migration." *Human Organization* 19, no. 3 (Fall): 159–63.

Hailey, Lord. 1938. *An African Survey*. London: Oxford University Press.

Harris, Marvin. 1959. "Labour Migration Among the Mozambique Thonga: Cultural and Political Factors." *Africa* 29, no. 1 (January): 53.

Kirk-Greene, A.H.M. 1956. "Tax and Travel Among the Hill Tribes of Northern Adamawa." *Africa* 26 (October): 369–78.

Kuper, Hilda, ed. 1965. *Urbanization and Migration in West Africa*. Berkeley and Los Angeles: University of California Press.

Ledange, Paul-Louis. 1922. "Une Colonie Nouvelle, La Haute Volta." *La Revue Indigene* 17, nos. 157–59.

L'Express. 1981. "Diara, loin des bulldozers." March 7:72–75.

Londres, Albert. 1929. *Terre d'Ébène (La Traite des Noirs)*. Paris: Albin Michel.

Macquet, Jacques J. 1956. "Motivations culturelles des migrations vers les villes d'Afrique Centrale." *Folia Sci. Afri. Centralis* 2 (December):6–8.

Mangin, Eugene P. 1929. *Les Mossi*. Paris: Augustin Challamel.

Mbatha, Mphiwa B. 1960. "Migrant Labour and Its Effects on Tribal and Family Life Among the Nyusa of Botha's Hill." Masters thesis. Durban: University of Natal.

New York Times International Economic Survey, The. 1978. Section 12, February 4:32.

Newsweek. 1983. "Nigeria's Outcasts: The Cruel Exodus." February 14:32–34.

Prothero, R. Mansell. 1957. "Migratory Labour from North-Western Nigeria." *Africa* 27 (July).

Richards, Audrey I., ed. 1954. *Economic Development and Tribal Change: A Study of Immigrant Labour in Buganda*. Cambridge, England: Heffer.

Schapera, Isaac. 1947. *Migrant Labour and Tribal Life*. London: Oxford University Press.

Shack, William, and Elliott P. Skinner. 1979. *Strangers in African Societies*. Berkeley: University of California Press.

Skinner, Elliott P. 1960. "Labour Migration and Its Relationship to Socio-Cultural Change in Mossi Society." *Africa* 30, no. 4 (October): 375–401.

Tauxier, Louis. 1912. *La Noir du Soudan, Pays Mossi et Gourounsi: Documents et Analyses*. Paris: Emile La Rose.

Thompson, Virginia, and Richard Adloff. 1958. *French West Africa*. Stanford University Press.

Watson, William. 1958. *Tribal Cohesion in a Money Economy*. Manchester: Manchester University Press.

3

THE ROLE OF YORUBA COMMERCIAL MIGRATION IN WEST AFRICAN DEVELOPMENT

NIARA SUDARKASA

The significance of migration in contemporary West Africa is attested by its role in shaping the demographic characteristics of all countries in that region; by its prominence, particularly, in the growth of cities; and by its role in the establishment and development of various economic patterns and institutions during the colonial and postcolonial periods (Gugler and Flanagan, 1978; Zachariah and Conde, 1981; Amin, 1974; Mabogunje, 1972; Riddell, 1978; Adepoju, 1979).

Most studies of migration in West Africa (and elsewhere on the continent) have dealt with labor migration, that is, migration associated with wage employment (Skinner, 1960; Kuper, 1965, Berry, 1970; Zachariah and Conde, 1981). It is important to remember, however, that *labor* migration is preeminently a twentieth-century phenomenon, whereas *commercial* migration—that is, migration associated with trade—has a much longer history and continues to account for much of the internal and international mobility of West African populations (Sudarkasa, 1974). The present distribution of ethnic groups in West Africa is an indicator not only of the twentieth-century mobility of labor but also of the past and present mobility of traders and others who have set out in pursuit of better opportunities to set up shop "on their own account" (Rouch, 1956, 1961; Charbonneau, 1962; Hill, 1970; Meillassaoux, 1971; Cohen, 1969, 1971; Sudarkasa, 1974, 1975, 1977, 1979; Eades, 1979, 1980; Arhin, 1979; Igue, 1983).

HISTORY OF WEST AFRICAN
COMMERCIAL MIGRATION

The origins of commercial migration in West Africa are rooted in the distant precolonial past. In fact, much of recorded West African history is the history of trade and associated population movements, particularly between the ancient kingdoms of the Sahel (of which Ghana, Mali, and Songhai are the best known) and those of the North African littoral (Bovill, 1958). Less popularly known but equally well documented in the scholarly literature, is the fact that from the earliest known historical times, and probably much earlier, West Africa itself constituted an economic zone wherein goods were traded through systems of periodic markets located in major towns as well as in rural areas (Meillassoux, 1971; Arhin, 1971). Cattle, textiles, and kola nuts were among the items traded across hundreds and thousands of miles. Timbuktu, Djenné, Salaga, Kano, Bida, and Oyo were among the major cities that catered to international trade at different periods in West African history (Skinner, 1964; Sudarkasa, 1974). In the Sahel as well as in the forest zone, a feature of all major West African commercial centers in the period between A.D. 800 and 1900 was the presence of stranger quarters or wards (often called *zongos*) that were populated mainly by migrant traders and their entourages (Skinner, 1963; Sudarkasa, 1979; Schildkraut, 1970, 1978).

In precolonial times as in the present, this intersocietal or international commercial migration was the specialty of certain ethnic groups, even though virtually all West African peoples had traders among them who carried on commerce within the nation or the group in question. Illustrative of the latter peoples are the Ibo, who have been very active in contemporary international West African commerce, but who in precolonial times were primarily traders within the borders of their own societies (Ukwu, 1969). On the other hand, the Hausa, Djoula, and Yoruba are three groups who have a history of continuous involvement in trans-West African trade over a period of centuries. There is written documentation that by the nineteenth century, Yoruba traders frequented the market at Salaga, in what is now northern Ghana, where they sold human captives, leather goods, cattle, and their locally made textiles. In turn, they purchased kola nuts grown in the Ashanti kingdom for resale on their return home (M. Johnson, 1966). This paper examines the role of Yoruba commercial migrants in contemporary West African regional trade—that is, in commerce dating from the late nineteenth century to the present—against the background of Yoruba trade in the

precolonial period. Attention is called to the activities of Yoruba traders
in various countries in the region, but the paper focuses on that group of
migrants who voluntarily left Nigeria to work in Ghana from the late
nineteenth century through the 1960s. Most of these traders were forc-
ibly repatriated to Nigeria between November 1969 and January 1970,
when the government of Ghana issued an official order for their expulsion
along with that of thousands of other West Africans from neighboring
countries, because they were living and working in Ghana without the
appropriate residence permits (Piel, 1971; Sudarkasa, 1979).

This paper examines the economic, political, and social factors underly-
ing the exodus to Ghana, paying attention to the specific economic niches
developed by Yoruba migrants. Light is thus shed on the important role
of Yoruba commercial migration in the development and integration of
West Africa over the last eighty to ninety years.

YORUBA MIGRATION FROM NIGERIA IN
THE EARLY TWENTIETH CENTURY

In the mid-nineteenth century, the Yoruba were a highly urbanized West
African people numbering in the millions, who formed a group of kingdoms in areas that now comprise parts of southwest Nigeria, northern
Benin (formerly Dahomey), and northern Togo. Each kingdom centered
around a capital city with a number of subordinate towns, villages, hamlets, and farmlands in outlying areas. A daily market catering to local
trade was a feature of each town, and throughout the kingdoms, various
periodic markets were held to facilitate long-distance trade. The Yoruba
were noted for the sophistication of their productive and distributive
activities and for the complexity of their state organization (S. Johnson,
1921; Bascom, 1955; Lloyd, 1953; Mabogunje, 1962, 1968; Sudarkasa,
1973; Akinjogbin and Ekemode, 1976; Igue and Yai, 1973).

Like most older West African states, the major centers of Yoruba
administration and commerce were located some distance inland from the
coast. Even during the eighteenth and nineteenth centuries, when European and American slave traders were most active along what is now the
Nigerian coast, the Yoruba kingdoms retained their inland focus. Of the
coastal settlements that had grown up in response to the slave trade, the
only Yoruba settlement was Eko, which became Lagos, the modern
capital of Nigeria. Although Yorubas could be found in Whydah and in
other coastal towns, Yoruba states themselves directed most of their
political and economic activities toward other inland kingdoms such as

those of the Hausa, Nupe, and Ashanti. It was not until the British at the turn of the century established Lagos as the political and economic capital of Nigeria that the Yoruba began to focus on Lagos as their most important commercial center.

The migration in the late nineteenth and early twentieth centuries of millions of Yoruba away from their homelands must be understood in the context of the general population upheavals caused by the overall redirection of economic activities away from many traditional inland West African administrative and commercial centers, toward the coastal cities and towns that became the focus of colonial economic and political activities.

> By the imposition of taxes, the introduction of various goods and services that had to be purchased with European currencies, and the passage of compulsory labor laws, colonial governments virtually and literally forced people to move away from those areas which could not provide them with adequate cash incomes. For most of West Africa, with the exception of Nigeria, the inland areas became virtual labor reserves for the coast. Something of the magnitude of the resultant population shifts is indicated by Samir Amin's (1974) estimate that between 1920 and 1970 there was a net population transfer (including migrants and their offspring) of at least 4.8 million persons from the interior to the coast. This number represented about 21 percent of the coastal population and 26 percent of the inland population of West Africa in 1970 (Sudarkasa, 1977:178–79).

Yoruba towns northward from Ibadan to Ilorin fell outside the "cocoa belt," which was the main area of economic development in inland western Nigeria during the colonial period (Igue, 1983). By the 1920s it was clear that weaving and other traditional crafts which had flourished in this area were doomed to near extinction by the importation of European manufactured goods. For most people, farming in yams, cassava, and other foodstuffs could not provide the monies needed to pay taxes and meet other expenses created by the burgeoning market economy; hence, young people who would normally have stayed in the area had to turn to the new colonial centers as sources of livelihood (Galletti et al., 1956).

Millions of Yorubas resettled in other parts of Nigeria. The main directions of the migration from the "backwater" Yoruba towns were toward other Yoruba cities such as Lagos and Ibadan, but also toward Kano, Kaduna, and Jos in the former Northern Nigeria, and toward Onitsha and Port Harcourt in the former Eastern Nigeria. Additionally, over the first four decades of the twentieth century, millions of Yoruba left Nigeria altogether to "try their luck" in West African cities such as Accra, Kumasi, Lomé, Abidjan, Niamey, Ouagadougou, Freetown, and Dakar. Some Yorubas even migrated to eastern and central Africa, where their descendants can still be found today.

Before World War I, some of the Yoruba migrants went abroad in response to the enticements of labor recruiters, such as those from Ghana (then the Gold Coast) who promised high pay for work in the mines and in roadway construction. When these Yoruba laborers saw the opportunities that existed in the *commercial* sector in Ghana, most of them abandoned the mines and the road gangs. There was still a demand in Ghana for Nigerian textiles, still opportunities to export Ghanaian kola to Nigeria, and a new, emerging niche for middlemen to distribute the imported goods being brought in by European wholesalers. These opportunities led many of the Yoruba migrants to eschew wage employment in favor of independent trade.

Their successes attracted others, and by the middle of the twentieth century the Yoruba were the most ubiquitous group of market traders in West Africa. Whereas Hausas and other trading populations tended to cluster in certain areas or at certain levels of commerce, in virtually every major West African town as well as in some villages in every country, one could find at least a small group of Yoruba traders. My studies in English-speaking West Africa in the late 1960s and early 1970s confirmed the Yoruba presence in Ghana, Sierra Leone, Liberia, and Gambia. Igue (1983) documents their spread throughout French-speaking West Africa from Benin to Senegal.

These Yoruba traders have played an important role in West African economic development throughout this century. They have served as intermediaries between African producers in different countries (as in the case of the Yoruba traffic in Ghanaian-grown kola nuts and Nigerian-manufactured cloth); as traders who bought goods manufactured overseas and sold them in increasingly smaller lots through networks of small shops and markets in urban and rural areas all across West Africa; as brokers who traveled the countryside buying cash crops (such as cocoa) from farmers and bulking them for resale to exporting firms and/or government marketing boards (Hill, 1963); and as craftsmen and -women who "traded with their machines" as tailors, seamstresses, vulcanizers (tire repairmen), pepper grinders, millers, mechanics, and so on, in rural areas as well as in cities and towns. The activities of these Yoruba traders have been responsible for generating incomes, bringing otherwise unavailable goods to consumers in remote areas, providing goods in quantities that consumers could afford to buy, and generally helping to distribute the material goods (such as patent medicines, canned foods, imported hardware and household utensils, textbooks, and school supplies) which to many West Africans are the tangible signs of modernization. The significance of the Yoruba commercial migrants throughout West Africa is illustrated by their economic role in Ghana, the country where they settled in greatest numbers during the first seventy years of this century.

OCCUPATIONS OF YORUBA MIGRANTS IN GHANA

As previously indicated, the earliest firsthand accounts of Yoruba traders in what is now modern Ghana describe their activities at Salaga (M. Johnson, 1966:33, 53, 144). Most of these traders came from Ilorin, the Yoruba town captured by the Fulani early in the nineteenth century. The oldest Yoruba settlements in present-day Ghana, including those in Kumasi and Accra, were founded in the late nineteenth century by Ilorin traders who had entered Ghana via Salaga (Stapleton, 1958; Oyedipe, 1967; Sudarkasa, 1979). After the turn of the century, the size of the Ilorin settlements in Kumasi and Accra was increased by Yoruba veterans who had fought for the British government against the Ashanti in the Yaa Asantewa War of 1900. (An important aspect of the establishment of European colonial rule in West Africa was the drafting or conscription of Africans from the "pacified" areas to fight in colonial wars against other Africans from "belligerent tribes." The military leadership was usually provided by Europeans, but the troops were predominantly or exclusively African.) After the war, many of the veterans (particularly those who had been wounded) remained in Ghana, where they received modest pensions. Married men had their families join them; single men had brides sent to them by their relatives in Nigeria.

Most of the Yoruba males residing in Ghana in the early 1900s (including the ex-soldiers) depended on trade for their livelihood. They continued to export kola to Nigeria and to import textiles (*aso ofi*, a type of heavy cotton cloth woven in Ilorin and other northern Yoruba towns, and *aso adire*, tie-dyed or wax-dyed printed indigo cloth made in Abeokuta and surrounding areas) for sale throughout Ghana. By this time the main West African trade routes had shifted from the interior to the coast, and the ports of Lagos and Sekondi (near Accra) became the main entrepôts for trade between Nigeria and Ghana.

During the 1920s, kola and cloth remained the principal items handled by Yoruba men, but some newcomers entered other growing businesses such as trade in dried fish, imported cloth, imported provisions, and cocoa. Those Yoruba who worked as "cocoa brokers" bought the harvested beans from Ghanaian farmers for resale to European exporting firms and, in later years, to the Ghanaian Marketing Board, which became the agency authorized to export this crop. These Yorubas remained active as middle men in the cocoa trade until 1960 when new Ghanaian laws prohibited foreign Africans from engaging in cocoa trade (Hill, 1970: 54).

Trade in kola declined during the early 1930s, by which time large quantities of the Ghana-variety of kola were being grown in Nigeria, and the Nigerian government moved to restrict imports from abroad. During the same time, trade in Yoruba cloth was dealt a severe blow by the influx into Ghana of cheaper cotton cloths from Britain. (According to men whom I interviewed in Kumasi in 1968–69, the patterns in most of these imported textiles had been deliberately copied from the *adire* designs.) Undaunted, Yoruba traders concentrated on other commodity lines, especially on the fast-growing trade in imported provisions (mainly canned and packaged foods, soaps, household cleansers, and the like) and sundries (small hardware and utensils, patent medicines, cosmetics, and so on). Perhaps also in the 1930s some Yorubas in Ghana began to act as "diamond diggers," even though as Africans they were at that time legally prohibited from mining for diamonds on their own account.

Yoruba women had started migrating to Ghana in large numbers in the 1920s. Before that time, when Yoruba males were mainly engaged in trade that took them back and forth between Nigeria and Ghana, many of them left their wives at home. Yoruba women who resided in Ghana before 1920 were typically wives and relatives of the first wave of traders who had come to Ghana via Salaga or they were wives of veterans of the Yaa Asantewa War. In the 1920s and 1930s, when an increasing number of Yoruba men began to handle commodity lines that kept them more or less permanently based in Ghana, they had their wives and fiancées join them from Nigeria. The tens of thousands of Yoruba women who were in Ghana in 1969, at the time of the expulsion order, had come to Ghana with their husbands; had come to join their husbands, fiancés, or relatives; or had been born in Ghana. As a rule, Yoruba women did not migrate to Ghana on their own (Sudarkasa, 1974; 1975).

The patterns of trade by Yoruba women did not change much over the fifty years of their sojourn in Ghana. According to most accounts, the Yoruba women who first came to Sekondi via ship brought with them baskets of red pepper which they sold in one-penny lots right at the docks or in the markets near their communities. Trade in pepper and other foodstuffs from Nigeria continued to be a favored line of trade for many Yoruba women throughout their stay in Ghana. Other women moved into

TABLE 1 Distribution of Yoruba population in Ghana compared with distribution of total African population in Ghana, 1960

Region	Total African Population	% of Total	Yoruba Population	% of Yoruba Population
Western	1,374,320	20.5	22,900	22.8
Accra C.D.[a]	483,510	7.2	9,260	9.2
Eastern	1,093,460	16.3	24,680	25.5
Volta	777,040	11.6	6,400	6.4
Ashanti	1,106,570	16.5	19,720	19.6
Brong-Ahafo	587,720	8.7	6,150	6.1
Northern	1,288,230	19.2	10,450	10.4
All regions	6,710,850	100.0	100,560	100.0

NOTE: Based on tables 1 and 2, *Special Report "E": Tribes in Ghana, 1960 Population Census of Ghana* (Ghana 1964b).

[a] Although legally a part of the Eastern Region, for Census purposes the area comprising Accra Municipal Council, Tema Development Corporation, and Ga-Dangbe-Shai Local council was considered as a seventh region of Ghana under the name of Accra Capital District. (See *Special Report "E"*, p. xcvii.)

the commodity lines their men had already begun to trade in, including imported provisions and sundries, dried fish, and Nigerian- and European-made cloth.

According to the Ghana Census of 1960 (1964a, 1964b), by that year the Yoruba population had grown to 100,560, which was 1.5 percent of the country's total African population (N = 6,710,850). The Yoruba were distributed (see table 1) throughout Ghana in a pattern that "more closely [resembled] that of the total Ghanaian population than [did the distribution of] any other ethnic group," including groups indigenous to the country (Hill, 1970:54). Moreover, the Yoruba had become a relatively settled group, of whom 39 percent were Ghanaian-born (see table 2). Women and children constituted 46 percent and 43 percent, respectively, of the total Yoruba population (see table 3). In other words, the Yoruba communities in Ghana were centered around sojourned families rather than around single male seasonal migrants, as was the case for the Mossi and some other stranger groups in Ghana (Skinner, 1960, 1965).

Data from the Ghana Census *Special Report "E": Tribes in Ghana* (1964b) show that nearly 84 percent of the gainfully occupied Yorubas (38,110 out of 45,590) were engaged in trade. Male traders (N = 13,360) constituted about 48 percent of the working Yoruba males (N = 28,080),

TABLE 2 Yoruba population born in Ghana and abroad, 1960

Region Born	Males	% of Males	Females	% of Females	Both	% of Both
Ghana	20,360	37.7	18,690	40.1	39,050	38.8
Nigeria	32,990	61.1	27,600	59.3	60,590	61.3
Elsewhere[a]	630	1.2	290	.6	920	.9
Total Born	53,980	100.0	46,580	100.0	100,560	100.0

NOTE: Based on tables 5 and 8, *Special Report "E": Tribes in Ghana, 1960 Population Census of Ghana* (Ghana 1964b).

[a] Ivory Coast, Liberia, Republic of Sudan, Upper Volta, Togo, Dahomey, Niger, and elsewhere in Africa and abroad.

N.B. The figures in this and other tables in this paper do not include the Atakpame, a Yoruba offshoot who were listed as a distinct ethnic group in *Special Report "E"* and whose present-day homelands are in Dahomey and Togo. Tables 5 and 8 in *Special Report "E"* show that of the 8,530 Atakpame in Ghana, 2,820 were born in Togo; 3,140 in Dahomey; 2,130 in Ghana; and 440 elsewhere in Africa.

TABLE 3 Yoruba population in Ghana classified by age and sex, 1960

Age	Males	% of Males	Females	% of Females	Both	% of Both
Under 15	21,980	40.7	21,470	46.1	43,450	43.2
15 and over	32,000	59.3	25,110	53.9	57,110	56.8
All ages	53,980	100.0	46,580	100.0	100,560	100.0

NOTE: Based on table 1, *Special Report "E"* (Ghana 1964b).

N.B. Males (N = 53,980) constituted 53.7 percent and females (N = 46,580) constituted 46.3 percent of the total population. However, there was a slightly different breakdown within the adult population, where males (N = 32,000) comprised 56 percent of the total adult population whereas females (N = 25,110) constituted 44 percent. A number of Yoruba males were married to women from other ethnic groups.

while female traders (N = 15,930) constituted 91 percent of the working Yoruba women (N = 17,510).

Yoruba traders were the largest group of nonindigenous traders in Ghana up to the time of their expulsion in 1969. Yoruba males ranked first among the male trading population in Ghana in 1960 (see table 4), comprising 20 percent of all male traders. Yoruba women ranked fifth among the female trading populations, totaling 6 percent of all the women traders. The fact that, despite their numbers, Yoruba women were a relatively small fraction of the female traders in Ghana only underscores the enormous size of the female trading population in that country, as indeed it is all over West Africa.

Those Yoruba in Ghana in 1960 who were self-employed outside of trade were mainly engaged in various craft and service occupations. According to *Special Report "E,"* 5,660 Yoruba males (approximately 20 percent of the working men) were "craftsmen and production process workers and labourers" (1964:C–43). Of course, not all of these were self-employed, but based on data collected in 1968–69, it is certain that in the specific job categories listed in the census report (for example, tailors, carpenters, weavers, and electricians) Yoruba males would have been primarily working on their own account or as apprentices preparing to work for themselves. Yoruba women who were not engaged in trade were primarily "family workers" who, no doubt, were involved in the operation of enterprises operated by family members.

TABLE 4 Leading trading populations in Ghana, 1960

Males			Females		
Ethnic Group	Number	Percentage	Ethnic Group	Number	Percentage
Yoruba[a]	13,360	20	Ewe[b]	57,490	21
Asante	6,820	10	Fante	44,990	16
Zabrama[a]	5,830	9	Ga	29,700	11
Hausa[a]	5,100	7	Asante	21,600	8
Ewe[b]	4,010	6	Yoruba[a]	15,930	6
Fante	3,510	5	Krobo	10,930	4
Others	29,180	43	Others	97,900	34
Total	67,810	100	Total	278,540	100

NOTE: This table is a condensation of data compiled by Polly Hill from *Special Report "E"*. A comparison of the leading immigrant trading populations with indigenous Ghanaian trading populations comprised two tables in the manuscript of Hill's *Occupations of Migrants in Ghana*. These tables were not included in the published monograph; however, an examination of *Special Report "E"* revealed that the figures were contained in table S–26, "Selected Occupations of Employed Persons," appendix C, pp. C–34 through C–50.

[a] These are non-Ghanaians: the Hausa and Yoruba are mainly from Nigeria and the Zabrama from Mali.

[b] According to table 5, *Special Report "E"*, just under 12 percent (N = 103,110) of the Ewes in Ghana (N = 876,230) were born abroad (mainly in Togo).

Only one-fourth of the Yoruba males working in Ghana in 1960 were employed as wage earners. The number of female wage earners (less than 500) was inconsequential. Over seventy-five percent of the Yoruba male wage earners worked for traders in the private sector as laborers, sales clerks, or bookkeepers; or they worked in agriculture as overseers. Those employed in the public sector were mainly messengers or laborers, but a small number were employed as teachers, hospital technicians, office clerks, typists, bookkeepers, managers, and higher-level civil servants.

From the foregoing, it is evident that the role of Yoruba migrants in Ghana remained essentially that of purveyors of goods and services throughout their stay in that country. Their success in commerce, like that of other important stranger-merchants in Africa and elsewhere in the world, depended on the strength of their kin and ethnic networks, which created economic opportunities while providing social support (Fallers, 1967; Cohen, 1971; Shack and Skinner, 1979).

THE ORGANIZATION OF YORUBA TRADE IN GHANA

Following twelve months of fieldwork in Ghana in 1968–69, I can compose a picture of the patterns of Yoruba trade in the period immediately preceding the Ghanaian government's expulsion of all illegal aliens from that country. By this time, the Yoruba population numbered probably close to 150,000 persons (Sudarkasa, 1974:95–98).

A list of specific commodities in which the Yoruba traded would comprise many pages; however, it is possible to provide a sense of the range of the items handled by listing a few of the major groupings encountered: (1) imported provisions (packaged and canned foods such as sugar, milk, tomato paste, margarine, sardines, Ovaltine, tea, etc.; soaps and detergents; cigarettes, matches, etc.); (2) imported sundries (flashlights, batteries, cutlery, stationery, school supplies, sunglasses, patent medicines such as aspirin and mentholated balms, toothpaste and other toiletries, cosmetics, etc.); (3) hardware and spare parts for bicycles, automobiles, etc.; (4) enamel pans, bowls, buckets, and other household items; (5) underwear, T-shirts, handkerchiefs, and children's ready-to-wear items, watches, etc.; (6) factory-made and/or handmade shoes and sandals; (7) fresh meat and fowl; (8) dried meat and fish; (9) garden vegetables such as okra, tomatoes, onions, and varieties of fresh red peppers; (10) herbs, spices, and medicinals (many of which were imported from Nigeria); (11) cloth of various types, including imported and locally made varieties; (12) bread and pastries; and (13) locally cooked foods, prepared and sold in the markets or at roadsides.

It was a rare commodity that was available in Ghana but could not be purchased from a Yoruba trader. In fact, Ghanaians had a saying that "if you want to buy anything at all, look for a Nigerian trader." (In everyday parlance, the term *Nigerian* was used to mean a Yoruba; Hausas and Ibos ["Biafrans"], the other two relatively large group of Nigerians in Ghana, were referred to by their ethnic labels.) Nevertheless, Yorubas and other strangers were almost totally excluded from *wholesale* trade in the major agricultural staples (especially yams and plantains). Apparently the market associations controlling wholesale trade in these foodstuffs did not permit non-Ghanaians to join their ranks. However, women from the stranger populations did buy from Ghanaian women for resale in smaller quantities.

Furthermore, imported textiles destined mainly for Ghanaian customers were usually handled in the markets by Ghanaians. (In shops such cloth was also sold by Middle Easterners and Europeans.) In fact, it appears that the textile market in Ghana was moving toward ethnic-specificity as regards to buyers and sellers. Yorubas handled cloth preferred by Yorubas; Ibos and Nigerians from what was then the "Midwest Region" handled cloth imported through Nigeria for their own ethnic groups; Ashantis and other Ghanaians handled goods preferred by their respective ethnic groups or by Ghanaians from their own regions. In 1969 *aso ofi* was still being imported from Nigeria for use by Yorubas on ceremonial occasions; *adire* was being made in Ghana by Yoruba women and sold mainly for decorative shirts *(dashikis)* made by local tailors for young people and tourists.

In the city of Kumasi, Yoruba traders could be found in all the markets as well as in shops and stalls throughout the town. The most successful of the general merchants had a row of shops along Princess Street in the heart of Kumasi's business district. In 1968 in the Central Market (which had the greatest concentration of traders from all ethnic groups) Yoruba traders, numbering 1,732, occupied approximately 23 percent of the 8,000 market stalls. They were the legal tenants of a smaller fraction (17 percent) of the stalls in the market because many of the stalls which they occupied were sublet from Ghanaians (Sudarkasa, 1975).

The most mobile group of Yoruba traders were the young men who hawked ballpoint pens, razor blades, sunglasses, and other small items in front of the post office, in the lorry parks, and wherever likely customers congregated. Young women hawking cigarettes, matches, kola nuts, peppermints, and the like usually plied the areas in front of supermarkets, in lorry parks, and near the city's various recreational clubs.

Yoruba men and women involved in craft and service occupations generally clustered together in specific areas. Mechanics (and the traders who sold automobile spare parts) could be found in the section of town where most of the African-owned vehicle repair businesses were located. Yoruba vulcanizers were located in the Zongo (specifically the Muslim stranger quarter) near the lorry park. Weavers, *adire* dyers, goldsmiths, barbers, tailors, roadside cooks, and other craft and service workers were mainly found in one of the Yoruba neighborhoods in Kumasi.

Although most Yoruba traders in Kumasi were small-scale operators whose capital ranged from a few cedis to a few hundred, there were some males in the community who owned fairly large general stores that stocked either provisions or the wide variety of goods termed "sundries" *(worobo)*. The capital of these general merchants ranged in the thousands of cedis. (In 1968 N₵1.00 was officially valued at US $.98; the unofficial value was considerably less.)

In an interview with the Kumasi sales manager for Lever Brothers (the corporation that owned the Kingsway stores and many other companies in West Africa), I was told that the company supplied fifty Yoruba wholesale-provisions sellers whose stock ranged in value from N₵6,000 to N₵16,000. Only one of the Yoruba customers had a stock worth about N₵20,000. A few of the general merchants who sold sundries had two shops, with combined stock valued in the neighborhood of N₵400,000. Probably most of the wealthy Yoruba merchants had a monthly turnover of a few thousand cedis. In an interview with one of the bank managers in Kumasi, it was revealed that the largest Yoruba account in the bank was for a man who turned over about N₵50,000 per month. The manager went on to say that "if a man makes N₵200 or N₵300 net profit per month on N₵50,000 turnover, then he would consider himself to be doing very well." Indeed, this would have been a very high income in a country where the average per capita income per annum was then N₵200. (University faculty salaries ranged from about N₵2000 to N₵6000 per annum.)

From the information available to the author, including data from the life histories of 217 male and female traders, not more than twenty Yoruba merchants in Kumasi had a net income of over N₵150 per month. Probably the traders who were considered "very successful" by other members of the Yoruba community actually had net incomes of well under N₵100 per month. The vast majority of Yoruba traders, of whom there were thousands, had incomes equivalent to those of low-paid laborers. They earned from about ten cedis (or less) to about thirty cedis per month.

Yoruba general merchants in Kumasi occupied a position in the distribution chain just below that of the Syrians, Lebanese, and Indians. According to the bank manager quoted above, "Syrian" (the general term used for Middle Easterners even though most of them were Lebanese) merchants usually had monthly turnovers of about N₵100,000 to N₵150,000. Many Yoruba traders, including those who owned the "large" stores, were supplied by "Syrian" and Indian merchants as well as by European and Ghanaian firms. Although the Nkrumah government had placed restrictions on the issuance of import licenses to expatriate traders in the early 1960s, there were still a number of Levantine (Syrian and Lebanese) importers in Kumasi in 1968–69 (Garlick, 1971).

Yoruba general merchants and other African middlemen never had an opportunity to compete on an equal footing with the Middle Easterners. During the colonial period, European firms accepted and promoted the Levantine merchants as intermediaries between themselves and the African traders. Institutional backing in the form of credit was given to the Middle Easterners while it was withheld from Africans. Even in post-Independence Ghana, Yorubas and other African merchants found it difficult, if not impossible, to obtain bank loans to expand their businesses. In fact, before some Middle Easterners started to leave Ghana in the early 1960s, Yorubas (and other Africans, including Ghanaians) in Kumasi had found it difficult to rent shops in the most favorable business locations because the Middle Easterners had gained control over most of the rental property in those areas.

The Yoruba general merchants in Kumasi in 1968 were the wholesale suppliers of most of the Yoruba retail traders in the city. They also supplied Yoruba retailers (and some wholesalers) from nearby towns and villages and from Ghana's Northern Region. It is worth remembering, in this connection, that the distinction between "wholesaler" and "retailer" is not exact in West African trade operations. The wholesaler often turns retailer whenever there is an opportunity to sell in small quantities, and the retailer will sell "wholesale"—that is, at an appreciable discount—whenever there is a customer willing to buy in bulk (Bauer, 1954).

Kumasi served as one of the two main supply centers (Accra being the other) that linked most Yoruba traders in Ghana with a distribution network that stretched to the remotest Ghanaian village. Yoruba traders who sold provisions, sundries, cloth, spare parts, and various other commodities in the outlying towns and villages made periodic trips to Kumasi or Accra to purchase their goods from other Yoruba merchants. Of course, in towns such as Tamale or Koforidua there were some Yorubas who bought directly from importing firms or, as in the case of textile dealers, who traveled to Nigeria to bring goods back to Ghana. In such cases, these traders, like their counterparts in Accra or Kumasi, served as suppliers for Yorubas who traded on a lesser scale.

As implied in the above statements, the trade networks established by Yorubas in Ghana were for the most part ethnically homogeneous, from the level of the urban-based Yoruba wholesaler, to that of the small Yoruba retailer in the remote villages. Generally, the Yoruba retail traders interviewed in Ghana said that whenever possible they preferred to buy from another Yoruba trader because of their common language and their understanding of each other's ways of bargaining and of generally doing business. A shared language was especially important because many of the Yorubas in Ghana who were over thirty years old were not sufficiently fluent in English to carry out transactions with Levantine or Indian merchants or with the European firms. These latter usually had Ghanaian representatives or salesmen who spoke English and Twi (and perhaps another Ghanaian language) but who did not speak Yoruba. Many older Yorubas had almost as much difficulty conducting extended transactions in Twi as in English. They were only able to quote prices and carry on relatively simple bargaining in the Ashanti language (commonly known as Twi).

Another reason the small-scale retailer preferred to buy from Yoruba wholesalers was that he or she might be able to buy on credit from those merchants, whereas it was usually impossible to do so when buying from Europeans, Ghanaians, Syrians, or Indians. (Of course, the large expatriate trading firms and the Ghana National Trading Corporation did extend credit to the "large-scale" Yoruba merchants whom they knew well.) Yoruba merchants could set up credit relationships with their compatriots (even with some of those who lived in places outside Kumasi) because their sociopolitical networks in Ghana (particularly the networks of kinsmen and town unions or *Parapos*) made it possible to locate, and put pressure on, delinquent debtors.

By and large, Yoruba market traders and general merchants operated as sole proprietors rather than as small companies or corporations. The businesses were usually owned, directed, and managed by one person. In fact, one of the Yoruba merchants who owned two stores in Kumasi complained that Yoruba businesses could not grow as much or as fast as they should because the store owners could not usually find trustworthy managers. Most Yorubas who wanted to go into commerce at all preferred to have their own businesses rather than work (even as managers) for others.

As a consequence of this type of business organization, the life of an enterprise was usually tied to the life history of a given person. When a businessman moved from one part of the country to another, he did not usually maintain a business in the place he had left unless one of his children or wives personally supervised that business. Even then, he might eventually choose to sell his "satellite" business and concentrate on one that he could personally oversee. When he died, his business was usually sold and the proceeds divided among his heirs. When a man left Ghana to return to Nigeria to live, he would usually sell his business because he did not intend to return to Ghana. Yorubas in Ghana did not normally have either the capital or the business organization to risk maintaining an enterprise in a country when they had no intention of returning there. Once a business was acquired by a new owner, that person needed to build up his own supply-distribution network; consequently, many reasonably successful operations became stagnant overnight.

Most Yoruba traders (women as well as men) had at least one person (though seldom the same person) working with or for them throughout most of their lives. Usually each trader would have, in addition to one of his or her own children, a young ward (normally the child of a relative) living and working with him or her. As indicated in a study of Yoruba traders in Nigeria (Sudarkasa, 1973), a structural correlate of the extensive involvement of women in trade is the Yoruba practice of dispersing their children among relatives. This practice frees mothers who are too busy or too poor to care for all their children and at the same time provides the guardians with reliable helpers in their work (Sudarkasa, 1973). For childless women or those whose children have grown up or gone to live with other relatives, the wards provide the much-appreciated presence of a child in the house.

Young relatives who assisted traders with their work were not usually given a salary but were provided with food, clothing, shelter, and some type of education. It was also expected, first, that when the time came for a dependent to get married, his or her guardian would pay most of the expenses associated with the wedding festivities and, second, that at the appropriate time the guardian would either provide the dependent with some money to begin a trade or finance a training course or apprenticeship that would eventually provide an independent living.

The failure of some guardians to live up to their responsibilities for young relatives who had worked for them for many years is one of the main causes of dissension within families. A number of males told me of having been disappointed at the time when they wanted to start trading on their own, by guardians who claimed that they had no money to put up as trading capital. It seemed that one reason the young males did not want to commit themselves to working as managers for relatives with fairly prosperous businesses was that they might never be fairly compensated by the older males and ultimately might find themselves without work and without sufficient trading capital to start work on their own. Hence, the young male store assistants tended to save as much as they could in as short a time as possible, in order to start out on their own.

Only a few Yoruba males spent their entire lives working in one occupation. (Many more females than males tended to pursue one occupation throughout their adult lives, but some female traders did report switching commodity lines after going bankrupt.) Most of the 185 males whose life histories I collected during my fieldwork in Kumasi reported that they had changed their line of work more than twice in their careers. Those who had been traders throughout their adult lives had usually switched commodity lines more than once in their lives; those who had learned a craft, such as tailoring or weaving, had often switched to another craft or skilled occupation, such as auto mechanics or tire repairing. What this indicates is that Yorubas were very responsive to the markets to which they geared their goods and services. Having to make their living by their wits, they would try one line of trade or one craft after another until they found a means of self-employment that could provide a livelihood. Although the majority of them were not nearly as well off as they were reputed to be, they were extremely hard working, and very few of the able-bodied among them did not find some means of earning a cash income (Sudarkasa, 1975).

Yoruba traders sought to take advantage of every opportunity that emerged in the world of the market. Whenever they perceived a consumer preference for a commodity, they sought to meet the demand. They also created new demands by introducing new commodities into the different localities where they traded. Reference has already been made to their early trade in dry fish. They were the first vendors to peddle this item in the interior villages of Ghana. Reportedly, the first Nigeria-to-Ghana lorry service was started by Yorubas. Persons interviewed in Kumasi recalled that the first pepper-grinding machines in the Central Market were introduced by Yorubas, and that the first vulcanizers in Kumasi were Yorubas who had acquired the skill in Nigeria. The first embroidered cotton *(joromi)* shirts were made by Yoruba tailors who brought the style from Nigeria. Some of the first African exporters of scrap metal from Ghana to England during World War II were Yorubas who answered advertisements sent out by overseas companies.

No distance was apparently too great for Yoruba traders to cross in their efforts to make a living in commerce; the long journeys they undertook to procure dried fish from Mopti on the River Niger in Mali is a case in point. When Ghanaian import restrictions limited the supply of various goods from Europe in the 1960s, Yorubas traveled to Nigeria, Ivory Coast, Upper Volta, Sierra Leone, and elsewhere to indirectly import European-made goods that were still in great demand in Ghana. The importation and sale of these "smuggled" goods was widely known and, apparently, widely sanctioned as the only alternative to a situation of widespread scarcity. The resourcefulness of the Yoruba traders who sold imported goods was proclaimed throughout Ghana until the failing economy of the late 1960s led the country to use the foreign traders as a scapegoat for the country's economic woes.

In November 1969, the Ghanaian government issued an Order aimed at ridding the country of African aliens who were perceived as occupying jobs that legitimately belonged to Ghanaians (Piel, 1971; Sudarkasa, 1975, 1979). According to newspaper accounts, the main intent of the Compliance Order, which called for the deportation of aliens without valid residence permits, was to end "foreign domination of [Ghanaian] commercial activity" (Oppong-Agyare, 1969).

> The anti-alien sentiment in the country was at such a pitch that shops and market stalls were looted, many people . . . physically assaulted, and lives . . . threatened. By all accounts, the prime targets among the foreigners thought to "dominate" retail market trade were the Nigerians, in particular the southern Nigerians, of whom the Yoruba were the most numerous, the most widely dispersed throughout Ghana, and the most easily identified because of their mode of dress and, in many cases, because of their facial "tribal marks." Moreover, they were easy targets in many cities and towns because of their . . . concentration in specific residential areas and in specific areas within the major daily markets. (Sudarkasa, 1979:142)

Estimates of the number of African aliens expelled from Ghana in 1969 range from 500,000 to 1,000,000. Probably about 150,000 of approximately 225,000 Nigerians who fled the country were Yorubas (Sudarkasa, 1974:94–98). The vast majority of the Yorubas who left Ghana returned to Nigeria, but some subsequently migrated to Togo and to the Ivory Coast.

In decrying the "dominance" of Ghanaian trade by Yoruba traders, most Ghanaians mistakenly equated visibility and numbers with economic exploitation. Yoruba traders did fill many of the niches within the distributive sector, but most of these traders were small-scale operators whose role in the economy was virtually that of self-employed laborers for the large importing companies. Except for a small number of well-to-do merchants, Yoruba traders made a very modest livelihood from their commercial activities. In a sector where the opportunity costs were very high, Yoruba traders created jobs for themselves and Ghanaians by the income they generated and spent in Ghana (*West Africa Magazine*, 1969:2). Operating without access to credit facilities, they assumed most of the risks involved in supplying goods to the Ghanaian consumers, and had to generate capital through their own kin networks or self-help associations whenever they sustained substantial losses in the course of their trade (Sudarkasa, 1974, 1975).

That the expulsion of Yoruba and other West African traders and migrant laborers was not a panacea for economic recovery soon became painfully obvious in Ghana as the economic and political situation worsened during the 1970s. In the wake of the Yoruba exodus, those Ghanaians who aspired to "take over the markets" began to appreciate the difficulties that the strangers had had to overcome in order to build reliable and (marginally) profitable trading networks.

INTEGRATIVE ROLE OF YORUBA TRADERS THROUGHOUT WEST AFRICA

The pattern of Yoruba emigration illustrated by the Ghanaian case was repeated on a smaller scale in other countries of West Africa. The Yoruba who immigrated from Nigeria over the first fifty years of the twentieth century spread from Dahomey (now Benin) to Senegal. Ghana (then Gold Coast) was the main port of call because it was a British colony to which Nigerians could go freely as "British subjects" (Sudarkasa, 1979). Ghana also happened to be one of the most prosperous of all the British colonies in Africa. Nevertheless, there were opportunities in other countries, especially the Francophone countries of Ivory Coast and Niger, and Yoruba enclaves quickly developed throughout the West Africa region (Igue, 1983).

This twentieth-century Yoruba migration from Nigeria to Francophone West Africa must be distinguished from the ancient population movements which led to the establishment of Yoruba kingdoms in areas now included in the north of Benin and Togo, thought to have taken place sometime between the tenth and fourteenth centuries. These ancient Yoruba populations are part of the indigenous peoples of Benin and Togo, and although their presence no doubt attracted the later Yoruba-speaking migrants, the communities of twentieth-century migrants are distinct from the older ones. The situation in Togo is also complicated by the fact that in the 1880s a number of "Brazilian" Yorubas who had repatriated themselves to Dahomey moved to Lome, the Togolese capitol. These Yorubas, like those who settled in the northern part of Togo, became Togolese citizens, quite distinct from the migrants who came in the twentieth century (Igue, 1983).

According to Igue, the modern Yoruba migration to French-speaking West Africa dates from the first decade of the twentieth century. Between 1900 and 1925, Yoruba settlements were formed in Atakpame,

Palime, and Badou in Togo; Abidjan in Ivory Coast; Niamey in Niger; Ouagadougou in Upper Volta; and Dakar in Senegal. Reliable demographic data on these Yoruba populations are not available. However, on the basis of membership lists kept by the Parapos (Yoruba/town unions) formed in each major city where Yoruba migrants reside, Igue (1983) estimates that there are about 45,000 adult Yoruba migrants in Ivory Coast, Upper Volta, Mali, Niger, Senegal, and Togo. It is virtually impossible to estimate the size of the Yoruba population in Benin because of the ease of movement back and forth between Nigeria and that country and because of the large indigenous Yoruba population there. Roughly one-third of the Yoruba migrants in Francophone West Africa (outside Benin) live in the Ivory Coast, and slightly more than another one-third live in Niger.

The importance of the Yoruba in West African development is understood when one not only looks at their role in commerce in the countries where they live, but when one considers the vital role they play in integrating trade throughout the entire West African region. Since the 1960s, when they moved goods between Nigeria, Ivory Coast, Togo, and Ghana, they have been mainly responsible for the transnational distribution of certain consumer goods manufactured in the West Africa region. For example, plastic dishes, containers, and sandals manufactured in Nigeria and Ivory Coast are distributed throughout West Africa by Yoruba traders, who purchase their wares in the countries of origin or from Yoruba wholesalers in the countries where the commercial migrants are based (Igue, 1983). Radios, portable tape players, records and musical tapes, textiles, ready-to-wear clothing, and other consumer goods are regularly moved from one country to another by Yoruba traders. And, whereas they are not the only ethnic group involved in such international activities, they are certainly one of the most active.

The important role played by the Yoruba in currency transfer within the region is often overlooked or undermined because the transfers take place within the "black market." In fact, in a region where only Liberia (which uses U.S. dollars) and countries in the franc zone (CFA) have convertible currencies, sustained international trade within the region would be virtually impossible without this "parallel currency market" (Igue, 1983). By placing themselves in the markets and at the frontiers where currency transfer is mandatory if business is to take place, the Yoruba "money changers" provide a service that is utilized by all West Africans, including persons from the governmental agencies that decry this practice. In fact, many people prefer to use these "parallel banks" because of their accessibility, the fair rates of exchange, and the reliability of those involved in the trade.

Another important role played by Yoruba migrants has also been noted with reference to those in Ghana—namely, the role of distributing products from the urban areas into the rural villages and hamlets. One might expect that such commercial activities would be carried on by indigenous peddlers, but, remarkably, it is the Yoruba immigrant who fulfills this role in many rural areas in West Africa. In the beginning, with only a minimum acquaintance with the local language, Yoruba traders set out to sell in periodic rural markets or to hawk their wares throughout the farmlands. Normally, the women and younger family members are primarily engaged in these activities. Yorubas say they quickly gain a working knowledge of the language(s) of the areas where they work, and, indeed, when I was in Ghana, I found that most Yorubas under fifty years of age spoke between three and six languages regularly and fluently.

As a result of their trade activities, Yoruba migrants are virtual market researchers for the wholesalers whose goods they distribute. Some become experts on comparative ethnic consumption patterns, and as such know which goods should be promoted in different areas. Of course, these traders are also the harbingers of innovations and themselves influence trends and tastes by their choices of wares. Thus, they facilitate the transfer of styles and preferences across ethnic and national lines. This has happened, for example, through the introduction of different styles of recorded popular music and types of textiles from one country to another. Thus, these migrants are often at the forefront of popular cultural change and/or diffusion through their trade activities.

CONCLUSION

The Yoruba are not the only commercial migrants in West Africa. The Djoula, Hausa, and Ibo are also widely dispersed groups whose members are involved in trans-West African trade. The importance of the activities of any one of these groups is enhanced by the fact that all of their interlinking trade networks help West Africa toward its goal of becoming an integrated economic region.

Although studies of some of these migrant trader enclaves have been undertaken in recent years, certainly additional studies which directly explore the role of these traders in regional integration and development would be of enormous value to governmental efforts to consolidate the Economic Community of West African States (ECOWAS). Not only are these migrants a valuable source of market information, but they are also living testaments to the fact that ethnic and national differences are not insurmountable barriers to long-term economic cooperation and integration.

Despite the waves of xenophobia which seem to accompany serious downturns in the economies of West African countries—the most recent example being the Nigerian government's expulsion of over two million Ghanaians and other Africans in 1983 and another 700,000 Ghanaians in 1985—significant numbers of Yoruba and other commercial migrants have remained abroad in West Africa. These populations, more than labor migrants, tend to be long-term residents of their adopted countries, and have evolved lifestyles incorporating many elements that "belong to" or are "derived from" the cultures of the peoples among whom they live. In most cases, the migrants are in close proximity to other strangers as well as to citizens of the host country, and their lifestyles also reflect the influence of these stranger groups.

Because of the influence of the formal institutions (especially schools) in the host society, and because of the dominance (and associated prestige) of the host culture, the offspring of commercial migrants often develop behavioral characteristics that mark them as children of two (or more) worlds. When they return to their countries of origin, they often become agents through whom the foreign culture is apprehended and comprehended. Upon their return to Nigeria, for example, the "Made-in-Ghana" Yoruba were admired as much as they were chided for their foreign accents and their different ways of doing things (Oyedipe, 1967). Such migrant groups can provide an understanding of critical thresholds of different West African cultures, and of the mechanisms of boundary maintenance and dissolution between cultures and communities in the region. By studying the social as well as the economic activities of the migrant traders, insight can be gained into the ways in which they have served as cultural transmitters, translators, and transformers through whom intergroup communication has taken place in the past and can be facilitated in the future.

REFERENCES

Adepoju, Aderanti. 1979. "Migration and Socio-economic Development in Africa." *International Social Science Journal* 31, no. 2:207–25.

Akinjogbin, I.A., and G.O. Ekemode, eds. 1976. *The Proceedings of the Conference on Yoruba Civilization.* 2 vols. Ile-Ife: University of Ife Press.

Amin, Samir, ed. 1974. *Modern Migrations in West Africa.* Oxford: Oxford University Press.

Arhin, Kwame. 1971. "Atebubu Markets: ca. 1884–1930." In C. Meillassoux (ed.), *The*

Development of Indigenous Trade and Markets in West Africa. Oxford: Oxford University Press.

———. 1979. *West African Traders in Ghana in the Nineteenth and Twentieth Centuries.* London, New York: Longman.

Bascom, William R. 1955. "Urbanization Among the Yoruba." *American Journal of Sociology* 60, 5:446–54.

Bauer, Peter, T. 1954. *West African Trade.* Cambridge: Cambridge University Press.

Charbonneau, J., and R. Charbonneau. 1962. *Marches et marchands d'Afrique noire.* Paris: Ed. la Colombe.

Cohen, Abner. 1969. *Custom and Politics in Urban Africa: A Study of Hausa Migrants in Yoruba Towns.* London: Routledge and Kegan Paul.

———. 1971. "Cultural Strategies in the Organization of Trading Diasporas." In C. Meillassoux (ed.), *The Development of Indigenous Trade and Markets in West Africa.* Oxford: Oxford University Press.

Coleman, James S. 1963. *Nigeria: Background to Nationalism.* Los Angeles: University of California Press.

Eades, Jeremy S. 1979. "Minorities and Entrepreneurship: Yoruba Enterprise and Community in Northern Ghana." In William Shack and E.P. Skinner (eds.), *Strangers in African Societies.* Berkeley and Los Angeles: University of California Press.

———. 1980. *The Yoruba Today.* Cambridge and New York: Cambridge University Press.

Fallers, L.A., ed. 1967. *Immigrants and Associations.* The Hague: Mouton for the Society for the Comparative Study of Society and History.

Galletti, R., K. D. S. Baldwin, and I. O. Dina. 1956. *Nigerian Cocoa Farmers.* Oxford: Oxford University Press for the Nigerian Cocoa Marketing Board.

Garlick, P.C. 1971. *African Traders and Economic Development in Ghana.* Oxford: Clarendon Press.

Ghana. 1964a. 1960 Population Census: *Special Report "A": Statistics of Towns.* Accra: Census Office.

———. 1964b. 1960 Population Census: *Special Report "E": Tribes in Ghana.* By B. Gil, A.F. Aryee, and D.K. Ghansah. Accra: Census Office.

Gugler, Josef, and W.G. Flanagan. 1978. *Urbanization and Social Change in West Africa.* Cambridge: Cambridge University Press.

Hill, Polly. 1963. *The Migrant Cocoa Farmers of Southern Ghana.* Cambridge: Cambridge University Press.

———. 1970. *The Occupations of Migrants in Ghana.* Anthropological Papers no. 42. Ann Arbor: Museum of Anthropology, University of Michigan.

Igue, John O. 1983. "Migration et Integration Regionale: Les Yoruba en Afrique de l'Quest Francophone," Draft monograph. Ann Arbor: Center for Afroamerican and African Studies, University of Michigan (December).

Igue, John O., and O.B. Yai. 1973. "The Yoruba Speaking People of Dahomey and Togo." *Yoruba, A Journal of Yoruba Studies* 1, no. 1:5–29.

Johnson, M. 1966. *Salaga Papers.* Vol. 1. Legon: Institute of African Studies, University of Ghana.

Johnson, Samuel. 1921. *The History of the Yorubas.* Edited by O. Johnson. Lagos: CMS (Nigeria) Bookshops.

Lloyd, Peter. 1953. "Craft Organizations in Yoruba Towns." *Africa* 23, no. 1:30–44.

Mabogunje, Akin. 1962. *Yoruba Towns.* Ibadan: Ibadan University Press.

———. 1968. *Urbanization in Nigeria.* London: University of London Press.

———. 1972. *Regional Mobility and Resource Development in West Africa.* Keith Callard Lectures. Montreal: McGill-Queen's University Press.

Meillassoux, Claude, ed. 1971. *The Development of Indigenous Trade and Markets in West Africa*. Oxford: Oxford University Press.

Oppong-Agyare, J. 1969. "Test Case of Credibility." *The Pioneer*, November 28.

Oyedipe, F.P.A. 1967. *Some Sociological Aspects of the Yoruba Family in Accra*. Masters thesis. Legon: Institute of African Studies, University of Ghana.

Piel, Margaret. 1971. "The Expulsion of West African Aliens." *Journal of Modern African Studies* 9:205–29.

Riddell, J. Barry. 1978. "The Migration to the Cities in West Africa: Some Policy Considerations." *Journal of Modern African Studies* 16, no. 2:241–60.

Rouch, Jean. 1956. "Migrations au Ghana." *Journal de Société des Africaines* 26, no. 9:fasc. i–ii.

———. 1961. "Second Generation Migrants in Ghana and the Ivory Coast." In Aidan Southall (ed.), *Social Change in Modern Africa*. Oxford: Oxford University Press.

Schildkrout, Enid. 1970. "Government and Chiefs in Kumasi Zongo." In Michael Crowder and Obaro Ikime (eds.), *West African Chiefs*. Ile-Ife: University of Ife Press.

———. 1978. *People of the Zongo: The Transformation of Ethnic Identities in Ghana*. Cambridge and New York: Cambridge University Press.

Shack, William, and Elliott P. Skinner, eds. 1979. *Strangers in African Societies*. Berkeley and Los Angeles: University of California Press.

Skinner, Elliott P. 1960. "Labour Migration and Its Relationship to Socio-Cultural Change in Mossi Society." *Africa* 40, no. 4.

———. 1965. "Labour Migration Among the Mossi of the Upper Volta." In Hilda Kuper (ed.), *Urbanization and Migration in West Africa*. Berkeley and Los Angeles: University of California Press.

Stapleton, G.B. 1958. Pp. 159–63 in "Nigerians in Ghana, with Special Reference to the Yoruba." *NISER Conference Proceedings*. Ibadan: University of Ibadan.

Sudarkasa, Niara. 1973. *Where Women Work: A Study of Yoruba Women in the Marketplace and in the Home*. Anthropological Papers no. 53. Ann Arbor: Museum of Anthropology, University of Michigan.

———. 1974. "Commercial Migration in West Africa, with Special Reference to the Yoruba in Ghana." *African Urban Notes*. News Series 1 (Winter 1974–75): 61–103. East Lansing: African Studies Center, Michigan State University.

———. 1975. "The Economic Status of the Yoruba in Ghana Before 1970." *Nigerian Journal of Economic and Social Studies* 17, no. 1: 93–125.

———. 1977. "Women and Migration in Contemporary West Africa." In Wellesley Editorial Committee (ed.), *Women and National Development*. Chicago: University of Chicago Press. Also *Signs* 3, no. 1:178–89.

———. 1979. "From Stranger to Alien: The Socio-Political History of the Nigerian Yoruba in Ghana, 1900–1970." In William Shack and Elliott P. Skinner (eds.), *Strangers in African Societies*. Berkeley and Los Angeles: University of California Press.

Ukwu, U.I. 1969. "Markets in Iboland." In B.W. Hodder and U.I. Ukwu (eds.), *Markets in West Africa*. Ibadan: University of Ibadan Press.

West Africa Magazine. 1969. December 20:2.

Zachariah, K.C., and Julien Conde. 1981. *Migration in West Africa: Demographic Aspects*. Oxford: Oxford University Press for The World Bank.

4

VILLAGE-LEVEL RESTRAINTS ON THE EXODUS FROM RURAL MALI

John Van D. Lewis

The aggregate flow of migrant labor from the agricultural savanna of the West African Sahel to wage employment along the West African Coast has received much attention from planners (Zachariah and Conde, 1981), politicians, and social scientists (Amin, 1974; Harris, 1978). The policies developed by village-level authorities to confront this phenomenon in the migrants' home, the Sahelian communities, have received less attention. A closer look at the conceptualization and implementation of these policies reveals some interesting and important features of the operation of village-level government in the contemporary Sahel. A better understanding of these features should help Sahelian planners to deal more effectively with the drain of emigrant labor from their countries by using the relevant village-level structures to assist in re-employment at home.

Too often, however, it is assumed that "traditional" village-level institutions are falling by the wayside in the modernization process, or, if not yet disintegrating, then they are unduly retarding that process. It will be shown there how some of these so-called traditional institutions are, in fact, mitigating some of the most disruptive and costly of contemporary changes: those associated with migration. Moreover, it is not one village-level institution but rather a balance among such institutions that needs exploration.

This chapter analyzes the case of a village in rural Segu, Central Mali.[1] There, as in most Mandenkan-speaking villages throughout Mali, some of the elders' authority over the juniors is deflected into age-set institutions that assert peer group pressure over the male youths to fulfill their farming responsibilities at home. The authority of the elder males is reinforced by their senior position in a patrilineage (Meillassoux, 1975). However, when their younger brothers and sons organize themselves by age into small clubs of contemporaries, or age sets, that cut across the genealogically vertical lines of the lineage with horizontal linkages that do not respect the chain-like lineage boundaries, then the elders are restrained from imposing their absolute will on these juniors. This transformation of the gerontocratic authority of the elders into a viable age-set system, giving the juniors a ramifying organization of their own, has resulted from a long history of outside threats to village economic and social security, not the least of which is the contemporary demand for the wage labor of village youths (Lewis, 1979).

Paradoxically, these age-set associations attain their greatest vitality in those villages where the gerontocratic authority of the elders is greatest. That authority appears to become more legitimate because of the contradictory relationship between the gerontocratic hierarchy and the egalitarian age sets of the youths. A sufficient balance of tension between them serves to mediate the disruptive influence of outside market pressures. This mediation would be less successful if each was left to deal with outside economic demands on its own.

In other villages, the authority of the elders can be weaker where economic inequalities have become manifest among them. Without a countervening reciprocal grouping based on age, it is more difficult for any elder to use age as opposed to economic influence as a basis of authority. Inevitable in such villages, inequalities also appear in the younger generations, frustrating the development of egalitarian, age-mate relations among them. In these situations the elders heading patrilineages have difficulty retaining control over the labor of their lineage juniors. Often they have had to activate or set-up family structures in those employment areas frequented by the out-migrating youths in order to retain any control over them. However, this effort further serves to fragment the home village. This second sort of village is in the minority precisely because such villages do not last (Lewis, 1978).

In the majority of villages in the district (circle) of Segu, including the one examined here, the leaders have been able to retain a much stronger hold on the young laborers. First, reciprocal relations between the elders make it more difficult for any one youth to break with any one elder in order to migrate out, however temporarily. Therefore, out migration from these villages is less frequent. Because equalitarian age-set institutions have developed as an echo of the reciprocal relations between the elders, however, migrants usually have age-mates to look out for them in the foreign employment situation. Youths from the same home age set are apt to undertake temporary wage employment together. This experience unites them not only to face the uncertainties of wage-labor employment in the Ivory Coast but also to bear the hostility of the elders upon their return home.

This "buddy system" obviates the necessity of any other family members having to leave the village with the migrants. Furthermore, it enables the migrants to maintain links with the village without having to establish a domestic unit where they are. Hence, a separate domestic unit does not develop into a countervening pull, making a return to the village more difficult. Meanwhile, the age-set organizations back home provide the migrants with a framework through which they can confront and placate the elders without the authority of the latter being tarnished. Much of this ability to placate the elders comes from the efficiency of the age-set associations as farming organizations.

In spite of these checks and balances, out-migration, however temporary, remains as much of a threat to the solidarity of the age-set associations as it is to the lineages. It is the age set which provides the most effective check on the prolongation or even the permanence of the out-migration experience, even if, at the same time, the lineage benefits equally from this check. This is not to say that the age-set associations cannot be said to facilitate temporary out migration by making it less disruptive. The evidence from rural Segu is that where the age sets are stronger, there is less out-migration; where they are weaker, there is more.

Two questions will be addressed in this chapter. First, why do strong age-set bonds develop in the context of lineage politics at the village level? Second, how do the lineage elders view these age sets and the contemporary lure of wage-earning opportunities in the Ivory Coast?

There are important historical reasons why some villages have strong patrilineal structure, and therefore the restraints on migration outlined above, while others have less incorporated local authority and therefore are more often shattered by the call of wage labor opportunities from the south. Where there is stability, the proliferation of patrilineal descent ties within the village is significant; where local authority is shattered, differences in the accumulation of commercial wealth within the community affect the outcome.

While the elders in this first type of Malian village condemn the emigration of youths for wage labor, they have long encouraged the autonomous mobilization of these youths into age-set associations for farming. The elders realize that age-set bonds ease the migrant labor experience for these youths, but, at the same time, these bonds involve the working youth more intimately in the life of the village. Rather, strong age sets provide a link back into the village without which emigration might be prolonged. The elders recognize that they cannot provide the same face-saving link back to the village, so they are obligated to encourage the autonomous age-set bond. While vertical patrilineal and horizontal age-mate ties operate on some contradictory sets of principles, they complement each other in situations in which both are equally threatened by the external demand for village labor. As it projects a greater organizational continuity over time, the lineage principle ultimately gains from their associations.

COOPERATIVE LABOR AND THE PROPENSITY TO MIGRATE

In attempting to identify some of the development benefits of the "migrant labor system" in West Africa, Elliot Berg cites the role of "communal work arrangements" in maintaining productivity on the farm of the absent migrant: "Where kinship organization, cooperative work societies, and other village institutions play an important role in production, the migrant's family is likely to benefit from mutual aid, and per capita output of staples is less likely to fall" (1969:171). For all the criticism (cf. Amin, 1974:98ff.) that Berg's "cost-benefit" analysis of West African migration has received, I have not seen this particular statement challenged. Berg discounts Skinner's (1960) and Lombard's (1960) observations to the contrary, that migration sabotages rather than encourages cooperative work arrangements: "These appear to be the only studies for West Africa which do not give the cooperative work group an important place in village economic life" (1969:172).

Lombard's and Skinner's are also the only studies cited which trace the migrants back to their actual villages of origin. Among the other studies cited by Berg, not even Watson's (1958) masterful work does this adequately; hence his implication throughout that cooperative farm labor favors migration. Of those studies cited for Mali (Malgras, 1960; Braseur, 1961) attesting to the significance of cooperative farm groups in West Africa, none gives any evidence for high levels of emigration from the actual villages where these forms of cooperation were strong. (Cissé [1970], Leynaud and Cissé [1978], and Lewis [1979] have elaborated more recently on the status of communal work groups in Malian village organization.) The correlation between migration and cooperative labor is made most frequently on a regional or a national level, and therefore cannot tell us what Skinner's and Lombard's studies tell us about village-level processes.

In this paper I will attempt to explain a pattern observed in rural Mali between villages with lower rates of emigration and villages with strong cooperative farming groups. Besides exposing the ethnographically inaccurate "cost-benefit" calculation of the abstracted migrant, an examination of the cases of this pattern has an important bearing on more recent perspectives in African migration studies (e.g., Caldwell, 1975).

The effect of temporary migration in fostering the continuity of traditional rural institutions has long been asserted in Southern Africa (Watson, 1958; Van Velsen, 1960). More recently those institutions have come to be viewed as the product of the migrant-labor system itself, with the "traditional" elements being no more than a caricature of another precolonial reality (Palmer and Parsons, 1977). The migrant's supportive institutions back in his home village serve as an important basis for the supply of "cheap labor power" to capitalist enterprises in South Africa (Wolpe, 1972). In all of these studies the extended family and communal work groups are considered to be among the supportive institutions in question. When we examine village by village (Bates, 1976), however, we find that, as in rural Mali, while the extended family may be reinforced by high rates of absence among working males, communal work groups are not.

In making a similar argument for West Africa, Meillassoux (1975) is more explicit about how rural patrilineal institutions facilitate the inexpensive provision of laborers to capitalist enterprises on the coast. Patrilineal descent groups organize the reproduction of this labor through marriages between themselves, validating each other's claims on that labor for the provision of their own subsistence. With descent group subsistence thus taken care of outside the cash economy, the labor of its members is that much less expensive to the wage-paying employer. However, those institutions that unite these patrilineal segments into regularized, communal work efforts not only help to keep lineage labor focused on subsistence; they also serve to restrain the emigration of this labor from the village economy.

I have already suggested that the restraining role of cooperative labor groups can be explicated by tracing migrants back to their home villages where it will be found (according to our hypothesis) that most of them come from villages with fewer cooperative labor practices. In rural Segu (central Mali) this is certainly the case: more migrants tend to come from villages where community work associations have broken down (Lewis, 1978). Those villages where community-wide groupings still thrive tend to lose fewer youths to the migrant labor system.[2] It is not unusual for these contrasting kinds of villages to appear side-by-side in a given zone of the rural Segu hinterland. In fact, to the extent that the village suffering from a high emigration rate hires a work group more energetic than its own from a neighboring village with, necessarily, a lower emigration rate, a certain symbiosis can be detected between them (Lewis, 1978).

Thus, the decision to migrate appears to vary by village as much as it does according to opportunity structure (cost/benefits) at the individual level. (Bates [1976:193ff.] perceptively adds the individual's family domestic cycle to the economic criteria usually considered when an individual's decision to migrate is analyzed.) This evidence requires that we elaborate an alternative to the individualist approach to the migration choice question without forgoing the utility of micro-level data.

In as much as it restrains emigration, the vitality of these community-wide work associations should be seen as a kind of political response to the migrant labor system. Unlike the more familiar political response carefully measured by Bates, the solidarity of these groups cannot be attributed to a "low elasticity of demand for rural living" (1976:254) on the part of the individual members. These groups are part of a structure that was stimulated, in some villages, by the modern threat before it could be absorbed, in other villages, by local entrepreneurs stimulated by the same process.

THE LINEAGE MODE OF PRODUCTION

In savanna West Africa the patrilineal production framework enables the migrant laborer to absent himself during his most productive years without losing old-age security back home (Hart, 1974). As a lineage member he automatically has rights to the fruits of lineage-held land (Hart, 1978). Nevertheless, few writers would maintain that the earnings remitted to the home village by the migrant would compensate for the labor lost to the village. Berg maintains that the benefits of migration outweigh the cost, for the village as well as for the individual migrant, under a perhaps unfortunate "specific set of economic circumstances" that "cannot be wished away" (1969:181). Amin (1974:98ff.) argues that Berg underestimates the value of dry-season (off-season) labor back at the village. Rey (1976:53–57) emphasizes the drain on craft production, particularly on the village-level production of agriculture equipment, caused by the dry-season emigration. These off-season absences leave the farming community more dependent on the outside market for their tool supply. This in turn stimulates further out-migration and/or nonsubsistence cash cropping in order to obtain the money for these purchases.

Even before this stage is reached, however, the internal dynamics for the "lineage mode of production" become vulnerable to the penetration of commodity relations. In this "mode" elders are sharply differentiated from the farming juniors by their exclusive, elder-to-elder reciprocity system:

> Government by elders is therefore determined by the structure of reproduction itself. Like in all corporate systems, it is because reciprocity between elders only ceases to operate at the death of a particular elder, that the chiefs are not eliminated after middle age: and it is because all juniors become elder, (as long as no appropriate methods of administrative control are activated), that every old man is nearly always replaced at his death by another old man. (Rey, 1975:58)

The elders preside over the reciprocal circulation of brides between their lineages. Because only they have access to this reciprocity network, they are in a position to arbitrate these marriages. Being in that position, they come to accumulate the surplus wealth used as bridewealth to guarantee these marriages. However, when off-farm, extralineal sources of wealth become available to the junior, he may wish to bypass this form of control by the elders by paying his own bridewealth, or at least seeking to have fewer elders assist him with it. Such an attempt leads rapidly to an inflation of bride-wealth rates that further stimulates off-farm migration with its call for cash (Rey, 1976:61–65). Thus, the competition internal to the lineage mode of production provides a point of entry for the capitalist wage-labor market to the labor power within.

Rey notes how reluctantly most West African peasants have participated in this development of a wage-labor market or proletarianization process, attempting, rather, to maintain an autarkic form of economic as well as political autonomy (1976:55). He stresses the study of the specific ways in which peasants are distracted from these attempts at convert resistance:

> This detailed knowledge of the internal contradiction of rural societies and the diverse modalities through which capitalism comes to dominate them (the basis of an understanding not only of the difference in attitude between different groups facing the migration option but also of the processes leading to that migration in

each case) therefore, has no resemblance to gratuitous specula-
tion, neither for the present nor for the future. (1976:53; transla-
tion mine)

In this chapter I am concentrating on the Malian, specifically the Segu-
vain (usually referred to as the "Bambara"—see Lewis, 1978), peasants'
form of resistance to this process of incorporation or "capturing" into the
wage labor market, also referred to as a process of proletarianization. I
have suggested that the vitality of cooperative labor groups protects the
lineage mode of production from its inherent vulnerability to the penetration of commodity relations. I will investigate whether this is true in
neighboring patrilineal societies.

The Guro, patrilineal speakers of a Mande language who occupy the
North Central Ivory Coast, as described in Meillassoux's well-known
monograph (1964), have a community-wide organization, the *klala*, that
closely resembles the *ton* of their fellow Mande speakers to the north in
rural Segu. Farm production, and food consumption, is managed at the
level of the minimal lineage segment comprising a patrilocal compound.
Nevertheless, much productive activity is performed by this community-
wide cooperative group. In reflecting on Meillassoux's study, Terray outlined how these two "modes of production" might be seen as operating
simultaneously as "simple" and "complex" forms of cooperation respectively (1972:115). Rey is less inclined to accord to both modes a simultane-
ous degree of influence:

> This [lineage] structure is defined essentially by the nature of the
> only permanent economic activity, namely agriculture, and by the
> mode of co-operation that agriculture implies; it is clear that the
> reproduction of the structure will be carried out by completely
> different mechanisms in a society with age classes where co-
> operation defines groups other than the lineage as labor groups.
> (1975:54).

For the Guro, at any rate, Rey is clear about which mode of production is
dominant: "The mode of production determines the unit, the lineage,
which must serve as the base on which the structure of society is built,
that is, the only unit where there is a permanent hegemony of function"
(1975:59).

In the Bambara villages, however, if the cooperative labor mode is so
well developed as to be able to resist the threat to the lineage mode of
production by the migrant labor system, has it then become dominant
over the lineage mode? If so, what are the implications of this for the

reproductive arrangements still mediated through the lineage structure? The conventional wisdom, following Eisenstadt (1966), is that well-developed age-set systems and their associations compensate for a lack of political range in the existing descent-based institutions. In the Malian case we shall see that outside circumstances dictate that the lineage structure will continue to lose what political and economic range it does have without the over-arching reinforcement provided by the age-set-based cooperative labor associations.

THE *TON*

In rural Segu most community-wide cooperative labor groups are made up of series of adjacent age sets depending on the size and complexity of the task to be performed. Most village wards with over 200 people, or associations of smaller wards, will have a youth group *(ton)* comprising all of the age set below a certain age.[3] The age of the oldest age set in the ton will be a function of the community's demography. With fewer youths, that age will be set higher; with an adequate number of laboring youths, the age of the oldest age set in the ton can stabilize between 30 and 35. With too many youths absent as migrant laborers, those remaining will have to be kept in the ton longer—as late as the age of 40—to get the work at home done. Yet, even if full numbers can be maintained, the absence of too many age-set members saps the working vitality of such a ton. Most villages have ton work groups—not all of which use their ton equally as effectively.

In the village in which my wife and I lived, the 32- to 33-year-old age set was heading up the ton. By the spring of their thirty-fourth year, they mobilized the ton to spend their accumulated (mostly in a livestock form) collective earnings, staging the customary, week-long festival that marks the graduation of an age set from the ton. During this festival, besides providing almost continuous dancing, the ton cooked for and fed the entire village.

Once graduated from the ton, this age set might only be brought out of the working context of their minimal lineage and exchange labor *(d'ama baara)* groups to participate in a more informal ton work group if the size of the task required more hands than were present in the formal ton. In the village being presented here, this was only the case for the millet-threshing activities. For tasks smaller that those requiring the full force of the formal ton, there were two younger *ton prieri* (from the French *prier:* to invite) that could be hired. The divisions between the memberships of these two junior ton correspond to the ancient division of the village into two wards, each centered on a maximal lineage segment of the founding clan—the oldest member of the oldest generation of which inherits the chieftaincy itself. This did mean that these junior ton were subordinated to the politics of lineage rivalry between these maximal lineage segments, as appears to be the case for the Malinke ton studied by Leynaud (1966—see footnote 5).

However, the senior ton overarched the whole village, and its solidarity had serious implications for the routine functioning of the patrilineal structure as well—but then so did the encroaching capitalist economy.

The *Ton* and the Lineage Mode of Production

Thus, the question of the conflicting loyalties of the young laborer between his community-wide ton and his lineage segment has come up again. Most writers cited, from Leynaud (1966) to Rey (1975), see a contradiction between these two forms of affiliation, a contradiction that ultimately has to be resolved in favor of one or the other. The status of age sets in West African villages has been given its most detailed treatment in a volume edited by Paulme (1971). Here the functionalist position of Eisenstadt (1966) is followed—namely, that age-set associations assume an increasing importance as formally defined or corporate descent, or kin, groups fail to provide an adaptive measure of one arching political order to the society in question. The way in which age sets fulfill this integrative function within the West African village is set down by Smith in the Paulme volume: "The main problem for these little egalitarian village communities is, at bottom, to divide the man himself adequately so that the desirable equilibrium between the different social forces is already achieved inside each individual" (Smith, 1971:204). Whether at the village or the individual level, no one seems to deny the tension between these two forms of social organization.

This would suggest that tension becomes tolerable to the elders heading up the lineage mode of production to the degree that the organization of production is threatened by a greater source of tension from outside of the community. In his Guro monograph, Meillassoux (1964) notes the increasing importance of the community-wide *klala* work association as one moves from the forest Guro to the savanna Guro. He attributes this increasingly dominating influence of the klala to the greater need for a community-wide organization for defense on the precolonial savanna. Terray (1972) makes more of the greater technical need for cooperation in hunting in the savanna as opposed to in the forest environment.

These military and technical constraints would also explain the predominance of the ton in Mande villages of the Malian savanna. However, Ernst makes more of the need for cooperative labor just to produce an adequate subsistence output there: "The low level of the productive forces demanded collective subsistence guaranteed by the community. Thus the decisive relationship in the traditional community is that of the individual as a member of the community—and only as such—to the naturally existing conditions for the realisation of his labour" (1976:53). Certainly, the farming season is so brief on the Malian savanna that important economies of scale can be achieved by having the weeding and other key labor bottlenecks performed collectively. This requirement has not put the ton in a position of domination over the elders because each field is still managed, if not always labored, by the minimal lineage unit— the compound.[4] Historically, it was by converting their farming role into an elaborate dry-season military role that the ton came to dominate the elders along the Niger and thus to form the Segu state (Monteil, 1924).

To the above explanations for the importance of the ton in Malian village life I (Lewis, 1979) have added an interpretation that combines the causes of collective defense requirements with those of the collective farming requirements: conditions of state domination. Either a village defended itself against the conditions of warfare that were favoring state formation all around it, or it maximized its agricultural productivity, through cooperative work groups, to pay the taxes of the state that protected it.

While the demand for slaves, and the conditions of warfare produced by that demand, no longer prevail, the demand for young villagers as migrant laborers is seen as an analogous sort of threat to village security.

The *Ton* and Migrant Labor

The tax burden remains and increases, and labor is needed at home to produce the surplus that is needed to pay that tax. The villager's preference is not to have the tax paid out of migrant earnings. If their social organization came to rely on outside earnings to pay its tax requirement, it would become dependent upon the fluctuating availability of those earnings for its survival. Furthermore, the elders, who control the agricultural surplus but not the youth's wages, would become more directly dependent on the whim of the youths for their own security. Where this has been steadily the case, the elders' position has become untenable and the village community has eventually disintegrated. The less dependent migrants too often forget the source of their survival as infants, not to mention the locus of their security as elders, and fail to remit adequate amounts of tax money back to their village. As a result, a next generation of potential migrants is not produced there.

A village becomes dependent on these cash remittances at its own peril. We have already noted the disruptive inflationary effects of having bridewealths paid from outside cash earnings. Paying taxes out of agricultural surplus cannot control their inflation, but it does enable the elders, as opposed to the employers of wage labor, to control more of the value of their youths' own labor.

In rural Mali, particularly in the Segu hinterland, the ton plays a decisive role in keeping the young laborer back on the farm, producing an agricultural surplus rather than earning wages elsewhere. Berg (1969) and others cited above, however, see such cooperative labor groupings as facilitating the out-migration of farming youths. Admittedly, the cooperative of labor performed by the ton, through its economies of scale during the bottleneck periods, could compensate for some absent labor. But it does not work that way.

Too many absences undermine the very operating premise of the ton as an organization that remains independent of the lineages by maintaining discrete organizational purposes. Individualized income—if it is to be had at all in such a village—is found within the framework of the lineages. The ton can only produce a collective income, to be consumed, in the spring festival, collectively. Any other format would bring the ton into serious conflict with the authority of the lineages, which would be to neither of their advantages. The ton cannot operate on this basis if too many of its members are away earning a personalized income.

Thus, despite Berg's logic (1969), not too much cooperative labor can arise if too many youths are away, even if such cooperative labor might mitigate the effects of their absence. The presence of a strong cooperative farm labor organization usually indicates that fewer rather than more youths are migrating out. In villages that I have observed in rural Segu this certainly appears to be the case.

It is not just the youths remaining at home that build a strong ton. A strong ton may be one of the primary reasons why they remain. This is not the place to deal with the ritual, initiatory, and educational activities of the age sets and of the ton. The elaborate socialization procedures of these institutions have received more attention (Zahan, 1960; Cissé, 1970; Leynaud and Cissé, 1978) than their precise economic implications. It is worth noting, however, that Upper Volta (now Burkina Faso) may end up sending more migrants to the Ivory Coast than Mali (even though the *lingua franca* there is the Dyula dialect of the Mande language and not the More language of many Voltaic migrants) because age-set-based initiatory institutions are not as important a part of the social structure there (Skinner, 1964).[5] Certainly, with present migratory trends there is little cooperative labor left back in the Mossi villages (Skinner, 1960).

MIGRATORY TRENDS FROM A SINGLE BAMBARA VILLAGE

By examining these processes in the more minute context of a single village, we can see how the contradictions between the patrilineage system, the ton, and the demand for migrant labor came together in a discrete situation.

The table below shows the use of the ton of each compound in the village studied; it also contains evidence of the use of reciprocal exchange-labor *(d'ama baara):* an alternative to the ton used for overcoming key labor bottlenecks. We see that remittances from the Ivory Coast are highest when absences are also more frequent, which indicates that the compounds that restrain migration are characteristically less willing to take, or acknowledge, any benefit from it. It is also indicated that labor is most frequently used by those compounds that lose fewer migrants and receive less in cash remittances from those that they do lose. Because their youths are absent less often, it is easier for them to be used to access an exchange-labor group, and it is considered more legitimate for them to hire the ton again because they are contributing a family member to that organization.

The first figure under "Average Annual Remittances" in table 1 shows the number of compounds receiving various amounts; the number in parentheses shows how many of the compounds farm with more ton and/or exchange-labor than with labor from their own eligible migrants.

A review of the subsistence production of each of these compounds in 1974 (Lewis, 1979) also reveals a correlation between lower rates of out-migration and higher yields per worker.

POLICY PLANNING FOR VILLAGE DEVELOPMENT

I hope I have demonstrated why Sahelian policy makers seeking to retard labor migration from their nations should seek to understand the operation of age-set associations. At the micro-level these associations appear to contradict the authority of the lineage elders. When looked at in a

TABLE 1

Absences per Male Migrant	Average Annual Remittances of Migrant Earnings, in Malian francs				
	5,000	10,000	15,000	20,000	25,000
1	3(2)	2(1)		1(1)	
1.5			1(0)	1(1)	1(0)
2		1(1)	2(2)	1(0)	2(0)

macro perspective, however, it can be seen how they bolster that authority by keeping more youths at home to farm and marry in the lineage sphere.

These age-set organizations, and the lineage authority structures they buttress, are differentiated by village—or, in larger villages, by ward. Some villages (or wards) have strong age sets, strong lineage-based command structures, and, therefore, few out-migrants. Other villages (or wards) have more individuated households, each fending for themselves, with no obligation to work for or be helped by another (either through an age set or a lineal relation); therefore, many of their migrants spend the better part of their working lives outside of Mali.

Significantly, it is these latter villages that are most ready to change. Their existing food production system is less stable or secure. They have less to lose if a risky innovation does not work out. Their household heads are freer to choose to participate in a project offering innovations than a household head in the more cooperative village. Furthermore, however little capital may be at their disposal, they have more independent control over the use of it.

Thus, as long as projects choose the household production unit as the target entity, and as long as analyses are performed accordingly (sampling households without looking for the larger and, as we have seen, stabler linkages between them), then the resulting project design will be better suited to villages with the more individuated, "stranger" household. Yet these are precisely the villages that lose the most labor to the outside.

Until the ward or village is treated as a significant unit for rural development planning, then it will be difficult to recognize, at the household level, the economic strengths of the peasant farming group that is reluctant to innovate. Yet it is these conservative peasants (Hutton and Cohen, 1975) who, in coordinating their labor allocation and their technology choices with their neighbors and relatives, have a system for keeping youthful laborers at home and, therefore, a greater amount of grain is needed and harvested. The significance of this interhousehold networking is difficult to detect from a random sampling of households, but, rather, appears more forcefully when analyzed at the village level.

If villages were treated as units of development analysis, the production strengths of these less cash-oriented communities would be better appreciated, and projects could be designed to build on and develop those strengths. Instead, projects are gravitating to the most easily changed peasants and these, as we have seen, are the same peasants who are already seeking much of their welfare beyond the projects in towns or on plantations, often, in other countries. Eventually, projects should provide incentives that counter this emigration, rather than targeting those individual households most likely to reproduce emigrants. If projects were targeted on households tied into community networks that serve to keep young laborers at home, they would have as their foundation a much more productive system with a social base that induces its members to spend their working years in Mali.

The first step for development planners, in taking advantage of these more stable and productive villages, would be to identify them and the institutional basis of their stability and productivity. They can be identified visually by the number of mosque minarets that appear on the skyline. An inward-looking, millet-producing village, the success of which is based on cooperative labor, will have only one mosque. All of the senior villagers will pray together under the auspices of the same brotherhood or sect of Islam. A less-united village producing a higher rate of out-migration will immediately manifest its internal divisions with two or more mosque minarets. These rural mosques will correspond to rural sects or brotherhoods, at large, among the village faithful. Such rivalry goes far beyond the cooperative competitiveness of the age mate in the ton; rather, it lessens the cooperative basis necessary for overcoming personal labor bottlenecks (Lewis, 1979) in millet-farming production. Such many-mosqued villages may be anxious to innovate, but they are not in an equally good position to sustain an innovation in the production sector.

Once identified, the more cooperative, unitary, single-mosqued village should receive closer investigation as to its farming system. I hope I have shown that the strength of that farming system can neither be recognized nor analyzed through household-level data. Data on labor input, capital input, and crop input needs to be collected and evaluated on a community-wide basis. Then the basis for introducing a socially, politically, and economically sustainable innovation in these more stable communities will be better understood.

NOTES

1. Anthropologic field research was pursued in this village over a period of sixteen months in 1974–75 under the auspices of L'Office Malien du Betail et de la Viande (L'OMBEVI) while two components of a Mali Livestock Development project were implemented in the vicinity. The project and the research were financed by the U.S. Agency for International Development, the latter as contract No. AID/AFR–1045 through the Research Foundation of the State University of New York (RFSUNY). I am grateful for the support and guidance given to my efforts by Dr. Boubaca Sy (director, L'OMBEVI), Dr. David Shear (director, USAID/Abidjan), and Dr. Michael M. Horowitz (professor of anthropology, SUNY at Binghamton). While I was in the village, the day-to-day contributions and advice of Dangui Sissoko (sociologist, L'OMBEVI) and Brihima Coulibaly (Service des Eaux et Forêts, Duna) were indispensable. The views and conclusions in this paper are mine and not those of any individuals or institutions listed above, including USAID, which funded my research and where I am presently employed.

2. See Kohler, 1971, 1972; and Remy, 1973 for analogous evidence from Upper Volta (now Burkina Faso). Finnegan, 1980, argues contra Amin, 1974, that migration has served to stabilize Mossi social structure. His findings are not necessarily inconsistent with those reported for the Malian case here, once the precise aspects of social structure being stabilized are identified. I suspect that, while migration may reinforce the patrilineage (à la Hart, 1978), it serves to break down, as in Mali, cooperative labor work for agricultural production.

3. As these wards, among most Mande populations, correspond to lineage segments, Leynaud (1966:54) for a Malinke area takes the differentiation of ton groups between wards to indicate a subservience of the cooperative age-set principle to the politics of interlineage rivalry. These appear to be less true of the Segu "Bambara" area discussed here.

4. The Socialist policies of the Modibo Keita regime, however, interpreted the ton's importance to this production system as a basis for collectivization. This interpretation neglected the role of the lineage segment and the lineage elder in farm management. This ethnographic mistake was to prove troublesome for the regime (Jones, 1976).

5. Amselle (1976) questions this practice of distinguishing varying propensities towards migration by ethnic groups. I agree that this propensity should not be attributed to the psychological characteristics of an ethnic culture. However, to the degree that local-level social organization (which, as we have seen, does effect migration rates) affects the assignment of a given community to this or that ethnic group, one can speak to general migratory trends that *correspond* with ethnic categorizations.

REFERENCES

Amin, Samir, ed. 1974. *Modern Migrations in West Africa*. Oxford: Oxford University Press.

Amselle, J–L. 1976. "Aspects et Significations du Phenome Migratoire en Afrique." In *Les Migratoire Africaines*. Paris: François Maspero.

Bates, Robert. 1976. *Rural Response to Industrialization: A Study of Village Zambia.* New Haven: Yale University Press.

Berg, Elliot J. 1965. "The Economics of the Migrant Labor System." Pp. 160–84 in Hilda Kuper (ed.), *Urbanization and Migration in West Africa.* Berkeley and Los Angeles: University of California Press.

Braseur, Georges. 1961. "Etude de Geographie regional: le village de Tenetou (Mali)." *Bulletin de l'IFAN*, no. 3–4.

Caldwell, J. C. 1975. *The Sahelian Famine and Its Demographic Implications.* Washington, D.C.: Overseas Liaison Committee.

Cissé, Diango. 1970. *Structures Malinkes de Kita.* Bamako: Editions Populaires, collection "Hier."

Eisenstadt, S.N. 1966. *From Generation to Generation: Age Groups and Social Structure.* New York: Macmillan Free Press.

Ernst, Klaus. 1976. *Tradition and Progress in the African Village: The Non-Capitalist Transformation of Rural Communities in Mali.* London: C. Hurst & Co.

Finnegan, Gregory A. 1980. "Employment Opportunity and Migration Among the Mossi of Upper Volta." *Research in Economic Anthropology* 3. George Dalton, ed. Greenwich, Conn: JAI Press Inc.

Harris, John R. 1978. "Economic Courses and Consequences of Migration Within the Context of Underdevelopment in Africa." Boston University, African Studies Center Working Paper no. 6.

Hart, Keith. 1974. "Migration and Opportunity Structure: A Ghanaian Case Study." Pp. 321–42 in S. Amin (ed.), *Modern Migrations in West Africa.* Oxford: Oxford University Press.

———. 1978. "The Economic Basis of Tallensi Social History in the Early Twentieth Century." Pp. 186–216 in G. Dalton (ed.), *Research in Economic Anthropology.* Vol. 1. Greenwich, Conn.: JAI Press Inc.

Hutton, Caroline, and Robin Cohen. 1975. "African Peasants and Resistance to Change: A Reconsideration of Sociological Approaches." In Ivar Oxaal, T. Barnett, and David Booth (eds.), *Beyond the Sociology of Development: Economy and Society in Latin America and Africa.* London: Routledge & Kegan Paul.

Jones, William I. 1976. *Economic Policy and Planning: Socialist Mali and Her Neighbors.* Washington, D.C.: Three Continents.

Kohler, Jean-Marie. 1971. *Activités Agricoles et Changements Sociaux Dans l'Ouest Mossi.* Paris: Memoires de l'ORSTOM, no. 46.

———. 1972. *Les Migrations des Mossi de l'Ouest.* Paris: Travaux et Documents de l'ORSTOM, no. 37.

Lewis, John Van D. 1978. "Small Farmer Credit and the Village Production Unit in Rural Mali." *African Studies Review* 21, no. 3:29–48.

———. 1979. "Descendants and Crops: Two Poles of Production in a Malian Peasant Village." Ph.D. dissertation, Department of Anthropology, Yale University.

Leynaud, Emile. 1966. "Fraternités d'âge et sociétés de culture dans le Haut-Vallée de Niger." *Cahiers d'Etudes Africaines* 21:41–68.

Leynaud, Emile, and Youssouf Cissé. 1978. *Paysans Malinke du Haut-Niger: Tradition et dévelopment Rural en Afrique Soudanaise.* Bamako: Edition populaire de Mali.

Lombard, J. 1960. "Les problèmes des migrations 'locales': Leur rôle dans les changements d'une société en transition (Dahomey)." *Bulletin de l'IFAN* 22, no. 1–2.

Malgras, R.P.D. 1960. "La condition sociale du paysan Minyanka dans le cercle de San." *Bulletin de l'IFAN* 22, no. 1–2.

Meillassoux, Claude. 1964. *Anthropologie économique des Gouro de Côte d'Ivoire*. Paris and The Hague: Mouton & Co.

———. 1975. *Femmes, Greniers et capitaux*. Paris: François Maspero.

Monteil, Charles. 1924. *Les Bambara de Segou et Kaarta*. Paris: La Rose.

Palmer, Robin, and Neil Parsons, eds. 1977. *The Roots of Rural Poverty in Central and Southern Africa*. Berkeley and Los Angeles: University of California Press.

Paulme, Denise, ed. 1971. *Classes et Associations d'âge en Afrique de l'ouest*. Paris: Librarie Plon.

Remy, Gerard, et al. 1973. *Les Migrations de Travail et les Mouvements de colonisation Mossi*. Recueil Bibliographique Paris: Travaux et Documents de L'ORSTOM.

Rey, Pierre-Philippe. 1975. "The Lineage Mode of Production." *Critique of Anthropology* 3:27–79.

———. 1976. "Introduction Theorique" to *Capitalisme negrier: la marche des paysans vers le prolétariat*. Etudes présentées par Pierre-Philippe Rey. Paris: François Maspero.

Skinner, Elliot R. 1960. "Labor Migration and Its Relationship to Socio-Cultural Change in Mossi Society." *Africa* 30:375–99.

———. 1964. *The Mossi of Upper Volta: Political Development of a Sudanese People*. Stanford: Stanford University Press.

Smith, Pierre. 1971. "Les échelons d'âge dans l'organisation sociale et rituelle des Bedik (Senegal Oriental)." Pp. 185–204 in D. Paulme (ed.), *Classes et Associations d'age en Afrique de l'ouest*. Paris: Librarie Plon.

Swinell, K. 1978. "Family Farmers and Migrant Labor: The Stranger Farmer of the Gambia." *Canadian Journal of African Studies* 12, no. 1:3–17.

Terray, Emmanuel. 1972. *Marxism and "Primitive" Societies*. New York: Monthly Review Press.

Van Velsen, J. 1960. "Labour Migration as a Positive Factor in the Continuity of Tonga Tribal Society." *Economic Development and Cultural Change* 8.

Watson, William. 1958. *Tribal Cohesion in a Money Economy: A Study of the Manbwe People of Northern Rhodesia*. Manchester: Manchester University Press.

Wolpe, H. 1972. "Capitalism and Cheap Labour-Power in South Africa: From Segregation to Apartheid." *Economy and Society* 1, no. 4:425–56.

Zachariah, K.C., and Julien Conde. 1981. *Migration in West Africa: Demographic Aspects*. A joint World Bank OECD Study, published for the World Bank by Oxford University Press.

Zahan, Dominque. 1960. *Sociétés d'initiation Bambara: Le N'domo et le Kore*. Paris and The Hague: Mouton & Co.

5

THE WOMEN POTTERS OF LUSAKA: URBAN MIGRATION AND SOCIOECONOMIC ADJUSTMENT

BENNETTA JULES-ROSETTE

The abrupt entry of all sectors of African life into the international economic system has stimulated urban migration throughout the continent. In central Africa, contract migration among lone males was prevalent during the preindependence years. Urban employment increased with the industrialization of the colonial infrastructure. Those individuals who did not have fixed wage labor opportunities were formally dissuaded from migrating. Contemporary Zambia, the subject of this discussion, has the highest rate of urban growth in Subsaharan Africa, with the exclusion of South Africa. Currently, Lusaka is one of the fastest growing cities in the world. As of 1978, over 40% of Zambia's population was estimated to be living in cities and towns. Although it has only light industry, Lusaka, Zambia's capital, is the most rapidly expanding city in the nation with an annual population increase of between 16% and 42% in its satellite townships.[1]

Lusaka has a population of over 450,000.[2] Most of this growth has taken place since the attainment of national independence in 1964. The Zambian cities of the Copperbelt mushroomed after World War I with a heavy migration of men into the colonial mining areas. The migration of lone females and families is a more recent phenomenon and entails distinctive patterns of urban socioeconomic adjustment. The socioeconomic adaptation of recent urban migrants with few marketable skills is a critical problem for national development. This chapter is concerned with the migration to Lusaka of rural women with little formal education and the adjustment of a special category of self-employed craftswomen to urban economic life. The data that form the basis for this analysis were collected from 1974 through 1979 as part of a longitudinal study of urban change in three of Lusaka's squatter areas.

By virtue of both education and employment preference, women in Central Africa were barred from the wage labor force under colonialism and were legally prevented from establishing stable residences in town. Recently, self-employment has been a major means of urban economic and social adjustment among women. The employment patterns set by the first women migrants are now shared by men in Zambia's peri-urban areas where wage employment has become increasingly scarce. Marketeering, small business entrepreneurship, and cottage industries are the principal outlets for these urban marginals. Migrant women have played a significant role in developing informal employment networks and strategies in Lusaka. Excluded from formal jobs by education and opportunity, women in the city had to find other means of support. Their situation emerges in perspective through a historical overview of the motives for urban migration in Zambia.

ZAMBIAN MIGRATION PATTERNS DURING THE POST-INDEPENDENCE PERIOD

From the mid-1920s to the present, copper production has dominated Zambia's economy and has accounted for much of the urban migration outside of Lusaka. The industrial "pull" that characterized urban migration in Zambia is, thus, much more typical of the Copperbelt than it is of Lusaka. It is difficult to make a clear-cut causal argument about the reasons for labor migration. The colonial economy is, nevertheless, an obvious factor, producing a need for cash exchanges in the "traditional" sector. The earliest patterns of labor migration to the Copperbelt involved contract migration by village men (cf. Du Toit and Safa, 1975:50–53). These migrants were hired by mines and other industrial concerns for periods of two to five years. They came to the towns and cities alone and lived in dormitory-like conditions provided by the mining companies. By the late 1950s there were an estimated 50,000 African migrants living in Ndola, one of the major Copperbelt cities (Epstein, 1961:30). Some of these migrants had been residing in Ndola for fifteen or more years, but most had come to town within the past five years on labor contracts. They included not only Northern Rhodesian nationals, but also migrants from the neighboring colonies who intended to return to their village homes after their contracts expired. The permanent squatters and stabilized migrants were products of the postcolonial period.

A preponderance of adult males living in culturally rootless but highly supervised urban settings in Zambia was characteristic of the period from World War I to the 1960s, despite the increasing migration of families and lone females in the decades preceding independence. Contract migrants usually sent cash back to their villages and oriented their lives toward the kin who stayed at home. Meanwhile, the women who remained in the rural areas assumed the responsibility for agricultural production and marketing. They constituted an important category of potential migrants. In his classic study of Xhosa migration in South Africa, Philip Mayer (1971:210–23) argues that education and attitudes toward external culture contact modified rural displacement patterns.[3] Mayer asserts that the preference for male migration among the more conservative Xhosa was culturally as well as economically motivated. Those more progressive Xhosa who could bring their families to town did so. The fact remains, however, that male migration was the norm in this case and throughout southern Africa (cf. Magubane, 1975:230–35).

Two further migration patterns result in temporary urban residence: regular movement between rural and urban areas, and seasonal migration. While these options are viewed as typically West African, they are found in concert with contract migration in Zambia. Under the first pattern, individuals live on the fringes of the city where they engage in agricultural labor. They sell produce on a weekly basis. The commuting pattern is critical to this analysis because it has always involved large numbers of women. Left with their families, the spouses of migrants bring produce to town both to feed their husbands and to sell. Even in regions minimally affected by contract migration, women are able to engage in town marketeering through commuting. This transient pattern gives them temporary access to the economic life of the city without the necessity of establishing permanent residence there. During the colonial era, Zambian men without labor contracts were not able to obtain legal passes for long-term residence in the city.[4] Their movements were restricted, and they also used commuting as one means of adapting to this confining situation.

Seasonal migration facilitated adjustment to colonial restrictions without interrupting the flow of village social and economic life (cf. Prothero, 1957). Unlike commuting, which is characteristically a woman's activity, seasonal migration involves young males who leave their villages after the agricultural planting and production season. They use a chain of communications, including kin and ethnic network ties, to find casual-labor in the city. These seasonal migrants return to the urban area on an annual or biannual basis. They enter the informal economic sector and can be viewed as the predecessors of the new self-employed migrants.

A final type of migration has been significant in southern Africa: mass migration. This involves the movement of entire social groups or village complexes from the rural areas to town. Mass migrants include refugees and displaced people. In Lusaka a significant number of those migrating en masse have been members of religious and political groups who were forced to move from country to country for ideological and legal reasons. The Apostles of John Masowe, a syncretic Christian sect, migrated en masse from then Southern Rhodesia to Port Elizabeth, South Africa, in 1947. The millenarian doctrine of this group, coupled with its entrepreneurial success, made the Masowe sect a target for suspicion among colonial administrators. As a result of their unconventional religious attitudes, the Apostles were officially repatriated to Rhodesia in 1962 (Dillon-Malone, 1978:28–29).[5]

MALE VERSUS FEMALE MIGRATION PATTERNS IN LUSAKA

The urban experience for many of Lusaka's men began with employment elsewhere, particularly in the Copperbelt towns and cities; for example, Karen Hansen (1975:780) found that 12% of the men interviewed in a Lusaka township had lived in the Copperbelt or in provincial towns. In most cases, these men were accompanied by their wives. By the mid-1950s, two-fifths of the male population of the Copperbelt had at least ten years of urban experience and, again, nearly two-fifths of them had brought their wives to the city (Little, 1973:16). The income of the Zambian urban male was more than twice that of his rural counterpart in the 1950s and was at least seven times that of his rural counterpart by 1964 (Heisler, 1971). This situation has led Kenneth Little (1973:17–28), along with other students of urban change in Africa, to conclude that "the men followed the money and the women followed the men" in Zambian migration patterns.

Although Little's hypothesis appears to be sustained by the basic demographic movements from village to city in Zambia, it does not investigate the full range of women's incentives to migrate or the distinctive characteristics of their economic adaptation. In addition to the women who migrated with spouses, many also came to town, initially as widows and divorcees, who could no longer function well in the village context. They migrated to earn a living in the city, just as the men had. Mayer

TABLE 1 The Zambian population working in the formal sector
and seeking work through the labor exchange, 1969–1975

	Total Adult Population	Working (Formal) Sector	Seeking Work	Registered at Employment College	Found Work at Employment College
Men	1,037,202	588,597	293,509	48,893	19,011
Women	1,121,122	141,297	178,419	2,541	659

SOURCES: Population Census, 1969, Annual Report of Department of Labor, 1969–1975.

(1971:233–34) suggests that younger women swelled the ranks of urban migrants in South Africa after World War II. This pattern is typical of Johannesburg, where a 500% increase took place in the female population between 1921 and 1951 (Koornof, 1953:29). These women worked primarily as domestic servants, but they also entered small-scale commerce.

Observation indicates a similar pattern for Lusaka, where women in the city outnumber men. Lusaka's women migrants, however, are largely excluded from domestic work, where the preference is for older men.[6] The 1969 Lusaka census demonstrated that nearly as many women as men were seeking work in Lusaka, but only a small fraction of them were ultimately employed in the wage-labor sector. This situation prevails throughout Zambia. Table 1 shows a breakdown by sex of the country's population seeking work at the various Labor Exchange Offices located in Zambia's major urban areas and provincial capitals.

In Lusaka as of 1975, 45% of the adult female population sought work. According to Labor Exchange figures, males placed in both unskilled and skilled jobs outnumbered females in Lusaka by a ratio of 29:10. Younger women who felt restricted by the lack of opportunities in village life migrated to the city for jobs, money, and what they perceived as freedom of choice. The "bright lights" and fast pace of the urban lifestyle had a particular appeal for these younger women. There are, thus, four major categories of women migrants from the Zambian rural areas: (1) the older divorced and widowed women with little formal education; (2) the younger single women with some primary school training; (3) the women with mixed training and skills who came to accompany their husbands; and (4) the town-born daughters of first-generation migrants. At some point during their careers in the city, women from each of these categories needed to work. They have all, however, been equally cut off from the Zambian wage labor force until very recently. Table 2 is an overview

TABLE 2 General occupations taken up by women from the employment exchange services between 1963 and 1973

Occupational Groups	Years										
	1963	1964	1965	1966	1967	1968	1969	1970	1971	1972	1973
Professional	—	—	—	—	—	—	—	—	—	—	1
Managerial, administrative	—	—	—	—	—	—	—	—	—	—	—
Clerical	7	13	13	14	96	168	155	266	—	408	453
Sales	—	—	43	39	78	62	74	55	—	122	128
Services	—	—	615	658	664	610	430	232	—	398	466
Agricultural	—	—	—	—	—	—	—	—	—	20	2
Productional	—	—	—	—	—	—	—	—	—	53	78
Total vacancies filled by women	7	13	671	741	838	840	659	553	—	1,001	1,128
Total women registered	18	62	1,763	1,592	1,465	2,076	2,541	2,896	—	3,419	3,454

SOURCE: Annual reports of the Department of Labor, 1963–1973.

of available data concerning women's employment in Zambia, including the subelite professions.[7]

TRADITIONAL FORMS OF EDUCATION FOR WOMEN

In recent years there has been an increase in the town-born population of women who receive compulsory primary school education and go on to secondary school in the urban centers. These young women, trained in and for the modern sector, still are not in the majority, and they will not constitute the primary focus for this discussion. Rather, I shall concentrate on the transitional generation of migrant women with little formal education. First-generation migrant women were usually married shortly after the onset of puberty. For many of them, a major source of instruction was the *chisungu*, a generic term for female initiation among the Bemba and in other Zambian ethnic groups.

Through chisungu (Richards, 1956: 52–111), young women were taught the appropriate norms of respect toward their elders and husbands. They were also instructed in basic agricultural and homemaking skills, including basketry and potting. Ceramic work is a basic part of the chisungu rites. *Mbusa* (clay figurines) were used to provide graphic examples of parables and moral instructions, and were employed in mimetic performances that depicted the ideal relationships between males and females. The *banacimbusa* (ceremonial mistresses) and their novice trainees acted out these moral standards in the initiation rite. Traditionally, chisungu was a three-year ceremony among the Bemba of northern Zambia. Similar initiation ceremonies lasted from one to three years in other groups. With the pressures of formal education and urban migration, however, the entire chisungu performed in the city has now been condensed into a one-week, highly abbreviated ceremony (cf. Jules-Rosette, 1980).

For women of the transitional migrant generation, chisungu has remained the most salient educational experience in which the adult female participated. Many women became ceremonial mistresses and traditional teachers after chisungu. One qualification for teaching was the mastery of potting and ornate ceramic work. Hence, many women with little formal education who migrated to the cities of the Copperbelt and Lusaka possessed at least one potentially marketable skill: ceramic work. This accomplishment could easily be combined with other informal skills such as cooking and beer brewing. Cooking and selling *chitumbowa*, or "fat cakes" consisting of fried corn flour, became the basis for informal marketing among many new migrants. Far more lucrative, however, was the brewing of *chibuku* (local beer) and of stronger illicit gins, *kachiasu,* and *seven days.* Brewing was also combined with potting. The home-brewed beer was prepared during the week and served at weekend *shebeen* parties in homemade clay pots. Brewing was linked with the conventional forms of prostitution that grew up around the mining centers. These migrant women, known as shebeen queens, would entertain single migrants in their homes on a regular patronage basis.

The shebeen queens were found across southern Africa, initially in the mining centers and eventually in provincial and national capitals. Social anthropologists (Mayer, 1971:117–18; Pauw, 1963) noted the appearance of shebeen houses as early as World War I in South Africa. The shebeen parties were not just frivolous forms of entertainment. Through the shebeen trade, women gained control over small-scale enterprises and solidified new, multiethnic social ties in town. Shebeen queens grouped together, dividing tasks of beer brewing and entertainment among themselves. They took on younger apprentices and developed a self-conscious attitude toward entrepreneurship. The South African shebeen queens became the major patrons of local folk musicians. South African jazz was born and nurtured as a form of shebeen entertainment (Coplan, 1979:14–18).

The women potters of Lusaka emerge in perspective as an outgrowth of the local shebeen trade and the communal society that surrounded it. The *mikotokoto,* or weekly beer-drinking network, was a multiethnic group of urban men surrounding a shebeen queen or shebeen network. These individuals helped to retain aspects of the communal sharing that was so important to village life. They also became a steady consumer audience for the transitional women migrants. Recently, the shebeen trade in Lusaka has grown in scale. Men dominate the transportation and marketing of legalized chibuku, and the fruits of its commercialization are increasingly going to them. This development has resulted in the newly coined term *shebeen king,* meaning a middleman who organizes the transport and marketing of indigenous alcoholic beverages.

Before discussing the shebeen trade in further detail, it must be placed in perspective with relationship to other economic outlets for women in Lusaka. Women find it difficult to obtain licenses for market stalls. These licenses are restricted in number, and, until the late 1970s, official preference was given to male household heads who applied for business clearance. Thus, while the fee for licensing is minimal, women are weeded out through a bureaucratic selection process which is preferential toward men. Although some vegetable vendors set up mats in front of the neighborhood markets, market sales, even in the smaller townships, require licensing and a health check. As a result, many women sell goods from their homes. Because these sales are illegal, they must be intermittent. The clandestine and sporadic nature of home sales limits both the regular clientele and the profits that can be obtained. Home vegetable stalls are periodically raided, and their owners are arrested and fined. Thus, the colorful and prosperous situation of the West African market women is atypical in Lusaka (cf. Faladé, 1971:217–29).

Fishmongering and official market sales are more economically rewarding; official market vending is, however, still largely in the hands of men in Lusaka. The sale of homemade arts and crafts, including embroidery, crocheted articles, and ceramic work, is not subject to strict legal monitoring, despite a recent prohibition against street vending in Lusaka.[8] These sales can be conducted on a door-to-door basis with the assistance of middlemen and small children. Among the unlicensed forms of commerce, beer brewing is the profession with both the highest economic profits and the greatest legal risks for women.

THE LEGAL STATUS OF BEER BREWING

Zambian society unofficially fosters the brewing of home beverages by placing a positive social valuation on the beer-drinking circle. During the colonial period, Zambian migrants did not have access to imported alcoholic beverages. Moreover, the drinking circle was a significant part of village social life for men, and it was adapted to the urban industrial centers. Thus, home-brewed beer is culturally esteemed among recent urban migrants. At the same time, most home brewing is illegal in the city. In the late 1970s the Lusaka city council legalized the controlled brewing of higher grades of chibuku for sale in taverns to increase its own revenue. "Legal" chibuku is supposedly made according to specific health regulations and is marketed at fixed prices. Nevertheless, the sale of illicit chibuku and stronger beverages continues, though it is punishable by a nine-month jail sentence or a fine of up to K500 (U.S. $660). During the period of my field observation (1974–79), police raids were frequent in the squatter areas. Zambia law enforcement agencies associate the home beer trade with prostitution. A recent survey (Mwanamwabwa, 1977:42) claims that 70% of the home-brewed beer produced in Zambia is connected with prostitution.

Women who brew beer are therefore careful to cultivate good relationships with community officials. Like the illicit vegetable vendors, they must be circumspect about their activities. It is not, however, possible to hide the brewing process, as it entails long hours of outside cooking before the beer can be brought indoors to settle. Despite the sources of legal conflict, the shebeen queens do not now appear to have a collective consciousness. They cooperate in small brewing groups, but their produce is coordinated on a large scale only by the new middlemen who have entered their trade.

While beer brewing seems more profitable for women migrants with little formal education than are other trades, it and related enterprises require that women have freedom of movement. Therefore, these women do not consider a husband an immediate advantage. Although married women are engaged in the beer trade, as case studies will demonstrate, most of those whom I interviewed were widowed, divorced, or temporarily living alone. Their children and the immediate drinking circle constituted the primary social network. In her survey of a Lusaka squatter township, Hansen (1975:784) found that none of the married women whom she interviewed had paid employment. Husbands were reluctant to let their wives work outside of the home even when money was scarce. When these women did work, they engaged primarily in the illegal vending of vegetables, fat cakes, charcoal, and beer on only an intermittent basis.

WOMEN'S POST-MIGRATION ADJUSTMENT

The female migrant with little formal education has a peculiar form of autonomy. In many ways she is unprepared for urban life, yet she is not the incumbent of a rigidly fixed social status or position in enterprise. Because she is freed from some of the familial and kinship expectations of village life, she can experiment with new forms of employment and survival strategies in a limited economic niche. Moreover, she must forge innovative social networks in order to maintain her economic situation.

The African urban entrepreneur generally experiments with a variety of economic strategies in developing urban markets and supply sources (cf. Beveridge, 1978:2). Since women migrants are faced with the challenge of devising such outlets, they are in an ideal position to be successful urban entrepreneurs *if* they become sensitive to the basic needs and economic demands of their communities.

According to Marris (1968:31) the small enterpreneur in Africa demonstrates

> an ability to assemble and reassemble from what is available . . . a new kind of activity, to reinterpret the meaning of things and fit

them together in new ways. . . . In the African countryside, an innovation may not seem at the outset very remarkable—a wholesale business, a restaurant at a crossroad, a bus service, a saw mill. But to achieve it, the owner must have seen what others had missed—an unsatisfied demand, a way of raising money, a source of skilled labor—and put them together.

In certain respects, the women with basic agricultural and crafts skills are able to adapt these abilities to the expanding socioeconomic setting of the urban townships. These activities can be conducted much as they were in the village setting. However, the economic success of marketeering and crafts in the city depends upon the extent of a woman's urban experience. The illegal nature of much petty trading limits its economic viability. A women engaged in these activities must learn how to cope with the official obstacles that face her. Among craftswomen, lack of knowledge of the urban buyers' market is another major problem.

Initially, women potters conceived of themselves neither as artists nor as businesswomen. They confined much of their trade to the local beer-drinking circle and were unaware of the extent of tourist outlets for marketing ceramic works. Not only were potters largely unaware of the types of craft articles that would appeal to tourists and townspeople, but virtually no use was made of middlemen to canvass the market for crafts and sell these goods.

Women engaged in agricultural marketeering do not have the same problems. They purchase produce wholesale in the downtown markets or from growers located on the outskirts of the city. Although their consumers are regular, the profits are low. Even when these market women manage to obtain small stalls, competition with others engaged in home and public trading makes business difficult. The bureaucratic obstacles to formal licensing for women have already been mentioned. Street vending of agricultural produce and crafts among these women has become an increasingly risky alternative due to police and health checks. Many marketeers combine evening home trading with daily market sales and are still unable to profit substantially. Still, informal sector employment continues to have both social appeal and economic reward.

Successful marketeers have developed a community reputation and have organized women's unions to regulate prices. Some prosperous home and street traders are able to accrue enough expertise and financial backing to move into market stalls, the tea cart trade, and even small restaurants or grocery stores. This career pattern, however, is more typical of vegetable vendors, fishmongers, and charcoal traders than it is of women producing and selling crafts. The increased profits in craft sales come from a combination of ceramic work with beer brewing. While such a combination may be economically beneficial to migrant women, it effectively closes them off from extensive public trade and confines their activities exclusively to a township audience. Thus, craftswomen remain marginal because of their former limited educational attainment and their inability to make use of employment opportunities in the city. Their recourse to informal networks is restricted by a variety of legal and social barriers.

PROFILES OF WOMEN IN THE INFORMAL SECTOR

The home and public vegetable vendors are part of a larger chain of farmers and marketeers. Two major official markets in downtown Lusaka are key distribution points. As already emphasized, women need an established business history and the support of their husbands to work in those markets. Despite these conditions, however, the home vendors continue to buy wholesale produce there. Many of the smaller township markets are organized on a cooperative basis. Women may join cooperatives, and in some cases they have formed collectives within the cooperative markets. Even these market stalls, no matter how small, require licensing.

Women marketing from their homes use their minimal profits for the purchase of more vegetables and their immediate subsistence needs. Thus, trade expansion is difficult from this niche. It is not possible to compare this activity with the more innovative forms of entrepreneurship that develop in licensed marketeering. Married women who work from their homes are many times obligated to turn profits over to their husbands. This obligation further restricts the potential expansion of their enterprises. As a result, with the exception of the more lucrative beer brewers, married women in the home trades frequently abandon selling because of low and sporadic profits.

Most women who sell from home mark up produce sales to make a profit and are accused of overcharging. This situation is typical of township marketeers and grocers generally. Some women sell produce from their own gardens, but this type of activity tends to offer little more than subsistence. The following case study collected by Mwanamwabwa (1977:26) illustrates this point.

Clara Phiri

Clara Phiri lives in Chawama, a squatter area, and sells vegetables at the market. To obtain her daily supply, Clara starts off her journey at about 5 a.m., walking a 10 mile distance to the airport junction on Great East Road, a delivery point for the growers who come from adjoining farm areas. There is a stiff competition between Clara and other buyers for reasonable prices and a variety of produce. When the appropriate vegetable produce has been purchased, Clara walks back for another 10 miles to Chawama where she rearranges the product for retail sale in the market. There is no system of costing involved except that her experience in the urban market trade determines the price at which she sells her produce. In addition, she considers purchase price and seasonality.

Once at the market, Clara competes with other marketeers to sell her produce, which is very similar to that offered for sale by others. With limited demand from consumers in the area due to their income, Clara may end the day with half of her perishable produce unsold and without proper storage facilities or means of preservation. There is a great loss in economic and opportunity costs through inappropriate storage, method, and total activity time.

Other women who sell vegetables but do not belong to an organized market system like Clara are classified as unlicensed street vendors. They also re-package their produce and sell it at selected strategic points such as near a shopping area. Some of these street sellers are firmly established but are still subjected to continuous police raids which result in frequent confiscation of their produce. Criticisms of alleged overcharging because of the unspecified weights of their produce and also of the unhygienic conditions under which some of the produce is sold are made by the consuming public.

Clara's case emphasizes that even women with official stalls move into home and street vending to sell their surplus produce. These women continue to be the victims of police clean-up programs once they are licensed. Because the goods that they sell are part of their day's surplus or the surplus of another city vendor, their vegetables are of inferior quality and are sold to squatters at higher prices than the more wealthy city dwellers pay.

Home trade in vegetables is often combined with other commodities such as dried fish and cooking oil. It is not uncommon to find charcoal and vegetable trading together. These ingredients are used in preparing the staple diet of township dwellers, and there is always a need for purchasing one or more such items after regular marketing hours. The case of Mrs. Phiri is typical of the home vegetable trade in Lusaka's townships.

ADDRESS PHIRI

Twenty-year-old Mrs. Address Phiri is a Zambian Cewa. Her husband, Mr. Iwal Zulu, is a Cewa who married her by customary law marriage in a village near Katete five years ago. Before their marriage, he had been in Lusaka for three years, and soon after the marriage he brought his wife there. They lived in Kalingalinga squatter compound for two years. Mrs. Phiri's first born child passed away but she has now two living children. In addition to their own children, an eight-year-old child of the husband's sister lives with them and attends school in Lusaka. Mrs. Phiri has attended school for six years, whereas her husband has no education. Mr. Zulu's first job in Lusaka for four years was as a security guard. Later, he was employed at the construction of the International Airport in Lusaka where he worked as an unskilled laborer earning K12 (U.S. $15.84) per month. He is now employed as a brick-layer by a Lusaka construction firm, but the wife does not know his salary. Every month Mr. Zulu buys her a bag of mealie meal and gives her further K6 (U.S. $7.92) for the purchase of vegetables and sundries.

The family has lived at Mtendele for two years.[9] Their house, which they want to build with six rooms, has one room finished. Mrs. Phiri would like to contribute to the completion of the house and for that purpose she has been looking for work, and her husband has not objected. She has visited several private houses to get employment as a domestic servant, but has met no success. Then she started vegetable trading. She borrowed her original capital from her brother, who lives at Mtendele. Apart from the brother, she and the husband have many other relatives in Lusaka. She sells tomatoes and occasionally cooking oil in front of her house. She buys a box of tomatoes for K2,50 (U.S. $3.30) and sells the tomatoes in small portions. She reckons to make a profit of K2 (U.S. $2.64) on each box. She usually sells three or four boxes a month. Mrs. Phiri, too, hands all the profit over to the husband, who uses it on the construction of their house. (Hansen, 1973:136)

Women are easily discouraged by the obstacles and the minimal profits of the home trade. They sell vegetables intermittently when household finances are low. When husbands administer the profits of vegetable sales, the incentive to work is reduced. Charcoal trading, requiring a larger capital outlay with the promise of improved profits, is seen as a step up from the home vegetable trade. Beer brewing, already described as the most lucrative home trade, is not considered an option for many married women, who fear the risks and cannot obtain familial support for their activities.

Unlike vegetable vending, the beer trade originates in the local townships. The production of legalized chibuku became a permanent and open occupation in the late 1970s. Women producing "official beer" could easily engage middlemen to expand their commercial outlets. They produced not only for local beer parties but also for taverns and commercial outlets. Both men and women freely purchased legal chibuku without fear of arrest or fine. The illegal drinks were confined to underground trade and were bought chiefly by men in alcohol transport networks. Hence, legal brewing interfaced with the bar trade. Women who became involved in these networks also provided entertainment which is distinct from the "traditional" prostitution associated with the shebeen trade. As vegetable vending proved less lucrative, some married women in the townships moved into both permanent and temporary beer brewing in competition with the more established shebeen traders.

MARIA KHOSA: A HOME BEER TRADER

Maria Khosa is a 25-year-old Sotho from Botswana. She grew up in Johannesburg, where she married a Zambian Nsenga by civil marriage five years ago. While in Johannesburg, she worked as a domestic servant. They came to Lusaka three years ago (in 1970) where the husband, Mr. Elfas Phiri, has worked as a security guard ever since. Mrs. Khosa has attended school for seven years, her husband for eight years. She is a member of the Anglican Church, he of the Dutch Reformed Church. The couple have no living children; all of the four children the wife bore have died.

On their first coming to Lusaka, Mrs. Khosa and Mr. Phiri lived at Mandevu, a squatter settlement where they rented a house. After two years at Mandevu, they moved to Mtendele where they are now building a house of their own, two rooms of which are finished. The house is planned to have six rooms.

Mr. Phiri earns K50 (U.S. $66.00) a month, all of which he hands over to his wife. A good deal of the money is currently being spent on the completion of the house. Further, they send every month K10 (U.S. $13.20) to the husband's matrilineal relatives who live near Petauke. Because of these expenses, Mrs. Khosa started beer brewing, which she has done for three months. She brews ample supplies of beer every week from Thursday until Sunday. The kind of beer she brews is a South African beer, which she calls "Banba." The beer is consumed in one of the family's two rooms, which is not yet furnished, except for some odd chairs and tables which serve to accommodate the clientele. The beer is sold in metal cups for which 10 Ngwee (13¢) are charged. Mrs. Khosa reckons to make a profit on her beer sale of K10 ($13.20) every week.

Mr. Phiri did not interfere much with his wife's beer trade. Being a security guard, he was away from the township at work from four p.m. to twelve p.m., and returned to Mtendele on his bike at night conveniently enough to help his wife close down the trade. As the control of illegal beer brewing was becoming very much stricter, Mrs. Khosa was considering domestic work instead. (Hansen, 1973:130–31)

Mrs. Khosa's work may be described as permanent brewing insofar as she uses it as a daily source of revenue. Her trade remains largely confined to the home, but her basic income and community reputation could allow her to enter the more expanded legal trading network.

EMILIA CHOMBA: A TEMPORARY BREWER

The marriage of Mrs. Emilia Chomba and Mr. Hudson Chomba is a remarriage. She had been divorced by her former husband because she bore no children. She has since been treated with African medicine and has two children in her union with Mr. Chomba. Mr. Chomba himself divorced his first wife for reasons unknown to Mrs. Chomba. Mr. and Mrs. Chomba were married in church in Lusaka six years ago. Mrs. Chomba has lived in Lusaka since the early [1950s] Federal days; she was brought to town as a a a child by her Ngoni parents from Malawi. Mr. Chomba, a Ngoni of Malawi origin too, has not spent as many years in Lusaka as has his wife.

On their marriage the Chombas settled in Kalingalinga squatter compound. After three years there they moved to Mtendele, where they now live in a four-room house. In addition to the family, a child of the wife's sister, a girl of twelve, lives with them, her mother not being able to care for her. A family with three children has rented a room in the Chomba's house for the last six months. They are expected to pay a rent of K7 (U.S. $9.24) every month, but have paid nothing so far. The husband of the family, being away working in Livingstone, has not sent his wife any money.

Mr. Chomba has worked as a postcarrier for seven years and receives a monthly salary of K49 (U.S. $64.68). Mrs. Chomba did not know this when we asked her, but was able to procure a wage statement. She receives K20 (U.S. $26.40) per month for food, and he provides the clothes when needed. Further, Mr. Chomba every year pays K65 ($85.80) for the maintenance of the children from his first marriage.

Because of these obligations, times occur when money is scarce in the family, and Mrs. Chomba brews beer particularly at such times and has done so for the three years they were at Mtendele. The kind of beer Mrs. Chomba is brewing is "kachiasu" which is a strong distilled product that has always been strictly prohibited. She does not accommodate her clients, but makes them buy her product and take it away. When she brews kachiasu she makes a profit of K18 (U.S. $23.76) per month. Some of this she sends to her sister in the village whose child she is caring for in Lusaka. The rest of the profit she spends on food.

When we first met Mrs. Chomba, she had not brewed beer for three months. Beer brewing of one kind or another is an activity that most women are familiar with and can readily launch into when monetary resources are scarce. Mrs. Chomba had not started again partly because of competition and partly because of official control, which, as mentioned before, was heightened. (Hansen, 1973:131)

Mrs. Chomba's clientele was not the immediate community; however, her connections with the city-wide alcohol trade were also tenuous. Since she brewed kachiasu, she was restricted to illegal contacts. Hansen (1973:130–32) does not give a detailed description of the illegal networks operating in Mrs. Chomba's township. It is safe to conclude, however, that the transport of kachiasu is more restricted than that of chibuku and relies upon an underground network that is difficult for outside researchers to penetrate.

THE WOMEN POTTERS OF LUSAKA

The women migrant potters are a key population in Lusaka because they actively combine craftwork with the beer trade. Some surveys of women in the informal sector (cf. Hansen, 1973; Hansen, 1975; and Mwanamwabwa, 1977) conclude that women serially engage in a variety of production and marketeering endeavors. Little (1973:85–86) characterizes this type of lateral mobility and job switching as a product of urban opportunism. Where opportunistic attitudes prevail, both men and women have mixed career patterns ranging from farming and marketeering to unskilled labor.[10] Dry spells of unemployment for women and their spouses lead to the temporary forms of self-employment that have already been discussed. Vegetable vending, beer brewing, and prostitution are pursued on a temporary basis by many urban women while they wait for potentially more stable employment opportunities. Little's controversial statement (1973:85) that young African women exchange sexual services for cash during periods of unemployment is based upon the recurrence of this pattern.

Migrant women with craft skills, however, are much more inclined to combine occupational options than they are to switch from one to another. Potting, for example, can always be relied upon to bring in a steady, although small, source of revenue. If the potter improves her commercial skills to the extent that they become widely marketable in town, she can depend upon both township and tourist sales. In this case, she acquires some notion of the craft articles that appeal to an outside audience while she continues to produce a basic set of pots for use in home water storage and in the chibuku trade. Generally, the more experienced "master" potters are able to make this transition while the younger women who learn ceramic skills in town are not. Case profiles (such as that of Mrs. Kave which follows) suggest that this range of adaptation is a key feature of urban potting and that it may be characteristic of other women's trades.

Mrs. Kave, a Bemba widow in her forties, came to Lusaka twelve years before I interviewed her in 1975, shortly after the death of her husband. Some years prior to her migration, she had moved from a small village in northern Zambia to Ndola to accompany her husband, a worker in the mines. Trained as a Bemba ceremonial mistress, Mrs. Kave was already skilled in ceramic work when she came to Ndola. There, she began to experiment with pottery sales combined with home beer brewing.

When Mrs. Kave moved to Lusaka, she chose to reside near a stream that cuts across Marrapodi township. The stream contained natural clay deposits that facilitated her potting work. She continued beer brewing and was soon joined by a collective of townswomen in her neighborhood. Mrs. Kave's already competent potting skills improved as she taught the members of the collective how to make pots for shebeen parties. Although she monitored the brewing and potting activities, Mrs. Kave did not engage in prostitution.

With continued residence in Lusaka, Mrs. Kave gained a sense of the local crafts market. Although she did not regard herself as an artist, she learned marketing skills from the men engaged in the local art trade. Mrs. Kave modified the traditional chisungu figurines for sale in town. The figurines that she produced were rough renderings of fish and animals, and were portable and cheap enough to gain a certain appeal in the tourist consumer audience. The figurines sold for 50¢ apiece in 1975. Two years later, Mrs. Kave had more than tripled her price as she acquired a better sense of the tourist market.

PRODUCTION TECHNIQUES AND
CERAMIC MARKETING

The tools used in urban potting are adaptations of traditional materials to a new setting. The potters do not use a wheel. At the same time, they do not use the more laborious techniques of other African and Oceanic potters.[11]

Mrs. Kave taught her apprentices to shape pots on a metal bucket. The bucket is turned by hand. The initial pot is molded upward from a single lump of clay. A wet corn cob is used to shape and contour the pots, and the lip of the pot is turned down with a small stick. All pots have a standardized appearance; one skilled woman's pots can be distinguished from those of another only by the subtle hatchmarks under the lip. Standardization is important because it facilitates a rapid production process, though even more significant is the fact that pots for beer storage and drinking are expected to be uniform in appearance. They are functional rather than decorative objects. Individualization in ceramic work results from the tourist trade, where some variation is sought in figurine production. Even then, the potters do not sign or mark their works by name.

When interviewed, Mrs. Kave described her production and marketing process:

INTERVIEWER: How do you work on a pot?

MRS. KAVE: First I put down a paper. Then I shape the clay by hand and put it on a plastic. Next, I take a corn cob and mold it well. When I have finished, I put the dried pot on a fire (an open wood fire). I polish the pot with this small stone until it shines.

INTERVIEWER: How many do you make per day?

MRS. KAVE: Sometimes we make five per day if they are small; if they are large, we make three.

INTERVIEWER: If you make a hundred and take them to town to sell, can you sell them all in one day? Do you usually sell on credit?

MRS. KAVE: No, we just sell them here. We don't have any clients who resell them either.

INTERVIEWER: Can you ever have a client who resells your pottery in town or in a store while you go on working?

MRS. KAVE: No, we don't have even one.

INTERVIEWER: But if you see a client, you can give him a good price so that he can buy many?

MRS. KAVE: Yes, we can give him a good price so that he can buy.

INTERVIEWER: Can you find a child to help you with the work or to bring you water or wood?

MRS. KAVE: Yes, there are children. There are many of them.

INTERVIEWER: What do you pay them?

MRS. KAVE: I don't pay them, because they are my children.

After this interview, Mrs. Kave developed town marketing outlets through street vending in the city. She conducted all of her own sales, which chiefly involved figurines. Since her production rate (including the shaping and outdoor firing of the pieces) was low, she had no more than five or six pieces to sell at a given time. This slow production contrasted with that of male curio brokers, who made and sold twenty to thirty pieces a day (cf. Jules-Rosette, 1979a:225–38). While the women potters in town moved from ceremonial arts to standardized commercial production (cf. Graburn, 1976:5–6), their commodity bulk and visibility were minimal. The pots used in the chibuku circle had a regular community demand, but the niche for figurine sales was exploited on a more tentative basis.

It is revealing to contrast women's ceramic work with that of commercial male producers in Lusaka. The men, with broader commercial outlets and a more rapid production process, specialize in delicate figurines of people engaged in work activities—hoeing, hunting, and reading, for example. Ngandu, a Bemba sculptor, worked with six of his brothers in ceramic production in 1975. He had learned ceramic work from his grandmother and put it to new uses in the city. He and his apprentices worked from a set of templates, and then they used wire to reinforce the figurines and make them more sturdy for tourist transport. No individual completed a single figurine. One brother specialized in arms and legs, while Ngandu, the most experienced, made the heads. Approximately fifteen figurines could be completed for firing in a single day. Ngandu both used shops as commercial outlets and vended in the street. Two brothers were engaged only in sales. Prices started at $10.00 for a small figurine.

Ngandu's production and marketing skills were far more sophisticated than those of the women. His art was consciously produced for the African elite and tourists, and he took pride in craftsmanship and innovation. Few of the women potters were aware of Ngandu's work and marketing procedures. Their mixed career patterns and limited production and sales experience made them unable to compete with his enterprise.

In sum, the male and female ceramic workers of Lusaka occupied two distinct economic niches. Women's figurines were standardized, and the women's outlook was constrained by other community involvements.

THE WOMEN'S APPRENTICESHIP CIRCLE

Mrs. Kave was surrounded by four younger women who regularly worked in the potting and brewing trades. Two of these women made their primary incomes by brewing kachiasu and selling it to local residents. They were secretive about their work but acknowledged Mrs. Kave's training. The pots that they fashioned, the crude work of beginners, were uniquely pots for chibuku storage and several of those that I examined were defective. These apprentices had not expanded into figurine production.

Dora Chilumbwe was an exception to this group. She had come to Mrs. Kave three years before to learn potting. Unlike the other apprentices, she lives some distance from the stream where the clay was collected. She experimented with diverse potting styles and made an effort to individualize each piece. Dora viewed chibuku brewing as secondary to craft work. She explained: "The chibuku is there. Instead of staying without anything to do, it's necessary to work. The job gives you something to do."

Dora was in the process of becoming a craft entrepreneur. Unlike the other members of the apprentice circle, she was willing to make pottery the major source of her income and to experiment with stylistic presentation. However, the market open to her was limited, and she had not yet acquired the expertise to increase production for a larger audience.

FAMILY LIFE, EDUCATION, AND URBAN MIGRATION

The scant employment for women in the formal sector is a direct result of limited educational opportunities. Traditional forms of education provided the potters and brewers with basic skills which they could adapt to city life. Women with some marketable skills were definitely much better off than those without any training whatsoever. However, only the more active and entrepreneurial women trained in the village milieu realized that these skills were insufficient to enter most trades in the public sector.

While many girls attend primary school, which is now compulsory in Zambia, the educational system is oriented toward progress for boys. Early marriage patterns that persist in the rural areas are an incentive for girls to leave school before completing the primary grades. Still, despite cultural obstacles, some women migrants of the transitional generation placed a special value upon educating their daughters. Ilsa Schuster (1979:32) presents one young woman's words:

> We would have starved if my mother did not sell in the market when my father stopped working because of illness. She hated it because market women are known as prostitutes. After my father died, she stayed in the market. She feared going home (i.e., returning to the village of her birth), for then we children would die through witchcraft.[12] She bore the insults of older women because we would complete secondary school.

It was generally the mothers rather than the fathers of the transitional generation who saw education as a source of escape and advancement for their daughters. These townborn daughters were able to enter Lusaka's "subelite" of clerical workers and skilled trainees in the early 1970s. The situations of their mothers, however, changed very little. Mothers who pursued education for their daughters experienced deep cultural conflicts from peers who valued male education—if any education was sought— and saw the young woman as an asset through her marriage potential. Even with the advent of compulsory education for young women between the ages of twelve and sixteen, the adolescent drop-out rate in Zambia continued to be high. The townborn women lacked the home skills of their migrant mothers, and their adjustment was even more difficult with incomplete formal educations.

After independence, Zambian schools were nationalized. Government educational agencies stated that school training was intended to place females "on an intellectual level with men" (Schuster, 1979:52), despite the fact that this goal challenged many conventional African values and beliefs. School girls, whether in the rural milieu or in the city, had to reconcile traditional and modern attitudes toward family and education. Furthermore, the formal cut-off points in the Zambian educational system resulted in the exclusion of women from higher levels of advancement.

TABLE 3 Ratio of girls to boys in the Zambian school system in 1973

| | | Ratio | |
		Girls	Boys
Grade	I	1 :	1.05
	II	1 :	1.09
	III	1 :	1.12
	IV	1 :	1.21
	V	1 :	1.29
	VI	1 :	1.49
	VII	1 :	1.70
Form	I	1 :	1.70
	II	1 :	1.73
	III	1 :	1.85
	IV	1 :	2.92
	V	1 :	2.48

SOURCE: *Educational Statistics for 1973*, Ministry of Education, Lusaka, Zambia, September 1975.

Grades 1 through 4 (formerly known as Standard I and Standard II) constitute the terminal education for many of the urban poor (see table 3). By the time Zambian school children reach the seventh grade (Standard VI), young women constitute only 37% of the population attending school nationwide. At this point, the students must pass a comprehensive examination to enter Forms I and II, lower secondary school. The women who have not been excluded at the lower primary levels usually drop out at this point. If the women do enter Form I, they have to leave their village or smalltown homes to continue the educational process. As already indicated, familial pressures mitigate against this move for young women.

Upper secondary school (Forms III–IV) is the final cut-off point before Zambian university entry. Even fewer women make it this far, and virtually none of the transitional migrant generation is represented in this category. While university education is nationally subsidized in Zambia, the competition for women's entry is stiff. (The women who do enter are not our concern in this discussion, since most township residents who are recent migrants have no access to the higher rungs of education.) Male dominance, family pressures, and socioeconomic entrapment prevent many migrant women and their first-generation daughters from reaping the benefits of higher education and the employment opportunities associated with it.

The drop-out rate for urban women in the Zambian educational system seems more socially significant if it is examined with respect to familial values and the decline in traditional educational outlets. Young township women whom I interviewed in 1976 explained that their initiation rites had been reduced to a one-week period of instruction from elders. Extensive training provided by the initiation rites is no longer available. At the same time, the formal education that these women had received is inadequate for them to enter the wage labor market at a competitive level. They are caught between the traditional values of nonformal education and the pressures of a modern industrializing society.

Family structure also influences the women's employment prospects. Limited options for work makes township women into appendages of their husbands (cf. Hansen, 1975:799). The economic avenues associated with home trade are conducive to sporadic self-employment. Married women with children in the squatter areas are tied to their homes in ways which they had not been in the village context. Although the children that I observed were casually watched by neighbors, community organization among squatters was such that adults could not account for the whereabouts of these children at all times. While the township housewife is freed from the burdensome water fetching and agricultural tasks of the countryside, she is responsible for monitoring the children and preparing the food alone. These responsibilities were shared with kin in the rural milieu.

In the city, the presence of an extended kin becomes a burden. Family members arrive from the countryside and expect housing and support for indefinite periods of time with minimal household participation. These "parasites" place a particularly heavy responsibility on the squatter woman whose income and prospects for mobility are already low. The new arrivals also add to the urban adjustment problems of families that are not yet secure in their new environment.

Polygynous families are also among the transitional migrants in my interview sample of seventy-eight households in Marrapodi township. Few of the urban potters fit into this category, but the women marketeers and craft producers do. In the urban polygynous families, women assume the responsibility for the care and upbringing of their own children. In many cases, the husband's income falls far short of what is necessary to maintain each mother-child unit. Some wives share child monitoring duties. The first, or senior, wives are freed to work while younger wives watch their children. Home trades are particularly conducive to the support of the polygynous family. The sectarian religious families that I contacted insisted that wives in polygynous households sell homemade crafts or cooperate in the marketing of their husband's wares.[13] Polygyny in town also tends to change women's attitudes toward fertility (cf. Clignet and Sween, 1976). Multiple wives reduce the number of children in their unit because of the economic and time burdens of care and nurturing.

Polygyny can have positive benefits in the urban context. If at least one wife participates in a home trade, she may contribute to the household income as well as to that of her own unit. The members of urban religious groups have established collective businesses among polygynous wives. They run groceries and market stalls together. This type of cooperation with other women is more difficult for squatter housewives in nuclear families to obtain. According to my observations, polygyny is found in conjunction with small entrepreneurial activities and women's home industries. Family pressures and the religious values of many of the polygynous women whom I interviewed in the townships excluded them from the lucrative beer trade. Their family structure was, however, particularly adaptive for other forms of urban entrepreneurship.[14]

A preliminary review of the family situation among recent urban migrants suggests that the monogamous nuclear family is not as conducive to women's self-employment as the female-headed or the polygynous family. Hansen (1975:777–78) emphasizes that monogamous wives without entrée into formal jobs had little motivation and familial support to work on a regular basis. Single women were freer to enter self-employment and had a wider range of options and career patterns. The combination of potting with the shebeen trade among the women potters is a key example of this urban alternative and the economic incentives that it provides.

CONCLUSIONS: URBAN ALTERNATIVES FOR RECENT WOMEN MIGRANTS TO LUSAKA

New forms of production and marketing in the urban environment are critical to the growth of African entrepreneurship. Joseph Schumpeter (1961) emphasizes that innovation in economic adaptation should not be confused with invention. Very few entrepreneurs actually invent new techniques. Rather, they discover outlets for existing economic demands and methods. The women potters and marketeers of Lusaka are small-scale entrepreneurs. Their problems reflect the overall adjustment process of Zambian urban marginals. They are, however, plagued with legal restrictions and social barriers that hinder entry into larger scale enterprises. When they do obtain familial support and capital, home marketeers break away from sporadic petty trading into official trading and small shop enterprises. The conditions for advancement into this area of self-employment exist, but they are still difficult to exploit.

The most successful migrant women pursue several avenues of self-employment at once. The serial pattern of job shifting described in the literature on male migration does not explain the situation of women in combined trades. A prevalent argument used to account for the advancement of women migrants in the city revolves around kin and ethnicity. It is hypothesized that ethnic networks are transposed from the village context to the city (cf. Gutkind, 1965:48–60) and that by using these channels as sources of mutual aid and as economic networks, the recent woman migrant adjusts to her new environment. Women working in the informal sector in Lusaka come from a variety of regional and ethnic backgrounds and live in a wide range of family situations. Certainly, strategies of familial adaptation to town life vary, based upon ethnicity. Nevertheless, the cooperative associations and the apprenticeship circles established among women marketeers and craft workers are not limited by ethnicity (cf. Little, 1978:177).

The potters of Bemba origin train women from other ethnic backgrounds. The beer circles from which their consumers are drawn are also multiethnic in composition. A similar ethnic plurality is characteristic of the women's marketeering collectives. In Lusaka, urban life, particularly among the squatters, juxtaposes individuals from a variety of backgrounds. The most viable community networks are based upon residence and the exchange of goods, ideas, and services. Some women entrepreneurs are able to exploit these immediate community networks and to move beyond them to consumer markets that transect social class and regional background.[15] Women's collectives and voluntary associations are far more important than ethnicity and social class in urban adjustment.

Isolated women in home trades, however, seldom operate on a collective basis. They must keep a low community profile. In their case, kin and ethnic ties are often an obstacle because they result in added home responsibilities. Many squatters attempt to maintain anonymity and social distance from their neighbors because of their tenuous legal status and transient residence in the townships. Even the beer-drinking circle described above is not stable in its composition and does not offer a constant support network.

It has been emphasized that women with traditional skills find the beer trade and related craft outlets among the most lucrative urban alternatives. The economic reasons for this choice are clear: beer is popular and its sale brings in more revenue than produce vending. The chain of associations involved in both legal and illegal sales is based upon the local community and also includes outside networks that can be combined with other remunerative enterprises. The flexibility of the shebeen trade makes it an important occupational category in southern African urban life. The position of women migrants is, thus, a critical area for new research.

Women have long been neglected in the migration literature. Their motivations and status in the migration process have been treated as a by-product of male urban adjustment. The statistics on lone women migrants and their independent economic motivations for participating in urban life overturn these assumptions.[16] In fact, first-generation townswomen have been pioneers in establishing informal sector entrepreneurship because they have had few other alternatives. As formal education and employment opportunities increase for town-born women, marketeering and home entrepreneurship will undoubtedly decline in importance as urban socioeconomic patterns. The hopes and aspirations of many women in the transitional generation will be realized as their daughters gain greater access to formal educational opportunities that will allow them to reap the benefits of urban social and economic life.

In terms of national development, the absorption of recent migrant women into the urban economy is a major problem. Legal and educational restrictions bar the untrained underclass of women from pursuing legitimate channels of business entrepreneurship. In Zambia no social welfare system currently exists to aid these women. The cooperative movement in Zambia has concentrated on the rural sector and has not systematically focused on the activities of women (cf. Quick, 1978:115–17). The Zambian case suggests the importance of policy planning that takes into account the short-term entrepreneurial options that migrant women generate in the urban context. This goal might be accomplished through both informal training or apprenticeship programs and the growth and licensing of small-scale home enterprises. In an urban economy characterized by poverty and massive underemployment, however, the local market for small-trade items is rapidly saturated.

Formal education is only a partial solution to the migrant women's employment and adjustment problems because continued education remains out of the reach of the masses of urban poor. In Zambia and other nations where a substantial gap persists between the technoeconomic goals of development and urban women's opportunities for improved economic conditions, there is a critical need for further investigation of the home trades and crafts with regard to their income-generating potential, technological level, and the sexual patterning of job activities. Understanding how women of various strata adapt to the urban economy is an important prerequisite for the assessment of policy issues related to women and development on an international scale.

NOTES

1. This chapter is based upon a study of squatter relocation in Lusaka, Zambia. The study took place from 1974 to 1979 and was funded by the National Science Foundation, Grants Soc. 76–20861 and Soc. 78–20861. This chapter was written during my tenure as a fellow at the Center for Advanced Study in the Behavioral Sciences at Stanford University. My fellowship was funded by NEH Grant #FC–262–78–1030, sponsored by the Andrew Mellon Foundation. I am solely responsible for the content and conclusions of the study.

2. The 1969 Zambian census records Lusaka's population as 262,425. By 1974 Lusaka's population had nearly doubled. As a result, the municipal boundaries of Lusaka were expanded to handle more of the suburban population. Lusaka now encompasses 57 satellite townships with thousands of new residents annually.

3. Cf. Mayer (1971:210–23). He emphasizes that those Xhosa migrants with some education and urban aspirations brought their wives to town because of money, land tenure, and kinship considerations. The less-educated migrants followed the lone male pattern that characterized early twentieth-century rural-urban movements in South Africa.

4. Little (1974:15–16) notes that a similar labor pass system was prevalent in the Belgian Congo. Subsidized housing was provided for clerical and unskilled workers in the urban labor force (Minon, 1960:2–29). The majority of Congolese were expected to reside in town on a temporary basis and to provide a constant labor resource for urban economic enterprises.

5. Several recent studies have been conducted on the forced migration of the Masowe Apostolic Sect (also known as the Apostolic Sabbath Church of God). Margaret Kileff (1973) and Kileff and Kileff (1979:151–67) have studied the return of the Masowe migrants from South Africa to Rhodesia during the 1960s. Clive Dillon-Malone (1978:28–45) discusses the adjustment of the insulated Masowe migrant community in Lusaka, Zambia. All of these studies suggest a need for further research on mass religious and political migrations in southern Africa.

6. Ilsa Schuster (1981) reports that women seeking work as domestics in public institutions in 1971 and 1972 had great difficulty and were accepted only after male applicants had been selected.

7. Many Zambian men seeking employment register with the government Labor Exchange. While women register as well, they are given less incentive to do so and there is a wide discrepancy between the actual numbers of men and women who register. As of 1973, 38.9% of the men who registered with the Labor Exchange were placed in a variety of urban occupational positions, as opposed to 25.4% of the women. In absolute terms, the male placement is highly disproportionate, though the number of women entering skilled and semiskilled occupations is increasing (see table 2). These women are primarily town-born and have had access to formal education. Many of the transitional women migrants discussed here never reach the Labor Exchange rosters. Data for 1971 are not available from the official files to which I had access.

8. Street vending in the downtown area was prohibited in Lusaka by a 1976 city council ordinance. This ordinance had a particularly devastating effect upon street vegetable and produce sales. It also curtailed the activities of street curio and tourist art salesmen. Art and craft producers and their middlemen suffered from this legal prohibition.

9. Mtendele, a squatter township east of Lusaka, is a stopping place for many new town migrants. Karen Hansen surveyed unemployed women in Mtendele in 1971.

10. Cf. Little (1974:32–39). Urban opportunism is the product of multiple outlets for casual labor and semiskilled work in the African city. As a result of this pattern, new migrants to the city may hold several completely different jobs over a short period of time.

11. Jehanne Teilhet (personal communication, 1978) has described techniques used by Oceanic potters. They walk around the pots to shape them without the aid of a wheel. Nepalese potters use hand-driven wheels which are slightly more efficient. The women potters of Lusaka achieve a similar effect by rotating the pots by hand on top of a metal bucket.

12. Cf. Mitchell (1965:192–203) and Mayer (1971:150–51). These authors emphasize the prevalence of southern African witchcraft beliefs in the urban area. Mitchell (1965:200) stresses that witchcraft is used as a major causal explanation of misfortune and illness in town, while Mayer (1971:150) acknowledges that townsmen view city life as a possible source of escape from vengeful ancestors and witches. Both studies point out that beliefs in the "long arm" of witchcraft extend from the village context to the city.

13. During the course of my research in the Zambian townships, I interviewed wives in polygynous religious households (Jules-Rosette 1979b:127–44). Polygynous wives in these households were encouraged to become economically self-sufficient in order to support their children as part of a separate unit.

14. Cf. Oppong, et al., eds. (1978) and Jules-Rosette (1978:123–44). There is a great need for current research on the polygynous African family as an urban adaptation. The polygynous family functions differently in town than it does in the village context. Multiple wives help out with agricultural productions but may be a hindrance in the urban environment if they are not self-employed or working outside of the home.

15. Cf. Little (1978:177–85). Little's argument suggests that urban voluntary associations are more important than kin and ethnic ties in moving beyond insulated community networks. Through these means, women are able to mobilize occupational, religious, and other social groups to their advantage.

16. Cf. Hansen (1977:13–20). Data collected in surveys of Lusaka households suggest that married women are less likely than single household heads to engage in steady self-employment. A further breakdown of these materials in terms of polygynous versus nuclear families would be helpful when considering women's incentives to work both within the home and in the wage labor force.

REFERENCES

Annual Report of the Department of Labor. 1969–1975. Lusaka, Zambia: Government Printing Office.

Beveridge, Andrew. 1978. "Indigenous Entrepreneurs, Development and 'Formal' Independence: The Zambian Case." Paper presented at the Annual Meetings of the American Sociological Association (September).

Clignet, Remi, and Joyce Sween. 1976. "Interaction Between Historical and Sociological Times in the Analysis of Fertility in West Cameroon." Paper presented at the 15th Annual Seminar on Family Research, Lome, Togo (January).

Coplan, David. 1979. "The Marabi Era: Social Implications of African Working Class Music between the World Wars." Unpublished paper, Indiana University.

Dillon-Malone, Clive M. 1978. *The Korsten Basketmakers.* Lusaka, Zambia: Institute for African Studies.

Du Toit, Brian M., and Helen Safa, eds. 1975. *Migration and Urbanization.* The Hague: Mouton.

Educational Statistics for 1973. 1975. Lusaka, Zambia: Ministry of Education (September).

Epstein, A. L. 1961. "The Network and Urban Social Organization." *The Rhodes-Livingstone Journal* 29:29–62.

Faladé, Solange. 1971. "Women of Dakar and the Surrounding Urban Area." Pp. 217–29 in Denise Paulme (ed.), *Women of Tropical Africa.* Berkeley: University of California Press.

Graburn, Nelson H. 1976. *Ethnic and Tourist Arts: Cultural Expression from the Fourth World.* Berkeley: University of California Press.

Gutkind, Peter C. W. 1965. "African Urbanism, Mobility and the Social Network." *International Journal of Comparative Sociology* 6, no. 6:48–60.

Hansen, Karen Tranberg. 1973. "The Work Opportunities of Married Women in a Peri-Urban Township, Lusaka, Zambia: An Exploratory Study." Unpublished thesis for the Magisterkonferens. Aarhus, Denmark: Aarhus Universitet.

———. 1975. "Married Women and Work: Expectations from an Urban Case Study." *African Social Research* 20:777–99.

———. 1977. "Prospects for Wage Labor Among Married Women in Lusaka, Zambia." Paper presented at the 20th Annual Meetings of the African Studies Association, Houston.

Heisler, Helmuth. 1971. "The African Work Force in Zambia," *Civilizations* 21, no. 4:1–29.

Jules-Rosette, Bennetta. 1978. "Family and Ceremonial Authority: The Sources of Leadership in an Indigenous African Church." Pp. 123–44 in Christine Oppong et al. (eds.), *Marriage, Fertility and Parenthood in West Africa.* Canberra, Australia: Australian National University Press.

———. 1979a. "Alternative Urban Adaptations: Zambian Cottage Industries as Sources of Social and Economic Innovation." *Human Organization* 38, no. 3 (Fall): 225–38.

———. 1979b. "Women as Ceremonial Leaders in an African Church: The Apostles of John Maranke." Pp. 127–44 in Bennetta Jules-Rosette (ed.), *The New Religions of Africa.* Norwood, New Jersey: Ablex.

———. 1980. "Changing Aspects of Women's Initiation in Southern Africa: An Exploratory Study." *Canadian Journal of African Studies* 13, no. 3:1–12.

Kileff, Clive, and Margaret Kileff. 1979. "The Masowe Vapostori of Seki: Utopianism and Tradition in an African Church." Pp. 151–67 in Bennetta Jules-Rosette (ed.), *The New Religions of Africa.* Norwood, New Jersey: Ablex.

Kileff, Margaret. 1973. "The Apostolic Sabbath Church of God: Organization, Ritual, and Belief." Unpublished Ph.D. dissertation, University of Tennessee, Chattanooga.

Koornof, P. 1953. "The Drift From the Reserves Among South African Bantu." Unpublished Ph.D. dissertation, Oxford University.

Little, Kenneth. 1973. *African Women in Towns.* Cambridge, England: Cambridge University Press.

————. 1974. *Urbanization as a Social Process.* London: Routledge and Kegan Paul.

————. 1978. "Countervailing Influences in African Ethnicity: A Less Apparent Factor." In Brian Du Toit (ed.), *Ethnicity in Modern Africa.* Boulder: Westview Press.

Magubane, Bernard. 1975. "The 'Native Reserves' (Bantustans) and the Role of the Migrant Labor System in the Political Economy of South Africa." Pp. 225–67 in Helen I. Safa and Brian Du Toit (eds.), *Migration and Development.* The Hague: Mouton.

Marris, Peter. 1968. "The Social Barriers to African Entrepreneurship." *Journal of Development Studies.* 5:29–38.

Mayer, Philip with Iona Mayer. 1971. *Townsmen or Tribesmen: Conservatism and the Process of Urbanization in a South African City.* Capetown, South Africa: Oxford University Press.

Minon, Paul. 1960. "Katuba: Etude Quantitative d'une Communaute Urbaine Africaine." Lubumbashi: CEPSI, Collection de Memoires, no. 10:2–90.

Mitchell, Clyde. 1965. "The Meaning of Misfortune for Urban Africans." Pp. 192–263 in Meyer Fortes and G. Dieterlen (eds.), *African Systems of Thought.* London: International African Institute.

Mwanamwabwa, Catherine. 1977. "Suggested Income Generating Activities for Women: Proposal for a Pilot Project." Unpublished manuscript, Lusaka, Zambia (August).

Oppong, Christine, et al., eds. 1978. *Marriage, Fertility and Parenthood in West Africa.* Canberra, Australia: Australian National University Press.

Pauw, B. A. 1963. *The Second Generation.* Capetown, South Africa: Oxford University Press.

Prothero, R. M. 1957. "Migratory Labor from North-Western Nigeria." *Africa* 27:251–61.

Quick, Stephen A. 1978. *Humanism or Technocracy: Zambia's Farming Cooperatives, 1965–1972.* Lusaka, Zambia: Institute for African Studies.

Richards, Audrey. 1956. *Chisungu: A Girl's Initiation Ceremony Among the Bemba of Northern Rhodesia.* London: Faber and Faber.

Schumpeter, Joseph. 1961. *The Theory of Economic Development.* New York: Oxford University Press.

Schuster, Ilsa M. Glazer. 1979. *New Women of Lusaka.* Palo Alto: Mayfield.

Zambian Labor Exchange Employment Figures. 1973. Lusaka, Zambia: Government Printing Office.

Zambian Labor Exchange Employment Figures. 1973. Lusaka, Zambia: Government Printing Office.

6

LESOTHO: A CASE STUDY OF MIGRATION AND HEALTH CARE DELIVERY

Nellie B. Kanno

The purpose of this chapter is to demonstrate that, in a country where migration plays a major role in its economy, the country's national health policy must consider the special needs of the migrants. The health status of a returned migrant from the Republic of South Africa is most often lower than when he migrated. The health of rural to urban migrants often declines. Therefore, an attempt must be made by the host government to identify the health needs of the migrants and to formulate national policies to satisfy their health needs.

Lesotho, the land of the Basotho, became an independent country on October 4, 1966. This small mountainous country, with an area of 11,716 square miles and a population of one and a half million, is an enclave completely surrounded by the Republic of South Africa. Elevation varies from 5,000 feet above sea level in the western plains to 8,000 feet in the higher eastern lands, where a steep leveling out in the direction of Natal begins. The highest peak reaches 11,425 feet.

The country consists of lowlands, foothills, and mountains. About one-half of the population live in the lowlands near main centers in the districts, with densities ranging from 200 to 2,300 persons per square mile. The lowlands consist of 2,160 square miles, of which 821 square miles are arable; 1,205 miles are grazing lands; and 134 square miles are rockly hills and roads (Smits, 1968:11). These are the main crop-producing areas of Lesotho. The mountainous areas of Lesotho consist of subsistence pastoral land, although some Basotho have turned to small farming as pastoral land has become exhausted by overgrazing. One may safely say that the mountainous areas are used chiefly for grazing, although 20% of the population live here. These areas of Lesotho are often referred to as the "roofs of South Africa" and are accessible only by light plane, by four-wheel-drive vehicle, or by horse. Because of the extensive mountainous areas in Lesotho, only about 12% of the land is suitable for cultivation.

Lesotho's economy is based on agriculture, animal industry, and man-power. There are no natural resources of great value in the country other than water. Lesotho has no large towns. The population of Maseru, the capital, was estimated in 1976 to be 36,000, rising to 75,000 by 1980. Since most of the country is mountainous, and thus not arable, the population is concentrated in the west, where there is considerable pressure on the cultivable land. There are no industries of any significance in the Lesotho; therefore, agriculture, with its limitations, is the mainstay of the economy. Only 7% of Lesotho's male labor force are able to secure consistent paid employment within the country.

MIGRATION TO SOUTH AFRICA OR TO URBAN AREAS

Reliance on agriculture as a principal source of income and wage employment has meant that Lesotho is unable to provide wage employment for its working age population. The Basotho supplement their income by migration for periods of time to the mines and other industrial centers in the Republic of South Africa. At any time as many as half of the adult male population may be absent from the country. According to Van der Wiel, "Lesotho has the highest relative involvement in, and dependency on, external labor migration of any African country" (1977:9). Income from the migratory laborers adds significantly to the overall economy of Lesotho. "The families of the majority of those working in South Africa live in Lesotho and depend on the money earned in South Africa. It is therefore clear that approximately 80% of the people of Lesotho are dependent on South Africa for their means of livelihood" (Van Wyk, 1967:40). In 1984 Lesotho sent 98,000 men to work in South Africa's mines, and their average annual income in U.S. dollars was $800.

Lesotho's involvement in migratory labor to South Africa dates back to the latter part of the nineteenth century when gold and diamonds were discovered. Recruiters from the mining industry sought cheap labor throughout central and southern Africa. By 1899 Lesotho had approximately 38,000 workers employed in the South African mines. Today, there are approximately 220,000 Basotho employed in South Africa and approximately 20,000 female migratory laborers employed in the domestic sector. The majority of the male Basotho are employed through 6- to 24-month contracts in the mining industry, although some do work for construction firms and in the domestic sector. They are classified as circulatory migrants—that is, they are employed for a short time and then return home only to seek employment again for short periods of time.

Basotho males employed in South African mines are usually between eighteen and thirty-nine years of age. The percentage of migrants between the ages of forty and sixty years declines from the earlier peak period. There is, however, a sizable number of men aged sixty and older who periodically migrate. It appears that most of the males between the ages of eighteen and thirty-nine who migrate to South Africa do so to get cash for bride prices, to build houses, and to buy cattle. Basotho males migrating to South Africa may also enable their families to have a supplemental income, perhaps even to survive. Between the ages of forty and sixty there is not the same demand as for those younger men. By the time a man is forty, he "may have accumulated enough stock through migrant labour, inheritance, or bride price *(bohali)* to warrant his staying home" (Van der Wiel, 1977:39). Males over forty-five are also likely to have sons old enough to be working outside of the country and in the Republic of South Africa.

Most of the males migrating to South Africa have very little education; oddly enough, however, Lesotho has one of the highest literacy rates in Africa. "This is largely a legacy of a century old missionary presence, reflected today in the fact that 55 of the nation's 62 secondary schools are operated by church organizations. The missions also run 98 percent of the 1,087 primary schools" (Lowther, 1978:11). Many of the more educated males attempt to find wage employment within the country, although there is little wage employment for even the skilled Basotho in Lesotho.

Each year more than 20,000 Basotho females work in South Africa, mainly as domestic servants. Wage employment, both in Lesotho and elsewhere, is limited for females. Females comprise only 10% of the migratory labor force to South Africa, although the figure is somewhat higher for rural to urban migration within Lesotho. Prior to 1963, when stringent controls (passes) were required by the South African government, the number of females migrating annually was increasing.

These women, who are part of the migratory labor force to South Africa and to urban centers in Lesotho, are usually single and their average age is thirty-eight. They are very often heads of households. The South African government classified these female workers as temporary migrants. One of the main reasons the females migrate, other than being the sole breadwinner in a household, is to have cash for school fees. (Education is neither free nor compulsory in Lesotho.) Of those females cooperating in a 1972 study and a follow-up study in 1975 (Kanno, 1973:48), over 90% seeking wage employment outside their villages reported they wanted to secure cash for school fees so their children would have a better life than theirs. Faith in education as the key to success has been expressed in many developing countries.

The harsh physical environment is another reason women migrate to the Republic or to urban areas within Lesotho. Living in rural areas, they are responsible not only for maintaining a household but also for cultivating the fields. Even though some of the women have never had conjugal ties, they must aid in supporting members of their extended household. Wages for domestic services are much higher in the Republic than within the country.

RURAL TO URBAN MIGRATION

Lesotho's population is approximately 95% rural, with the major developmental projects placed within centrally located large towns or districts. That is, unlike many African countries where there are several large major cities, Lesotho has one major city, Maseru. Most of the country's economic developmental projects are centrally located in Maseru. There are more varied types of wage employment available there (though these are limited) than in other parts of the country.

When discussing rural to urban migration, it is important to note that Lesotho is unique when compared to other African countries. There is only one major ethnic group, the Basotho, and one major language, Sesotho. Although there are a few other ethnic groups living in the country—the Xhosha are the most numerous—they have generally managed to speak the national language of Sesotho.

The Basotho see Maseru as a flourishing area which supplies many of their needs. There are numerous international organizations located in the city, since "the Lesotho National Development Corporation (LNDC) has encouraged foreign private investment" (Van der Wiel, 1977:61). Some small factories have been set up outside of Maseru near the South African border, but they do not have a large number of jobs to offer the Basotho. The majority of Basotho migrating from rural areas to industrial centers find wage employment in the modern sector—government, manufacturing, and construction industries—although a smaller number will be found in the domestic sector. However, the largest wage employer in Lesotho is the government, and the largest wage employer inside or outside the country is the South African mine industry.

In 1976 the minimum annual income for work in South Africa was about R800 (U.S. $1,600), and this was considered by government estimates to be below the poverty level. Although migrants to the South African mines receive free room and board, this should not be considered as a benefit since strict laws prevent the worker's family and children from accompanying him. Therefore, money still has to be sent home for family needs. This problem is even more profound in urban areas where the average annual income is under R500 and the migrant has to pay room and board. Cash payments for room and board may take up most of his wages. In rural areas housing and food needs could be taken care of much easier; for example, a small vegetable plot is more feasible in the rural area than in the urban centers.

BREAKDOWN OF TRADITIONAL VALUES

Two major values of residents of Lesotho are the traditional patriarchal family and a life style revolving around rural subsistence agriculture. There is much evidence in the anthropological literature that the breakdown of values held by a group of people places them into social and psychological conflict with serious consequences to their health and well-being. The World Health Organization (WHO) defines health as enhancement of the physical, mental, and social functioning of the individual (WHO, 1978:2); the breakdown of values resulting from migration of a large number of males and a somewhat smaller number of females to the Republic of South Africa puts all three of these health dimensions in jeopardy. Although the major movement of migration is southward and out of the country, the secondary migration from rural areas to Maseru and other centers further exacerbates problems arising from loss of values. A primary value in which the Basotho believes centers around the cohesive family dominated by the male members. The Basotho male has traditionally paid the bride price, saved to invest in cattle or improve his land, and is valued as a provider and protector of his family. The male who is traditionally the head of a household may lose his status in the family upon leaving, since the major responsibility for running the household falls upon his wife, traditionally under his care. A strong patriarchal tradition built up over centuries is suddenly strained and in many cases severed.

What drives the male Basotho south in great numbers is both tradition and economic necessity. The traditional rural occupations will not support the requirements of the bride price and the capital needed to invest in cattle and land upkeep. In order to maintain tradition, males between eighteen and forty must leave for extended periods to work for wages in the mines of South Africa. These migrants are forbidden by South African laws to bring their families with them. While migrants toil for money to improve their families' economic situation in Lesotho, new and difficult relationships often develop since the men are geographically isolated from their families. The shift in family relationships may find the wife taking full responsibility for family socialization practices while she is dependent on her husband's monetary remittances—but not on his presence.

A second value concerns the belief in a rural life style based upon traditional community support. A breakdown of this value is noted in both men and women migrants who are subjected to the much higher living standards available in South Africa. These standards, advertised in the media, create a demand for material goods among the migrants that is not part of their cultural heritage in Lesotho. For many of the migrants, aspirations are raised to a level where satisfaction is almost impossible. Some researchers have observed that traditional values no longer appear exciting to the returning migrants after witnessing urban life in Capetown and Johannesburg. In her study "Take out Hunger" Sandra Wallman states that there is an enormous gap between what the Basotho see in the city and what actually exists at home (1969:66). Van der Wiel adds further information on the reality of this situation: "Migration to the thriving industrial complex shows [the Masotho] that the poverty of his village is relative as well as absolute and, relative to something as rich as industrial South Africa, what chance can there be of alleviating that poverty?" (1978:3). Bridging the gap is often difficult since the migrants' perceptions are based on the harsh realities of economic and agricultural life in rural Lesotho. For example, much of the land is left idle because the men and women are not able to tend it. It is not unusual to find Basotho attempting to till land which is too hard for primitive tools. Yet they often make futile attempts to secure agricultural equipment appropriate for cultivating the land (Kanno, 1974:36).

Given these conditions of rural life, there is an increase in the number of women engaged in other cash-earning enterprises such as beer making and prostitution. A more serious breakdown of community structure occurs in the rural to urban migration. The crowded conditions in Maseru and other centers harboring the migrants soon contribute to the statistics on various diseases and crimes. Current figures are not available on the numbers of venereal disease cases or of crimes, but health officials will readily admit that a rise in the incidences of venereal disease, tuberculosis, and crime accompanies the influx of migrants.

There are no accurate figures on mental breakdowns of migrants returning from South Africa, although a study commissioned by the Agency for International Development (AID), conducted in 1978, reports that many of the Basotho workers returning from South Africa contacted tuberculosis and other communicable diseases while in the Republic. Their return home presents a constant source of infections to the local population. Given this sparse data, the call for reentry physical examination, diagnosis, and treatment is a commentary on the crisis nature of that form of migration and its effect on the physical health of the migrants.

Data on rural to urban migration is kept somewhat more systematically. They reveal significant increases in trauma (mental illness), venereal disease, infant mortality, and tuberculosis among this population.

The consequent loss of traditional values in recent years, especially reflected in the recently urbanized population, has affected both the birth rate and the nutritional level. Basotho mothers who have traditionally breast fed their infants through two years now resort to the use of infant formulas. This is especially true of the newly urbanized working mothers. The result is a rising birth rate (since breast feeding has a contraceptive effect) and a declining standard of nutrition. (Lesotho is currently experiencing a population growth estimated at 2.5 per 1,000.) According to the 1978 AID study, one out of five Basotho children now suffers from serious degrees of malnutrition. One must understand that the increasing amount of money available to the city children does not compensate nutritionally for their loss of the rural garden plots. Ready cash is spent on housing, always in short supply as a result of migration, and on material goods rather than on food. It becomes quite clear that having more money does not necessarily improve the quality of the migrants' life. According to Alan Berk, "Immigrants have more money than the rural poor, but they need more for rent, clothing, transportation, and other necessities of city life. . . . Their food costs more in the big city, and they no longer have access to the free wild foods of their village days" (Berk, 1973).

STRUCTURE OF HEALTH DELIVERY SYSTEM

During the British administration's tenure in Lesotho, little effort was made to develop a comprehensive medical program based on the needs of the indigenous population. Before independence, however, Catholic missionaries established eight hospitals and twenty-three health centers for the indigenous populations. These institutions were the only sources of health education and treatment until independence in 1966. The Government of Lesotho has now added nine hospitals, twenty-one health centers, thirty-one dispensaries, and thirty-five out stations. According to the second Five-Year Development Plan, all centers will ultimately be staffed by a team of village health workers, either directly or indirectly trained by a registered nurse or a trained midwife. This appears to be one way of decentralizing the present structure, of making primary health care more accessible and applicable to the Basotho.

Some forty medical doctors staff both government- and mission-operated hospitals. The government has stressed a need to increase this figure. Increasing the number of medical doctors will serve an immediate need but will not meet all basic problems in the health delivery system. In an effort to coordinate the dual health delivery system, the missions involved in health delivery systems organized the Private Health Association of Lesotho (PHAL) in 1974. One of the main goals of this organization was better communication with the Ministry of Health in Maseru. Since the Ministry of Health operates out of the capital and all statistical data dealing with health are located there, PHAL stressed a need for lessening the strong centralized powers. The cooperation of the PHAL makes possible the better dissemination of health information from the Ministry of Health through the PHAL, rather than through various fragmented units. Also, to a certain degree overlapping of programs and duplication of services by the missions can be more easily avoided and emphasis in the health delivery system can be shifted to other need areas.

In Lesotho, as primary health care shifts to rural areas, the unique needs of the returned migrants are not given adequate consideration. The government has stressed that the goals of the health delivery system should be directed toward rural areas; these goals, however, should also consider the unusual health needs of the returned migrants and the urban migrants. This emphasis neglects the fact that the rural population experiences a greater sense of family and community structure than is the case with the migrants. An overlooked factor is that in rural areas there is still considerable family support which the migrant loses in an urban area and a strong sense of community structure which is increasingly breaking down among urban migrants.

If a migrant does feel these losses, he may not, though services are assessible, take advantage of the health delivery system. Newly arrived migrants would then need an alternative to the modern health delivery system. Absence of the extended family, which provided assistance during times of crises, may pose more severe health problems for the migrant. The migrant may no longer have family members as a support base to provide treatment in some instances; nor is there an easy way to locate traditional healers. In addition, there is a shortage of cash to pay for various types of services. Due to the many stresses caused by migration, there may be an increased need for health care; however, the absence of funds poses problems. Many migrants who move from rural areas to urban areas attempt to live just as they did in the rural areas. In the urban setting this often creates additional problems for recent migrants. Of the many dimensions of health care which the immigrants lack, the most visible is adequate nutrition. Many migrants have been accustomed to small vegetable gardens and have special food preferences, and in the urban areas they discover they must buy nearly all their food. Their diets may become more restricted and their overall nutritional status less optimal.

Better coordination of existing health delivery services is needed for Basotho. The health delivery systems have failed (though unintentionally) to take into account the uniqueness of a country which is predominately rural, traditional in culture and folkways, and largely dependent economically on migration. Because of the close connection between the government's health delivery services and the missionary health delivery services, however, returned migrants are being looked at more carefully in terms of their overall health status.

Recently, a series of workshops has been conducted to address some of the most visible weaknesses in the current health delivery system; these looked at levels of accessibility and satisfaction, and reviewed the entire structure of the health delivery system. Some of these workshops clearly indicated that there should be more emphasis in the health delivery services on the special health needs of returned and other migrants in Lesotho. For too many years, prevention and cure of diseases have been the most significant aspects of developmental planning and have been considered indispensable features in the government's program to modernize the country. Prime Minister Jonathan declared: "Health services will be predominantly preventive rather than curative. . . . Improved sanitation in towns and villages and prophylatic injections are part of the preventions program to improve the health of all the people" (Lesotho, 1974:80). This appears to imply that the health delivery system will be changed from one context to another. For such a radical change, there must be a closer review of the type of needs which presently exist in Lesotho. In particular, a closer look should be taken at the needs of the migrants newly arrived in urban areas. Considering Prime Minister Jonathan's statement regarding prevention, a question arises whether prevention per se is applicable to migrants. Although the health delivery system may seem adequate after the shift, many Basotho may still believe it will not meet the special needs of the migrant. The vast problems encountered by the migrant would suggest that a different view of prevention is needed. Accessibility and satisfaction must be relevant components of health care delivery systems. Such components may provide coherence that links present and past health care systems to enforce opportunities for healthy migrants.

CONCLUSIONS AND POLICY RECOMMENDATIONS

This case study of migration and health care delivery in Lesotho has implications for the future of both the Basotho and other African people. It is important to state the uniqueness of conditions in Lesotho—namely, that the major health needs of the Basotho stem from the specific history and traditions of their homeland. The intersection of a history based upon a traditional patriarchal family and a rural subsistence agricultural life style, along with the current migration to the Republic of South Africa and to the city, has severely strained customary values. This breakdown of values has led to a decline in the mental, physical, and emotional health of the two sectors of the population most seriously affected: the migrants who have returned from the Republic of South Africa and the migrants to Maseru, the capital.

The Government of Lesotho has called for a redirecting of public health services to rural areas following the WHO model of selecting health workers from the community. Thus, the concept of the village health worker is now being implemented in rural and urban Lesotho. Village health workers are now regarded as a basic means of providing some type of health care to the most remote areas of a country. The use of village health workers in developing countries has also been considered one of the most important ways of getting community participation in health-related projects. The use of village health workers in Lesotho appears to be a manageable approach to meeting some of the basic health needs of a few migrants. Specifically, these workers could be used to involve community leaders in identifying returned migrants and other migrants with specific health needs.

This paper includes two further recommendations for the support of the village health worker concept in Lesotho. First, the concept of the village health worker should be maintained; these workers should not, however, be employed primarily in rural villages where the culture is intact, the rate of breakdown is relatively low, and culturally sanctioned healing arts are intact. They should be assigned or recruited, wherever and whenever possible, to work in those areas with a large number of migrants returning from the Republic. The presence of a village health worker would give these migrants the advantage of immediate physical examinations and referrals to other levels of health care and would provide the government the opportunity to set up a policy designed to seek compensation from the Republic for their illnesses.

A second recommendation is that village health workers be recruited from and/or assigned to the shanty towns in the capital where disease levels among migrants are high. This should have the advantage of providing this group with basic health care as well as offering entry into other levels of the health care system.

Finally, this shift of emphasis to the village health worker as a provider of primary health care would be less costly to a developing nation which has limited resources and can ill afford to develop a Western style of health care which is too costly as well as inappropriate. With this shift also would be the beginning of some forms of record keeping so that accurate statistics would be readily available regarding the health status of returned and other migrants. The Government of Lesotho could then begin to implement long-term policies for its large migratory labor force.

REFERENCES

Amin, A. 1974. *Modern Migrations in Western Africa.* Oxford: Oxford University Press.

Anderson, James. 1977. *The Current Status of Nutrition Education in Lesotho.* Maseru: Planning Assistance, Inc.

Ashton, Hugh. 1952. *The Basuto: A Study of Traditional and Modern Lesotho.* London: Oxford University Press.

Benjamin, Paul. 1955. *Health, Culture and Community: Case Studies of Public Reaction to Health Programs.* New York: Russell Sage Foundation.

Benyoussef, A., et al. 1974. "Health Effects of Rural-Urban Immigration in Developing Countries—Senegal." *Social Science and Medicine* 8:243–54.

Berk, Alan. 1973. *The Nutrition Factor: Its Role in National Development:* Washington, D.C.: The Brookings Institution.

Brownlee, Ann T. 1978. *Community, Culture and Care: A Cross Cultural Guide for Health Workers.* St. Louis: C.V. Mosby.

Bullough, Bonnie, and Vera Bullough. 1972. *Poverty, Ethnic-Identity and Health Care.* New York: Appleton-Century-Crofts.

Coates, Austen. 1969. *Basuto Land.* London: Her Majesty's Stationary Office.

Connell, John, D. Gupta, et al. 1976. *Migration From Rural Areas: The Evidence From Village Studies.* Delhi: Oxford University Press.

Djukanovic, V., and E. P. Mach, 1975. eds. *Alternative Approaches to Meeting Basic Health Needs in a Developing Country.* Geneva: World Health Organization.

Du Toit, Brian, and Helen Safa, eds. 1975. *Migration and Urbanization: Models and Adaptive Strategies.* The Hague: Mouton.

Fried, Marc. 1964. "Effects of Social Change on Mental Health." *The American of Orthopsychiatry* 34, no. 1 (January).

Gould, G. Clifford, ed. *Health and Disease in Africa: The Community Approach.* Kampala: East African Literature Bureau.

Gulliver, P. 1955. "Labor Migration in a Rural Economy: A Study of The Ngoni and Ndendeuli of Southern Tanganyike." *East African Studies*, no. 6. Kampala: East African Institute of Social Research.

Hailey, Lord, P.C.O.M. 1956. *An African Survey–Revised: A Study of Problems Arising in Africa South of the Sahara.* London: Her Majesty's Stationary Office.

Hinkle, L.E., Jr. 1974. "The Effects of Exposure to Culture Change, Social Change, and Changes in Interpersonal Relationships on Health." In *Stressful Life Events: Their Nature and Effects.* New York: Wiley.

Jennings, Peter, and Marlene Zuchr. 1976. *The Sociology of Mental Health and Illness.* Indianapolis: Bobbs-Merrill.

Kanno, N.B. 1973. *Effects of School Feeding Schemes Upon Learning Among Primary School Children in Lesotho.* Unpublished Ph.D. dissertation, Michigan State University.

———. 1974. "Comparative Life Style of the Black Female in the United States and the Black Female in Lesotho." *Journal of Afro-American Issues.*

Kingdom of Lesotho. 1974. *Second Five Year Development Plan.* Vols. 1 and 2, 1975–80. Maseru: Government Printing.

Leys, R. 1975. "South African Goldmining in 1974: The Gold of Migrant Labour." *African Affairs*, 74:295.

Lloyd, P.C. 1969. *Africa in Social Change: Changing Traditional Societies in the Modern World.* Baltimore: Penguin.

Lowther, Kevin, et al. 1978. *Health and Development in Southern Africa: A Review of Health Care in Lesotho.* USAP Aid Consultation Report, Washington, D.C.

Morgan, Robert. 1973. "Migration As a Factor in the Acceptance of Medical Care." *Social Science and Medicine* 7: 865–73.

Porsching, Susan, and Luding Garth. 1972. *A Behavioral Science Health Case Study: Central African Republic.* University of Pittsburgh.

Read, Margaret. 1966. *Culture, Health and Disease: Social and Cultural Inferences on Health Programs in Developing Countries.* London: Tavistock.

Richards, A. 1952. *Economic Development and Tribal Change: A Study of Immigrant Labour in Buganda.* Cambridge: W. Hitter.

Schopera, I. 1947. *Migrant Labour And Tribe Life: A Study of Conditions in the Bechuanaland Protectorate.* London: Oxford University Press.

Smits, L. 1968. *The Distribution of the Population in Lesotho and Some Implications for Economic Development in Basuto Land.* Maseru: Notes and Records, no. 7.

Spence, J.E. 1968. *Lesotho: The Politics of Dependence.* London: Oxford University Press.

Tabot, R., and H. Barnum. 1976. *Migration, Education and Urban Surplus Labour: The Case of Tanzania.* Kampbea: Employment Series no. 3.

Van der Wiel, A.C.A. 1977. *Migratory Wage Labour: Its Role in the Economy of Lesotho.* Maseru: Mazenoid Book Centre.

Van Wyk, J. 1967. *Lesotho: A Political Study.* Pretoria: Africa Institute.

Village Health Worker in Lesotho, The. 1977. Maseru: Ministry of Health and Social Welfare.

Wallman, Sandra. 1969. *Take Out Hunger.* London: Athlone.

———. 1972. "Conditions of Non-Development: The Case of Lesotho." *Journal of Development Studies* 8, no. 2:22–30.

Williams, J. 1972. *Lesotho Land Tenure And Economic Development.* Pretoria: Africa Institute.

Wilson, F. 1972. *Labour in the South African Gold Mines: 1911–1969.* London: Cambridge University Press.

World Health Organization. 1974. *Promotion of National Health Services.* Geneva: WHO, ECB55.

———. 1978. *Primary Health Care.* Geneva: WHO

7

INTERNAL BRAIN DRAIN AND DEVELOPMENT: A CASE STUDY OF SENEGALESE HIGHER EDUCATION

ROBERT C. JOHNSON

The formal system of higher education has been long and widely viewed as a means of human resource development in developing nations, and as a critical factor in social and economic reconstruction. However, an unintended and unforeseen consequence of higher education—and the entire formal educational system—may be that it contributes to the migration of domestic talent from rural to urban areas. This phenomenon can be termed "internal brain drain." If higher education contributes to internal brain drain, what are the implications for national development?

HIGHER EDUCATION AND BRAIN DRAIN

Brain drain is generally defined as the emigration of skilled and talented persons from their countries of birth to another country. Often, those persons who migrate leave poorer societies for richer ones, seeking to maximize their earning powers, to best utilize their talents and skills, and to be in the company of their professional peers. Much controversy exists over the net benefits to the host or receiving country, and the losses (or benefits) incurred by the country of emigration. It is disputed whether a person, by leaving his or her home country, contributes to the well-being of that country through whatever general contribution he or she makes to the stock of human knowledge, or whether the country of emigration suffers a loss of returns on investments made in human capital development, taxes on the potential earnings of the emigrant and his family, and other social and economic costs.[1]

Within a single country, the same question can be posed about the effects of the movement of human capital on the social and economic growth of the nation. This chapter uses this question as a starting point to examine the possible consequences that institutions of higher education could have on the national reconstruction of a developing society through their recruitment and subsequent placement of domestic talent within that society. To the extent, then, that human capital (in this case students) produced by local resources are attracted away from poorer regions of a country (usually the rural sector) to wealthier areas (usually urban centers) with little prospect of returning, internal brain drain is occurring. (On another level, internal brain drain can be a stepping stone to international migration, with skilled nationals emigrating to more developed countries after being recruited to urban areas within their countries.)

Within the national context, the question must be asked if the displacement of local talent serves the national good by producing greater returns than if that talent had remained in the local area. In other words, of what benefit is it to a local rural area to send its students off to an urban center for higher education? Alternatively, if local populations are not adequately represented in institutions of higher education in a country, do they benefit from their subsidization of these (and other) institutions? Several conceptual notions are central to this discussion: the theoretical relationship between higher education and national development; rural migration and rural development; urbanization in Africa, and its impact on African societies; and the attraction and distribution of domestic talent from and between rural and urban areas. These issues are examined in the context of the West African nation of Senegal.

Since human resource development primarily entails the training of students, this population is the focus of this study. More specifically, students (both foreign and Senegalese) at institutions of higher education in Senegal are looked at. This group is of interest because its ranks will produce the next generation of top-level professionals, managers, technocrats, and government officials who will be responsible for the development of their countries. Examined here are the students' social and geographical origins, their career aspirations, and their views on African development. Statistical data and analyses are used to study the interrelationships among their backgrounds, occupational desires, and development views. Using these analyses and empirical data on the larger society, conclusions and inferences are drawn about the relationship of higher education to the internal migration and distribution of students (as domestic intellectual talent) and national reconstruction (especially rural development).

Senegal is essentially a rural and agrarian country, with 70% of its population living in rural areas and 74% of its workforce engaged in agriculture. While lacking an abundance of natural resources, Senegal has an established system of higher education which supplies it with trained manpower. At the heart of this system is the University of Dakar, the oldest and most developed university in Francophone Africa.

As a French colony, Senegal enjoyed several advantages over other French-occupied territories in Africa: a relatively well-developed Western educational system, an established administrative and bureaucratic structure, a protected light industrial and manufacturing sector, and a somewhat developed infrastructure. Given this legacy, the challenge for Senegal (as well as other African countries) is to transform the former colonial institutions into instruments of national reconstruction. Thus, the experiences of Senegalese higher education as a factor in national development could be instructive for other African countries with emerging systems of higher education.

FORMAL SCHOOLING AND DEVELOPMENT

As African countries go about the business of nation-building (through modernizing and developing), a host of institutions and resources are marshaled and put into use by the leaders of the societies. Education, or at least the formal school system, is commonly accepted as the social institution through which human resource development most often occurs. In Africa, the Western-derived and -oriented system of formal education has been assigned both a high degree of importance in fulfilling this role by national leaders and, parenthetically, a great deal of social prestige by the general populace. These assertions hold true even though the Western model of formal education is fraught with difficulties and poses many problems for African societies. (For a discussion of the nature of these problems see, *inter alia*, Moumouni [1968]; Cowan, O'Connell, and Scanlon [1965]; Sheffield and Diejomaoh [1972], Coombs and Ahmed [1974]; and Ela [1971].)

Education does not operate in a social vacuum. Besides having many different social functions to carry out, education (as embodied in educational institutions) is subject to and affected by political, social, economic, and cultural institutions in the society. This point is of utmost importance and must be understood before a meaningful discussion can take place of the relationship between education and development. Thus, as changes and transformations occur in the larger society, education as a social institution is accordingly affected. Furthermore, in many instances, educational institutions are considered as vehicles of social change. This is particularly true in developing areas.

In Senegal the government places a great deal of emphasis on formal schooling of the Western variety in its development plans. Formal education expenditures constitute the leading item in the national budget of Senegal, accounting for 20% of the total. The officially stated role of formal education in Senegal is to provide trained personnel for socioeconomic development and a culturally enlightened citizenry.

Formal education in Senegal is modeled after the French school system, reflecting its roots in French colonial history in Africa. Today, partly because of this colonial legacy, formal education in Senegal suffers from a host of quantitative and qualitative problems: a lack of classrooms and teachers; overcrowding; high dropout rates; a large number of "repeaters"; poor job possibilities for primary and many secondary school dropouts; curricula poorly adapted to the needs of the country; a lack of adequate and relevant textbooks and other teaching materials; and the pull of youth from the countryside to towns and cities are just a few of these problems. Recently, the government appointed a national commission to examine formal education in Senegal and to make recommendations for changes in the structure and content of the system.

HIGHER EDUCATION AND AFRICAN DEVELOPMENT

In Africa the university has long been regarded as a key component in the development process of the continent (UNESCO, 1963). In more recent assessments (Altbach, 1982; de Kiewiet, 1971; McCain, 1980; Yesufu, 1973) the role of the university in African development has continued to be emphasized; this is a part that universities in America and Europe were never expected to play in the formative years of these industrialized states, and seldom are even today. Without a doubt, the African university occupies a very special and important position in modern African society, and is called upon to fulfill certain critical functions.

The following six social functions of the African university have been identified and deemed paramount by African educators, particularly, participants in the 1972 Association of African Universities' Workshop in Accra, Ghana; they are: (1) pursuit, promotion, and dissemination of knowledge; (2) research; (3) provision of intellectual leadership; (4) manpower development; (5) promotion of social and economic modernization;

and (6) promotion of intercontinental unity and international understanding (Yesufu, 1973:42–44). Such a list illustrates the wide range of activities and functions that have been set down for the university in Africa. Most, if not all, of these functions can be said to be central to the process of social transformation in African societies.

Formal higher education has a long history in Senegal, dating back to the colonial era when the French established institutions to train teaching, medical, and other personnel to service its West African colonies. In 1950 the forerunner of the University of Dakar, the Institut des Hautes Etudes de Dakar, was founded as an overseas branch of the Universities of Paris and Bordeaux. It was aptly described as "essentially an European, French university in the service of Africa" (Senghor, 1959). From its inception until the student rebellions of the late 1960s, a large proportion of the students at the institute, and later the university, were French nationals. Following the student disorders of the 1960s and 1970s, the Senegalese government, in direct response to these crises and to public criticism, embarked on a program of "Africanization" and "Senegalization" of the faculty, staff, and student body. Today, French students constitute 5% or less of the student population.

Over the years, government officials have identified the university as a key factor in the Senegalese developmental process: "The University is at the heart of the nation" (Senghor, 1974:1) and "The University of Dakar, with the totality of the Senegalese schools, is the first instrument of national economic development" (Camara, 1974:11). Until recently, however, the government failed to evaluate the relative contribution of the university to the country's development efforts, subjecting it to criticism from observers at home and abroad. Students in particular have been critical of the relevancy of their training to the developmental needs of their country.

For purposes of this study, students from two of the institutions of higher education in Senegal, the university and the Ecole Nationale d'Economie Appliquée, are included here to determine their perceptions of the relevance of their academic experience to the developmental needs of Senegal, especially in the rural sector. Other selected characteristics of the students will also be examined in this light.

RURAL DEVELOPMENT, URBANIZATION, AND MIGRATION

Three phenomena—rural development, urbanization, and migration—are intimately interrelated in Africa. Africa is essentially a rural continent. As Lele (1981:548) reports:

> . . . concern for economic development in Africa primarily means a
> concern about agricultural and rural development. Between 80 and
> 90 percent of the nearly 400 million people in sub-Saharan Africa
> live in rural areas. Most derive their subsistence from meager crop
> and livestock production and survive on annual per capita incomes
> of less than U.S. $150. Although production is largely geared to
> subsistence, the rural sector is also the major source of food for
> urban consumption and of raw materials for exports and for do-
> mestic manufacturing.

Despite rhetoric to the contrary, rural sectors of African countries are
generally neglected by governmental development policies in favor of
costly and capital-intensive industrialization projects in urban areas. (See
World Bank [1981] for an extensive discussion of the larger role that
agriculture should play in the development of Africa.) Rural poverty, lack
of cohesive and long-term planning for agricultural productivity by African governments, and the placement of major income-producing industries and activities and of most governmental services in urban areas
contribute to the flight of people away from the rural areas. Consequently, Africa has the fastest-growing rate of urbanization among the
regions of the world.

These conditions pose a double problem for African states. First, the
agricultural sector, which is the critical factor for development in Africa,
is decimated by the loss of needed labor and the lack of coherent governmental support (that is, policies and funding). Second, urban areas are
not prepared to receive the onrush of newcomers from the rural areas.
Basic necessities such as jobs, housing, sewage systems, transportation,
and the like are either in short supply or lacking for many parts of the
towns and cities. Prospects for the provision of such services are dim
because the agricultural sector, which subsidizes the urban existence
(through export commodities and by way of exploitive governmental
policies which pay rural producers extremely low prices for their goods),
suffers a decline in population and productivity. It would appear that full-
scale rural development is the way out of this problematic situation. (Lele
[1981] provides a broader discussion of this problem of rural development
in Africa and the actions needed to achieve it.)

Senegal is beset, in its own fashion, by these types of problems. By
African standards it is a very urbanized nation, with about 30% of its
population in 1976 living in urban areas (compared to a 20% average for
the rest of Africa). The population is badly distributed among the various
regions. In 1976 over 19% of the population lived in the Cap Vert region,
which had a surface area of about 550 square kilometers, only .28% of the
total land area of the country. This fact is reflected in the high population

density of the area (4,476 inhabitants per square mile in 1976, or 1,790 persons per square kilometer). On the other hand, some areas, such as the Senegal-Oriental region, are underpopulated. For the two decades since independence was achieved in 1960, the average annual rate of urbanization for the country was approximately 2.9% for the 1960s and 3.3% for the 1970s.

More recent population estimates (Paxton, 1984) indicate that the trend toward urbanization continues. Available statistics for some of the regional capitals show the following population increases in these cities between 1976 and 1979: Dakar, 22.3%; Ziguinchor, 8.9%; Diourbel, 8.5%; Saint-Louis, 9.8%; Kaolack, 9.1%; and Thies, 8.5%. For these cities the percent of change in the total population for the 1976 to 1979 period is 17.61%, or an annual average rate of 5.9%. These statistics would suggest that the trend is not only continuing into the 1980s but accelerating as well.

Thus, it is clear that the urban population is growing at a higher rate than is the national population. Furthermore, the growth of Senegal's urban population is largely due to the large numbers of newcomers to the capital city, Dakar. This city has had a growth rate almost three times that of the other regional capitals in the country (7% versus 2.5%). More recently, population estimates suggest that the rate of increase for Dakar is 7.44% and is 3% for the other large regional capitals, making the rate of growth of the capital city more than double that of the other urban areas. Almost 65% of the urban population of Senegal is located in Dakar.

In its early years Senegal followed a course of development commonly pursued by many African countries—industrialization. Over the course of several four-year plans, the development emphasis has shifted slightly towards rural development. Currently, the Senegalese government adheres to the objective of creating a semi-industrial state by the year 2001.

Analysis of the government's development plans shows that the urban areas continue to be favored, with the industrial and service sectors receiving considerably more funding than rural development, although close to 80% of the population earn their livelihood from agriculture and 70% of the population live in rural areas.

This long-standing imbalance toward the urban population points to the regional disparities that exist in the country. Clearly, the Cap Vert region, containing Dakar, is highly favored. More specifically, this region, representing .28% of the country's land area and containing 19% of the population has: 73% of all doctors; 37% of the primary school-age children; 32% of the primary school classrooms; 44% of the civil service; 80% of the industrial business; and 84% of industrial jobs. Furthermore, intraregional disparities exist, with the regional capitals being favored. While these data are for the 1970s, in all likelihood the disparities continue to exist and to grow in this decade.

The twin factors of urban attraction and poor rural conditions fuel internal migrations. Essentially, these migrations are either permanent or seasonal. Permanent migration is seen in the high rate of urbanization in the country. Seasonal migration comes about during the dry season in Senegal (January–May), when agricultural activity comes to a near stand-still and many in the agricultural workforce seek employment in the cities and towns, especially Dakar.

Exact figures on migratory movement are not available, but it was estimated that in 1971 more than 500,000 Senegalese lived in areas other than their region of birth. Close to 37% of the inhabitants of the Cap Vert region were born in other regions. Furthermore, it is estimated that 15% of the rural population moves annually, with one-third going to another region (Ministère du Plan et de la Coopération, 1977).

The problems of rural poverty, migration, and uncontrolled urban growth will have to be resolved if meaningful progress is to occur in Africa. Many observers view the development of trained human resources as one factor in tackling these issues. In particular, as already noted, higher education has been viewed as a primary means of addressing such problems. This study examines the extent to which higher education in Senegal affects rural development through the recruitment and training of students.

CHARACTERISTICS OF THE STUDENTS SURVEYED

In addition to using aggregate data compiled by various national, international, private, and bilateral agencies, this study relies on survey research conducted among the student body at the University of Dakar in 1974–75. Approximately 850 questionnaires were disseminated to students at the university and at the Ecole Nationale d'Economie Appliquée (ENEA), the latter used to serve as a comparison group.[2] Of these 850 questionnaires, 317 usable ones were returned; therefore, the return rate was about 37%. Considering that an estimated 6,697 students were enrolled in the various faculties and institutes of the university that year, and that 304 of the returned questionnaires were from university students, about 4.5% of the university student body were surveyed. About 20% of the ENEA student population participated in the study. Students from Anglophone African countries, enrolled in a one-year French language training program at the university, were also purposely included to serve as another comparison group.

The questionnaire was written in French and consisted of thirty-nine closed and open-ended items. Some questions asked information of a demographical, biographical, and scholastic nature, and other items were included to ascertain students' opinions of the needs of their country, the contribution of their education to fulfilling these needs, and their individual orientations and aspirations (in terms of career, future employer, choice of place of residence after graduation, and so on). A cover sheet was attached which explained the purpose of the questionnaire and included instructions for its completion.

A purposive sampling strategy was used so as to include students from the various schools, programs, and departments of the university. Students from all four of the faculties and all but one of the teaching institutes were included. In many respects the distribution of students in the sample on certain variables closely paralleled the distribution within the university on these characteristics. Males were 82% of the student population when this study was conducted and comprised 80% of the sample (85% when excluding Anglophone students in the French-language-training program). Senegalese students were 70% of the student population and 60% of the sample. Their percentage increases to 67% when those students enrolled in the French-language program are not included. The majority of the students (73%) in the university were in their beginning years of study (first cycle). For the sample 79% of the students were first-cycle students (76% without the students in language training). For the most part, enrollment patterns in the sample were fairly similar to those in the university as a whole. There was an overrepresentation of students from the Law-Economics Faculty, and an underrepresentation of students from the Faculty of Letters in the sample. The representation of students in the sample from the faculties of Medicine and Sciences and from the institutes approximated within a few percentage points their enrollment in these divisions of the university.

Because of the use of a nonprobabilistic sampling strategy, it cannot be claimed that this sample was representative of the total student body at the university at the time of this study. The research does, however, have indicative value.

While Senegalese students constituted 70% of the student body in the 1974–75 academic year, many other nationalities were represented. The continents of Africa, the South and North Americas, Europe, and Asia were represented by the 1,997 students from 46 countries. Fourteen Francophone African countries accounted for 68% of the foreign student population at the university, and students from these countries constituted 20% of the total student body.

French students comprised 5% of the total student body and 16% of the foreign student population. There had been a steady decrease in French student enrollment, down from 27% in 1967–68 to 5% in 1974–75. Foreign students from non-French-speaking countries were also 5% of the total student body and constituted about 16% of the non-Senegalese student population. Of these students, 38% were enrolled in the French language program for non-Francophone students (these students generally returned to their home universities after this training), and the others were enrolled in the different faculties.

About 82% of the students were males and 18% females. Among the Senegalese at the university, the male-female ratio was about 5 to 1, slightly higher than that for the total student body. This can be explained by the fact that Senegal and many of the other countries sending students to the university are Muslim societies, and in these countries most girls until recently either did not go to Western schools or they did not complete the full term of study leading to higher education.

Information on the religious affiliations and the ethnic origins of students is not available for the total student body. In Senegal this kind of information, if it is gathered, is rarely, if ever, published. (It has been speculated that this information is suppressed to minimize intergroup conflicts based on overrepresentation of some ethnic and religious groups in privileged positions. However, data I collected during field investigation will provide some insight into the backgrounds of the students.)

Given the regional disparities and, more pointedly, the urban-rural discrepancies in resource allocations in Senegal, it would seem plausible to find discrepancies in the enrollment of students from these different areas. Further, given the stronger attachment of some ethnic groups to traditional ways (for example, Serere, Toucouleurs) and the fact that some ethnic groups are primarily located in geographic areas which are not fully integrated in the development process, (for example, Peulhs, Diola, Manding), one could expect to find differences in the representation of the different ethnic groups in the university.

Data presented in the following tables shed some light on these questions. It appears that there are regional differences in the distribution of the Senegalese students at the university (see table 1).[3] The same regions—that is, Cap Vert, Fleuve, and Thiès—shown to be most favored on other indices are also the ones overrepresented in the university by students. This finding is not too surprising considering that most of the older and more prestigious secondary schools are located in these areas

TABLE 1 Sampled Senegalese university students' region of birth and population distribution in Senegal by region, 1973

Region	% of Students Born in Region	% of Population in Region	Difference	Selectivity Index[a]
Cap Vert	27.5	18.6	8.9	1.48
Casamance	11.2	15.5	−4.3	0.72
Diourbel	7.9	15.9	−8.0	0.50
Fleuve	13.5	9.7	3.8	1.39
Senegal-Oriental	1.1	6.1	−5.0	.18
Sine-Saloum	16.3	20.3	−7.0	.80
Thiès	14.6	13.9	.7	1.05
Students born outside of Senegal	3.9	—	—	—
No response	3.9	—	—	—
Total	99.9 (N = 178)	100		

[a] Selectivity Index is the percentage of sample divided by the percentage of population.

TABLE 2 Background of sampled Senegalese university students

Birthplace of Students	% of Sample (Adjusted for No Responses)
Dakar	27.6
Zingulnchor	1.8
Diourbel	3.5
Saint-Louis	7.1
Kaolack	4.7
Thiès	5.3
Noncapital town of 10,000 or more	11.8
Small town–village	34.1
Foreign locale	4.1
No response	—
Total	100 (N = 170)

and that higher percentages of the urban populations of these regions are better schooled than are other segments and other regions of the society.

Statistics show that 50% of the Senegalese students who responded to this item were born in the regional capitals of Senegal (see table 2). Another 11.8% were born in noncapital towns with populations of more

TABLE 3 Ethnic representation in the sample of Senegalese university
students and in the total population

Ethnic Group	% in Sample	Estimated % in Population	Difference	Selectivity Index
Wolof	41.4	36.2	5.2	1.14
Serere	19.5	19.0	.5	1.02
Peulh	4.6 ⎫			
	⎬ 14.9	21.5	−6.6	.69
Toucouleur	10.3 ⎭			
Diola	7.5	7.0	.5	1.07
Lebou	5.2	1.8	3.4	2.89
Manding-Bambara	0	6.4	−6.4	0
Sarakhole	3.4	2.1	1.3	1.62
Other Senegalese Ethnics	3.5	2.2	1.3	1.59
Other groups (non-Senegalese)	4.6	3.8	.8	1.21
Total	100	100		
	(N = 174)			

than 10,000 inhabitants. With a 70% rural population, the country seems
to have only about one-third of its student body from this sector.

The ethnic representation of Senegalese students in the sample and its
comparison to the ethnic distribution in the total population are presented in table 3. These figures show that the Wolof and Lebou are
slightly more represented than are other groups. On the other hand, the
Toucouleurs, the Peulhs, and the Manding-Bambara people are underrepresented in the university. Explanations for these distortions are
found in the history, the traditional location, and the social make-up of
these groups. Those groups which are underrepresented are generally
from regions which are slighted by the development process. The
Toucouleurs, the Peulhs, and the Mandings are found in these regions or
in the unfavored areas of other regions. The Peulhs are further characterized by their frequent nomadic life style. These combined factors account for the underrepresentation of these groups in the sample of
university students. However, tribalism, or deliberate discrimination
based on ethnic affiliation, appears to be in no way a factor in this matter.

Groups which would appear to be disfavored because of either regional
isolation (the Diola) or strong attachment to traditional beliefs (the Serere) are proportionally represented in the sample. There are two reasons for this situation. First, the Serere are found in those areas where
schools are accessible; second, both they and the Diola have been subject

to zealous Roman Catholic proselytising, resulting in Catholic mission education for some.

The Wolof and the Lebou have long been in contact with the French and were the first groups to frequent the French schools. The Lebou are long-time settlers of the Cap Vert region and therefore have had access to the better Western schooling opportunities available in this area. The Wolof, while found in most regions of Senegal, are mostly concentrated in the area between Saint-Louis and Dakar, and therefore profit from the many Western schools located in this stretch of the country.

Students at the university are generally from affluent socioeconomic backgrounds relative to the masses of people in Senegal (and Africa). Senegalese students in the university sample are almost as likely to come from high to middle socioeconomic backgrounds (based on the father's reported occupation) as they are to come from low socioeconomic groups. Almost 80% of the active population in Senegal are engaged in agriculture or related activities, and in other traditional occupations. In the sample less than 40% of the students' fathers earned their living in the traditional sector. On the other hand, 13.5% of the sampled university students from Senegal reported that their fathers' occupation would place them in the top 1% of the occupational hierarchy in Senegal. Students from middle-level socioeconomic groups also appear to be overrepresented relative to their numbers in the larger society.

These findings show that social background is an important factor in determining who will receive a university education, and thus who will have an opportunity to become a member of the privileged elite. While ethnic group origin does not readily appear to be a selection factor, geographical and social backgrounds seem to be key variables in the formation of future Senegalese leaders.

Data on the students at ENEA support this contention. In general, the backgrounds of the ENEA students approximate the national profile. Their families are more likely to have rural origins and to be Muslims, illiterate in French, lower in socioeconomic status, and not highly schooled. The basic exception to this rule is the fact that many of them come from families headed by low-level civil servants.

Senegalese university students in this sample generally reported that when not in school they live in the same area in which they were born. There is some movement away from the rural areas to the cities and from the regional capitals or large cities to Dakar.

Students who do migrate are more likely to move from rural areas to cities, or from large cities to the capital, than from urban areas to rural locales. There are not many students, however, who report having moved

TABLE 4 Senegalese university students' place of birth by fathers' socioeconomic status

| | SES | | |
Place of Birth	Low	Middle	High
Dakar	55.8%	27.9%	16.3%
	(24)	(12)	(7)
Regional capital or city/town	44.7	29.8	25.5
	(21)	(14)	(12)
Rural/semi-urban	93.9	4.1	2.0
	(46)	(2)	(1)
Foreign country	16.7	50.0	33.3
	(1)	(3)	(2)

Total Number of Responses: 145

directly from rural areas to the capital (less than 2%). For the most part, students still consider their birth areas their homes.

A highly significant association is found between the father's socioeconomic status (SES)[4] and the location in which the student was born. Over 90% of the students from rural backgrounds come from low-income families, whereas only about one-half of those from urban areas have low socioeconomic origins (see table 4). Almost 90% of the students from the high SES group are from urban areas.

STUDENT CAREER ASPIRATIONS

When asked where they wanted to work after leaving the university, 50% of the students indicated an urban location. Another 42% had no preference, and the remaining group indicated a rural location. These figures were fairly constant for students with the same birthplace. Also, in examining students' preference for location after school by current residence, the same distribution held: 52% elected an urban locale, 8% chose a rural location, and 40% indicated no preference.

Generally, students from the high socioeconomic group indicated a greater preference to work in the urban areas than did students from the middle and low SES groups. Middle SES students were most likely to indicate no preference, followed by the low SES group, and lastly by the high SES group. Among all three groups, postuniversity placement in rural areas was a distant third.

The data on students in the other subsamples (Anglophone and ENEA) showed similar patterns to those of the Senegalese students. About 57% of the Anglophone students desired to work in an urban area. Almost 36% had no preference and only 7% identified a rural locale as a preference. Students of the ENEA were evenly divided in their choices of locations; exactly 50% noted a preference for an urban location, and the other half said they had no preference, meaning that none specifically indicated a rural location. Furthermore, within these two subsamples, no significant associations were found between the students' geographic backgrounds and their preferences for posttraining placement. It is instructive to note, however, that although most of the 13 students from the ENEA are from low-income rural families, many of these students expressed a desire to work in an urban location. Anglophone students, on the other hand, generally reported being from high-level SES family backgrounds (55.6% high, 22.2% middle, and 22.2% low); over half (almost 59%) of this group preferred an urban location for posttraining placement. One-third (33%) stated no preference and the remaining persons indicated a preference for the rural area.

Students were asked a series of questions concerning their plans for the future in terms of both occupations and choice of employers. For the Senegalese students at the university, essentially no difference was found among the occupation aspirations of the students from the different geographical areas (for example, urban or rural). The most frequently cited career choices, by 27.5% of the students, were in education or education-related fields (teaching, research, administration, and so on), followed by commerce and industry (18%), technical fields (12%), foreign service (11%), and health professions (7%). A variety of other disciplines or plans were listed in addition to these.

When asked their choice of employers, many students (55.6%), regardless of their birthplace, indicated they would like to work for the government. Twenty-nine percent said they would like to work for a large private firm, and 9% showed a desire to be self-employed. The remaining students either had several choices or some other choice.

Almost two-thirds of the Anglophone students had career plans in the area of education. This is not surprising considering that many of the students were in teacher-training programs or were planning to become French teachers. Most of the remaining students planned to work for the government—either in the civil service or in the foreign service. Of the 29 students responding to this item, 25 or 86% identified the government as their choice of employer. Again, this finding is not surprising since most of these students identified jobs that are under government service (that is, education, civil service, foreign service).

All of the ENEA students expected to work for the government as civil servants. The nature of their training and their appointment to this institution essentially dictate that they work for the government for a period of time. The training these students received was supposed to prepare them for work in villages and small towns on development-related projects. While these students saw their future in government service, they did not necessarily view themselves working in rural areas.

STUDENT VIEWS ON DEVELOPMENT

Students were asked: "In your opinion, what are the most urgent needs of your country?" and "How can your education (training) respond to these needs?" Since the responses to these items were extremely diverse, no attempt at statistical tabulation or analysis will be made. The students' comments not only reflected a wide range of statements on needs but also revealed different levels of awareness of the developmental problems and conditions facing the countries. Student views on the most urgent needs of their countries vary from the suggestion of one or two priority areas (for example, education, technical manpower, or natural resources) to detailed, sophisticated elaborations on the causes and consequences of, and solutions to, underdevelopment. The principal themes expressed are (presented in no particular order): (1) literacy among the peasants—teaching them in indigenous languages; (2) raising the level of political awareness among the people; (3) training of high-level manpower; (4) ending the state of neocolonialism; (5) elimination of economic and social inequities; (6) removal of foreign influence, replacement of foreign technical assistants and advisors, reduction or elimination of foreign investments, and nationalization (of industries and companies dominated by foreigners); (7) Africanization (or Senegalization); (8) development of infrastructures in the countries; and (9) agricultural and economic development and reform, and mastery of the natural environment.

The single most frequently cited priority among the Senegalese students at the university was manpower development (15.8%). This was also cited in combination with other perceived needs. It is interesting to note, however, that almost one-fifth (16.3%) of the sample did not respond to this question. This could be because of the fact that this item was one of the last two on a nine-page questionnaire, or because many of the students who did not respond had no views on the problems of their country. Since this percentage of no responses is higher, on the average, than for most of the other questions, it is reasonable to speculate that many of these students had no opinion on the matter.

When asked whether their education was relevant to the needs that they identified, almost twice as many students did not respond to this question than the same to the previous one (28.1% versus 16.3%). Another 16% either said that they did not know how their training addressed the needs of their country or that it did not. Therefore, 44% of the Senegalese students in the university sample did not or could not identify the role their training could play in meeting the needs of their country or said it was irrelevant. Most of the students who did respond affirmatively said their training met manpower and educational needs of the country, which is not surprising given that these were the areas cited most frequently as the needs of the country.

CONCLUSIONS AND POLICY CONSIDERATIONS

Institutions of higher learning in Senegal do attract students from rural areas. However, there appears to be a differential recruiting pattern occurring within this level of formal education. It was noted above that the more prestigious institution, the university, tended to attract students from a higher socioeconomic (urban) background than did other postsecondary institutions (for example, ENEA). While students from urban areas are disproportionately represented at the university, rural students do attend.

Regardless of geographical and socioeconomic background or type of institution attended, students in higher education in Senegal express very little preference to work in rural areas. From the data in this study it appears that poorer students use nonuniversity postsecondary institutions as a means of social mobility. Other researchers have observed this same phenomenon in Senegal and elsewhere in West Africa (Flis-Zonabend, 1968; Clignet and Foster, 1966). Note that 50% of the students from the ENEA expressed a desire to work in urban locations and two-thirds of the ENEA students from low socioeconomic (rural) backgrounds selected urban locales as their choice of posttraining work locations.

While many of the university students also chose urban locations, they were more likely to be from urban backgrounds and the upper SES groups, and thus could be expected to have such a preference. Even among the low SES students at the university, very few (10%) explicitly indicated a rural location as their preference for an area to work in after finishing their studies.

The fact that almost half of the Senegalese students at both institutions indicated "no preference" may be seen as a positive sign. Some of these students wrote unsolicited comments to the effect that they were willing to go wherever they could be useful, wherever they may be assigned by their employer, and similar reasons. This could mean that a larger number of students are willing to locate in rural areas than those who specified such locations.

Not only do students choose posttraining urban locales (or express no preference), but most plan to work in occupations or fields that are not primarily related to agriculture or rural development (with the possible exception of teaching). However, the student's choices of occupation and work placement are not simply a function of individual preference. These choices probably reveal his or her awareness of the reality of both the employment situation in Senegal and government policy. The degree of regional disparity in resource allocation was noted earlier. The same problem exists with jobs. Of the jobs in the government 44% are located in the Cap Vert region (which includes Dakar); 80% of the industrial enterprises and 84% of industrial jobs are found in this region. The region of Thiès, located near Dakar, is the second-leading center of economic activity. Thus, much of the professional employment in both the public and private sectors is located in urban areas. This reality has its origins in the colonial history of Senegal and was perpetuated by the developmental policies of the government, which emphasized urban and industrial projects.

Other structural conditions may also explain the geographical preferences of the students. Not only are most institutions of higher education located in Dakar, but most of the secondary schools in Senegal are in urban areas. Therefore, most students who attend postsecondary institutions have spent a considerable part of their adolescent and young adult lives in urban environments, allowing them to be exposed to, and perhaps to acquire, Western tastes and life styles. In fact, the *schooling* process itself may be a major factor in shaping the students' outlooks, attitudes, and preferences. Studies in Senegal of the acculturation effects of Western schooling (Fougeyrollas, 1963, 1967; Sow, 1972) show that the higher the level of schooling, the more likely the adoption of some aspects of European life styles and attitudes. This acculturation phenomenon may explain some of the choice for urban locales, because these acquired tastes can best be satisfied in the cities and towns.

The type of training that the university students receive seems to do little to help them conceptualize the developmental needs of their country. The responses of many students to the question about their country's most urgent needs fell into single categories (28%), and most students (86.3%) identified three or fewer national needs. In the initial analysis of these data, responses were categorized according to the nature of the response. Seven broad categories were established. These are: (1) development of infrastructure (telecommunications, transportation, construction); (2) high-level manpower formation (training of professionals and skilled technicians); (3) mass education and literacy programs; (4) development of agriculture and rural areas, or of natural resources; (5) economic and social development (for example, freedom from underdevelopment, neocolonialism, and imperialism, and the need for health care); (6) political awareness, changes in values and value systems, commitment; and (7) technical and scientific development and research. Less than 30% made explicit mention of rural development as a priority.

Not only does university training not prepare future leaders to grasp the essentials of national development in conceptual terms, but it provides little in professional training that could assist rural development. For years the university has not produced enough graduates to meet the need for scientific, technical, and administrative personnel. Most students at the university are studying in fields other than those designated as priority areas by the government. There is no major university curriculum devoted to the study and teaching of rural development, and few of the university graduates, if any, become involved in agricultural research, extension work, agronomy, animal husbandry, or the other areas related to rural development. Even if governmental policy were to shift to recognize the priority of rural development, the university would be ill-equipped to play a role without undergoing substantial change.

In response to the question "Does higher education contribute to internal brain drain in Senegal?" the answer is certainly yes, it does. Higher (and secondary) education brings rural students to urban areas, exposes them to different and perhaps alienating life styles, and provides them with training that requires working in an urban setting. These factors help to steer these students away from returning to their rural homelands. Even if they were to return, they would have very little in the way of skills to offer the local populace and probably could not find a position outside of teaching or health care. In sum, since the educational and economic policy of the Senegalese government does not favor rural development, the rural areas which supply both people and resources to higher education get little, if any, benefit from higher education.

There are some actions that could be taken by governmental leaders to remedy this situation. The most obvious is to recognize the priority of rural development and to devote more resources to this objective. In line with this fundamental policy change are implications for manpower and educational policies. Future leaders need to be exposed to realistic, comprehensive, and relevant theories about African development, the causes of underdevelopment, and possible solutions. The curricula, structure, and nature of the formal educational system should provide skills and training, and should develop attitudes that allow the graduates of these institutions to serve the needs of many.

Decentralization of the institutions of higher education is another action that could make them more useful to the entire nation. Having such institutions located in rural or semirural areas could (1) attract more students from these areas; (2) reduce the amount of exposure to alienating foreign influences; (3) produce more meaningful responses to local needs; (4) provide students with more development-related training; and (5) expose students to and involve them in the needs of the majority of the populace.

In terms of human resource policies, more places in secondary and postsecondary schools can be reserved for students from rural backgrounds provided they undertake training in areas needed for rural development and that they spend a portion of their working careers in rural areas. This practice has recently been instituted in the Imo State in Nigeria (*Africa News*, 1981). Another practice that many African countries have adopted is "national service." Generally, persons benefiting from scholarships and formal schooling are required to serve the government for a given period of time (usually one or two years), doing work in underdeveloped communities. This type of service would permit students from urban areas to experience firsthand the plight of the rural masses, while making some contribution toward changing it.

These proposed actions or related ones will only be effective to the extent that basic changes are made in governmental and international donors' policies toward rural development in Africa. Not only will the rural-to-urban migration among students and would-be workers continue if there are not such changes, but damaging economic, political, social, and cultural consequences are likely to occur in African societies.

NOTES

1. Many statements and studies have been issued on the question of brain drain in the international context. Some works that the reader may want to consult include: Blaug (1969); Myers (1972); Glaser (1978); Trébous (1970); Aderinto (1978); and Yesufu (1978).
2. The ENEA trains persons for a number of positions in rural and urban development

projects and agencies. Students pursue an interdisciplinary curriculum which can be said to be "development oriented" and which creates development specialists. Students are also required to spend six months in a village to effect a group study of the village and the district in which it is located. The course of study is two years.

3. Since the time this study was conducted, 1974–75, the Senegalese government in 1976 reorganized the country into eight administrative regions, dividing the region of Diourbel into two regions called Diourbel and Louga. For purposes of this discussion, the seven regions that existed during the time of this investigation are used in the analyses.

4. In the previous discussion of socioeconomic status in this essay, father's occupation was the criterion used. For purposes of these analyses, a weighted measure consisting of father's occupation and level of schooling has been created. There is not a perfect correlation between these two variables, although they covary strongly in the same direction. Some fathers may have high occupational positions even though their level of schooling is only moderate or low. This is so because in earlier times, attainment of postprimary schooling was limited to few Africans and qualified them for positions in the civil service and the private sector. Upon independence, many of these men acquired high-level administrative positions in the government.

In the created measure, father's occupation has slightly more weight than level of schooling.

REFERENCES

Aderinto, A. 1978. "Toward a Better Understanding of Brain Drain." In V.G. Damachi and V.P. Diejomaoh (eds.), *Human Resources and African Development.* New York: Praeger.

Africa News, 1981. "Back to the Land." *Africa News* 16, no. 10 (March 9):12.

Altbach, P.G. 1982. "The University of Zimbabwe: Colonial No More." *The Chronicle of Higher Education* 23, no. 17 (January 6):64.

Blaug, M., ed. 1969. *Economics of Education 2.* Baltimore: Penguin.

Camara, O. 1974. "La Reforme de l'Enseignement Supérieur (Université et Etablissement de Formation)." Presentation to the Conseil National de l'Union Progressiste Sénégalaise, Dakar.

Clignet, R., and P. Foster. 1966. *The Fortunate Few: A Study of Secondary Schools and Students in the Ivory Coast.* Evanston: Northwestern University Press.

Colvin, Lucie G., et al. 1981. *The Uprooted of the Western Sahel.* New York: Praeger.

Coombs, P., and M. Ahmed. 1974. *Attacking Rural Poverty: How Non-Formal Education Can Help.* Baltimore: Johns Hopkins University Press.

Cowan, L.G.; J. O'Connell; and D.G. Scanlon, eds. 1965. *Education and Nation-Building in Africa.* New York: Praeger.

de Kiewiet, C.W. 1971. *The Emergent African University: An Interpretation.* Washington, D.C.: American Council on Education, Overseas Liaison Committee.

Dieng, A. 1975. "Les Migrations au Sénégal." Presentation to Réunion sur les Mouvements de Population et les Systèmes d'Education dans les Pays Sahelo-Soudaniens, Bureau Regional de l'UNESCO pour l'Education en Afrique, Dakar.

Ela, Jean-Marc. 1971. *La Plume et la Pioche.* Yaounde: Edition Clé.

Flis-Zonabend, F. 1968. *Lycéens de Dakar.* Paris: Librairie François Maspero.

Fougeyrollas, P. 1963. "Phenomènes d'Acculturation chez les Etudiants de la Cité Universitaire de Dakar." *Revue Française de Sociologie* 4, no. 4 (October–December):411–23.

———. 1967. *Modernisation des Hommes: L'Exemple du Sénégal.* Paris: Flammarion.

Glaser, W. 1978. *The Brain Drain: Emigration and Return.* Oxford: Pergamon.

Johnson, R.C. 1983. "Societal Implications of Changes in the University of Dakar (Senegal)." In P.T. Robinson and E.P. Skinner (eds.), *Transformation and Resiliency in Africa.* Washington, D.C.: Howard University Press.

Kane, P. 1975. "Analyse Comparative du Phenomène Migratoire dans Deux Zones du Sénégal: Basse-Casamance et Haut-Fleuve." Presentation to Réunion sur les Mouvements de Population et les Systèmes d'Education dans les Pays Sahelo-Soudaniens, Bureau Regional de l'UNESCO pour l'Education en Afrique, Dakar.

Lele, U. 1981. "Rural Africa: Modernization, Equity, and Long-Term Development." *Science* 211 (February 6):547–53.

McCain, J.A. 1980. "National Development and Higher Education in Ghana." *The Journal of Negro Education* 44, no. 1 (Winter):91–96.

Ministère du Plan et de la Coopération. 1973. *IVᵉ Plan Quadriennal de Développement Economique et Social 1973–1977.* Dakar: Les Nouvelles Editions Africaines.

———. 1977. *Cinquième Plan Quadriennal de Développement Economique et Social.* Dakar: Les Nouvelles Editions Africaines.

Moumouni, A. 1968. *Education in Africa.* London: Andre Deutsch, Limited.

Myers, R.G. 1972. *Education and Emigration.* New York: David McKay.

O'Brien, R.C., ed. 1979. *The Political Economy of Underdevelopment.* Beverly Hills: Sage.

Paxton, J., ed. 1984. *The Statesman Year Book.* New York: St. Martin's Press.

Pfefferman, G. 1968. *Industrial Labor in the Republic of Senegal.* New York: Praeger.

Senghor, L.S. 1959. "Inauguration de l'Université de Dakar." *Chambre de Commerce d'Agriculture et d'Industrie de Dakar* (December):199–201.

———. 1974. "l'Université est au coeur de la Nation." *Le Soleil* (November 5):1.

Sheffield, J.R., and V.R. Diejomaoh. 1972. *Non-Formal Education in African Development.* New York: African-American Institute.

Sow, F. 1972. *Les Fonctionnaires de l'Administration Centrale Sénégalaise.* Dakar: IFAN.

Trébous, M. 1970. *Migration and Development: The Case of Algeria.* Paris: Development Centre of the Organisation for Economic Co-Operation and Development.

UNESCO. 1963. *The Development of Higher Education in Africa.* Paris: UNESCO.

World Bank. 1980. *World Development Report, 1980.* Washington, D.C.: World Bank.

———. 1981. *Accelerated Development in Sub-Saharan Africa: An Agenda for Action.* Washington, D.C.: World Bank.

Yesufu, T.M. 1973. *Creating the African University: Emerging Issues of the 1970's.* Ibadan: Oxford University Press.

———. 1978. "Loss of Trained Personnel by Migration from Nigeria." In V.G. Damachi and V.P. Diejomaoh (eds.), *Human Resources and African Development.* (eds.), New York: Praeger.

Zachariah, K.C., and J. Condé. 1981. *Migration in West Africa.* New York: Oxford University Press.

8

MIGRATION AND NATIONAL DEVELOPMENT: THE KENYA EXAMPLE

ROBERT J. CUMMINGS

This chapter has two basic objectives. One objective is to attempt a reliable analysis of the primary advantages and disadvantges of the migration of people and of its relationship to national development in Kenya. Migration patterns in Kenya are characterized, as elsewhere, by shifts in population from the rural to urban or from the less prosperous rural to richer rural areas. The second objective is to examine the claim that national development in contemporary African societies must be assisted through planned migration—policies of accommodation—by governmental authorities who should now place the national interests of their nations above that of their former colonial masters. This view does not imply that officials should set out to control migration through legal constraints. Rather, geographic diversification of jobs and other economic opportunities and incentives, according to this view, must become a more obvious part of Africa's developmental planning process. Such a policy would serve to attract individuals into predetermined areas while providing agricultural and industrial schemes, when appropriate, to maintain people in the rural and urban centers. National and international firms and corporations would be expected to assist the planning process by locating employment opportunities more equitably, or selectively, throughout the country, rather than primarily in the major urban cities or centers. This process is starting to occur in places but at a notably slow pace. The Kenya case is instructive.

This chapter argues that a sustained effort and a more forceful advocacy posture should be assumed by government to achieve national goals. The local areas, as in the case of Kenya, should be encouraged to share management responsibilities with the national government. This sharing is vital because the urban sector is expanding both in scale and complexity beyond the management capacity of the Kenyan government. Although dormant, the structure for a two-level approach to national development exists and is familiar to most rural people through their several levels of local support groups and associations. Historically, local organizations provided needed distribution and exchange mechanisms for precolonial societies, with a highly structured management component and across ethnic lines. These associations, or economic "corporate" structures, imbibed and shared fundamental *managerial* skills which allowed such historic institutional arrangements to survive.

Employment of existing locally based organizations in Africa could provide policymakers with a broader range of developmental options. Community organizations are in possession of valuable lessons which could become more readily available to governments. Presently, for example, African decisionmakers often "attempt to modernize by changing the organization of traditional agriculture—that is, by establishing cooperatives or collective cultivation instead of encouraging individual farming; or by constructing modern silos for surpluses, instead of improving traditional storage methods" (Lele, 1979:33). In Kenya, smallholder farming is supported by incentives and services, which explains to a large degree the significant growth realized in both the productivity and incomes of local small farms over the past decades.

Many supportive economic communities still are available in rural Kenya. The Akamba of both Kitui and Machakos, among other Kenyan nationals, demonstrate through their local organizational histories and structures that Kenya has maintained a tradition of semi-autonomous rural/local institutions (Cummings, 1975). The basis for Kenya's "further development of local capabilities is one of the best in East Africa" (World Bank, 1982a:7). Polly Hill demonstrated that cocoa farmers in Ghana, by way of comparison, maintained their precolonial economic organizations right through the colonial period and into independence. Considerable national strength and economic growth-potential exist within local organizations and represent the internal basis for further development and employment of local capabilities for national economic growth throughout Africa.

Many local institutional arrangements with precolonial histories might provide supportive, African-centered solutions to contemporary African development problems. But they generally have not been used precisely because they are inherently independent of colonial-created institutions and parastatal agencies.[1]

Too often parastatal agencies, which represent the export-oriented approach to economic development in Africa, have played havoc with the Third World. Moreover, their policies and goals have failed to recognize the special needs and cultural differences of local populations that are significant to national economic planning. Soedjatmoko, an Indonesian scholar, published an article in the *Development Digest* less than a decade after Kenya received its political independence, observing that western theories of development and planning generally

> . . . overlook the importance of cognitive factors in development and growth. It is man's vision of the future, his hopes, fears and expectations that determine his actions in the present; his awareness of the past influences him as well. It is impossible to understand the dynamics of a social system responding to new problems and challenges (and this is what development is about) unless one also has an understanding of these hopes and aspirations as well as of the self image of the people within the system. And until we take into account how man in a certain system perceives his own problems, his interests and his goals, we really have no clues as to how and why he will react in a particular way or not in another (1971:45).

Kenya appears to have recognized the value of cognitive factors in planning, as demonstrated in its efforts to link its rural-urban economies and in its policies of accommodation, for example, towards urban migrants. Yet urbanization as a long-term issue had not received priority attention from the Kenyan government as of late 1982.

MIGRATION LITERATURE: A REVIEW

Human migrations usually are recognized as being related to processes of economic and social change. Such a relationship tends to vary in complexity depending upon the situation. J.A. Jackson, therefore, was able to observe correctly that "it may still not be possible to provide a completely satisfactory sociological model of migration which can adequately embrace its various types and implications" (1969:10). A general theory of migration is almost certain to be insipid or trite, and engulfed by variations and alternatives. Other inadequacies in migration studies are intrinsic in the nature of migration. A large number of the difficulties associated with migration studies have been isolated by sociologists and demographers and "include the selection of relevant political units, irregularities of the boundaries of such units, distinction of the motives and establishments of the permanence of movement and consequently identification of 'movers' as contrasted to 'migrants'" (Migot-Adholla, 1973:2). The inadequacies of census data in Africa only add to the frustration in the analysis of migration.

The need for an interdisciplinary approach to migration research is developing, since discipline-bound research has been limited to the conceptual tools and concerns of the more narrow intellectual traditions. Sociologists have focused upon the effects of migration on social and political structures at the points of departure and destination. Sociologists have concerned themselves also with what they saw as problems of social adjustment and accommodation. Demographers, on the other hand, tend to be concerned with age and sex ratios and structures, and with differential fertility rates. Economists, finally, seek to understand and explain the implications of migration as it is perceived to relate to the distribution of human resources throughout various regions.

Migration literature from the econometric field emphasizes the causes of migration in Africa and other developing world regions.[2] It has failed to examine the broader consequences of such migration, choosing, for example, to emphasize such narrow results as "the effect of rapid migration on farm output and rural incomes" (Knowles and Anker, 1981:205). The narrower disciplinary approach should be replaced by an interdisciplinary approach. Migration literature is divided generally into two categories of subject matter: causes and consequences.

Historians approach the review of migration studies from a historical perspective, tracing the growth in complexity of various theories about human migration as well as their methodological sophistication (see Migot-Adholla, 1973:3). According to early researches, migration was caused by "an expulsion and the attraction, the former nearly always resulting from dearth of food or from over-population which practically comes to the same thing" (Haddon, 1927:1).

Writing in 1937, the German Numelin saw all human migration as a result of "a wandering instinct," "a spirit of restlessness," or an "instinctive disposition." Food shortages, wars, and other such phenomena contributed to migration, but Numelin saw these as having only a secondary influence on the natural wandering nature of humankind. However, such work as Clausen's strongly counters the view of Numelin, stating emphatically that "it was not the 'roving spirit' of the Africans . . . but the economic push and pull between rural and industrial (urban) sources of income which made Africans migrate" (1971:111).

Students of migration in Africa agree that economic motives are basic (Gulliver, 1957; Mitchell, 1959; and Gugler, 1969). Others note that migrations go in search of new, productive economic bases, claiming that those areas which are unable to attract or develop sufficient economic opportunities are also unable to attract large supportive populations. Migrations, then, are usually away from such economically deficient areas (Kay, 1964:14–28; Udo, 1964:326–38; and Elkan, 1967:581–89). Yet, Shem Migot-Adholla observes, "It can be argued that migration for wage labour operates as a means of maintaining the standard of living which the migrants have come to regard as essential," which further "suggests that given comparable circumstances only the relatively badly off will migrate for economic reasons" (1973:7). It is also argued that even though migrants who respond to the push factors are negatively motivated, those who respond to the pull factors are motivated in a positive manner (Lee, 1966:47). The Nyakyusa migrants among whom P.H. Gulliver worked, who were in search of agricultural opportunities, would be responding most likely to "push" factors while the Kenyan school leavers studied by Henry Rempel were responding to the positive "pull" factors.

The great difficulty in interpretations of the motives of migrants has rendered generalizations in this area very difficult to make. J.C. Caldwell shows that in Ghana, for example, migrants who traveled to the urban regions usually came from relatively prosperous familial homes (1968:361–77). Their prosperity apparently emanated from the financial support given by family members who sent home regular monthly remittances gained from their city employment. Moreover, Caldwell observed that more than seventy percent of those youths planning migration were doing so clearly for reasons other than the pressures of social and economic factors (cf. Peterson, 1961:175).

Analysis of African migration forms a primary component of the study of social and economic change beginning with colonial control of Africa. Important patterns of mass movement have been associated with labor migration to the industrial, commercial, and mining centers, which grew into major cities, and to the agricultural plantations that were established by the white colonial settlers. Thus, for a considerable part of Africa—particularly East, Central, and South Africa, where there was not a notable tradition of urban living—migration has been the major mechanism for urban growth (Migot-Adholla, 1973:6).

Migration may be temporary or permanent and may result from personal, social, political, economic, or religious reasons. In Kenya, religious migrations have had relatively little historical impact, save perhaps the recent religious movement activity in western Kenya, *dini ya Masambu*. On the other hand, in Uganda the religious factor has been more pronounced than in all the rest of East Africa, as demonstrated by the Moslem-Christian conflicts. Often environmental conditions—for example, human and bovine diseases, soil exhaustion, flood and droughts—force migrations to relieve excessive pressures on affected lands.

There are other consequences of migration such as those motivated recently by the high influx of tourists in Kenya. Newspapers have reported that some young men and women from the interior migrate to the Kenyan coast and become prostitutes. The environmental conditions of Uganda, moreover, recently forced much of its labor force to migrate into Kenya to provide support labor for Kenyan growth while increasing the well-publicized brain drain from Uganda. Such out-migration from a country is clearly a loss of national investments in human capital. Finally, the movement of individuals from employment in rural communities to nonproductive activities or unemployment in urban areas create burdens on urban institutions as well as the national treasury.

Interpretive problems are accentuated by a scarcity of recorded measurements of migration and economic development. The causal relationship among population growth, population movement, and unemployment, for example, is very subtle and therefore, without proper records, difficult to establish.

COLONIAL INFLUENCE ON MIGRATION PATTERNS

In East Africa after World War I one of the primary aims of manpower development was attracting and maintaining a sufficient quantity of workers for the colonial labor force: a labor force not associated with local African development but entrapped instead by colonial enterprises, industries, farms, and coastal plantations. The rise of European settlers' large-scale farming effectively excluded Africans from cash-crop farming in Kenya and led to colonial policies designed to generate a cheap labor force. Roger van Zwaneneberg (1972:207–32) demonstrated the intense dependency of the settler community on Africans, for the expatriates usually had very limited farming skills as well as limited economic resources. Therefore, in addition to their struggle for survival in the interwar years, colonists were forced to generate a surplus out of African labor if they were to continue farming in greater security in future years. Lord Lugard summed up the matter by noting that "European ownership on a large scale has in all cases resulted in the demand for alien or compulsory labour by which alone large foreign-owned estates can be kept going" (1972:97). Thus, punitive registration measures and the infamous Kipande system of control were strengthened and statutory punishment of "deserters" was made easy in the rural areas, where labor was at a premium and associated with a backward sloping supply curve.

In urban Kenya there evolved a typical labor migration pattern characterized by a circular movement. Annual reports from the East African Statistical Department between 1945 and 1961 demonstrate this pattern while identifying migrant laborers as largely unskilled workers who migrated to the colonial capital, Nairobi, and were allowed to remain in the city only for prescribed periods of time. This permission did not extend beyond the labor force to dependents, wives, or other Africans, who were required, via the Pass Laws provisions, to remain in rural areas. "During this period," notes urban geographer J.W. Muwonge, "a very anomalous situation prevailed whereby a balance existed between housing demand and supply, employment and in-migration. . . . Perhaps more important as far as urban housing was concerned, a unique population structure became characteristic, wherein adult African males predominated" (1982:58–59).

Urban housing was simple and rents were low, yet the workers were unhappy. Crucial to the reactions and expectations of the migrant workers were the Pass Laws' exclusionary provisions. A low level of labor productivity was directly related to worker dissatisfaction and rapid worker turnovers. As soon as the unskilled laborer was trained to meet work requirements, his temporary period typically expired. This wastage was an unacceptable result for the colonial administrators. In an effort to reverse the trend, various research studies were initiated (Van der Horst, 1957:275–89; Elkan, 1960, 1967). High labor turnover rates were confronted by the Carpenter Commission, which recommended both an increased urban wage for African laborers and the establishment of economic incentives to assist in stabilizing African labor—that is, to create an urban proletariat. It was the responsibility of the Carpenter Commission to prescribe a system of incentives to induce the "native" to leave his homestead and make a commitment to wage employment.

> The statutory minimum wage based on the needs of a single man was to be changed to one based on the needs of a family unit. In addition, fringe benefits particularly the provision of cheap housing were to be substantially improved to help the new generation of urban workers fully to identify with their new way of life and sever the connections with the rural areas. "Stabilization of the labour force" became the key phrase (Henley, 1972:2).

Even though subsequent improvements in the wages of African migrant laborers and in urban social services extended the time periods of labor migrancy and increased labor productivity, there is limited evidence—save the report of the Carpenter Commission—that the colonial regime intended to create a permanent skilled urban African labor force. Research such as that of John Harris and Michael Todaro confirmed the functional relationship between the growth of industrial real wages and the growth of labor productivity, but it also noted the persistence of lower wages and lower productivity for a considerably larger industrial labor force (1970:29–46). The evidence "suggests that the measures taken to stabilize industrial labour and to increase labour productivity have probably led instead to a greater differentiation in urban real wages but more importantly between urban and rural incomes" (Migot-Adholla, 1973:11).

Independent Kenya thus inherited a tremendous population of unskilled workers, an institutionalized wage system, and an urban inmigration problem as its colonial legacy. The shift in colonial urban migration policy following publication of the Carpenter Commission Report in the mid-1950s preceded more radical changes in national urban policy after 1963 when Kenya was granted its political independence. Africans were allowed, via the general policy of postcolonial Kenya, to take on permanent citizenship as urban dwellers rather than as just transient laborers. With the repeal by the Kenyan government of the oppressive rural-to-urban migration laws, dramatic urban population growth began. This influx of rural residents into the urban centers was given added momentum by new policies in land adjudication and registration. A son of a land-wealthy father could find himself without his appropriate "share" of land upon leaving school and seek refuge in the cities.

The city was the natural place to go, for the government was in the process of replacing expatriates with Africans and reducing the striking disparities within the public pay scale. The pattern of government employees' wage increases spread throughout the modern urban sector ". . . partly through minimum wage legislation and partly through the trend-setting influence of the most rapidly growing sector of urban employment—the government and its various (inherited) parastatal agencies" (Acharya, 1981:17). The increase, moreover, of income and available employment opportunities for unskilled labor and clerical workers in the cities increased the flow of migrants from their rural locations to the urban centers.

Yet the fundamental problems were not at the policy level, as can be seen when one reviews the colonial influence on migration and urban growth; rather, these problems were at the institutional level. The independent government's acceptance of inherited institutions without considerable reconstruction also meant *de facto* maintenance of inherent problems created by the colonial regime. Recently, many African countries, including Kenya, have "encountered a major deterioration in the international environment which has exposed more clearly than before the *frailty of their institutional framework* and weaknesses in economic policies" (Gulhati, 1980:1, emphasis added). To do other than a serious reorganization of the inherited institutional arrangements was only to replace physically absent European *rulers* with psychologically distant African *governors*.

MIGRATION AND URBAN GROWTH PROBLEMS

The high volume of migrants into the African urban centers has caused national growth on that continent to become a major problem.

> In several countries of Africa, the combination of rural-to-urban migration and natural increase is producing unprecedented rates of population growth within the major cities. Caught unprepared and lacking both financial and technical resources, urban authorities are witnessing a gigantic stream of migrants who, given the shortages in accommodations meeting the legal minimum standards, resort to living in slums and squatter settlements both within the city and at its periphery, often in extremely hazardous health and sanitation conditions (Muwonge, 1980:595).

Before 1970, several factors reflected in immigration data illustrated the consequences of urban migration in Kenya. Among these were (1) decreasing employment opportunity coupled with a rapidly increasing number of school dropouts; (2) increase in capital intensive industries in an effort to respond to trade unions' demands for higher wages; and (3) a general pricing policy which tended to discriminate against agriculture and rural-urban linkages (Ghai, 1970:4–11).

Both the colonial and the independent governments in Kenya tried to battle the dual problems of migration and urban unemployment. Their actions resulted at different times in the creation of legal restrictions on migration into the cities as confirmed by the colonial regime's *Report of the Commission on Destitution among Africans* (1954) and the independent government's Vagrancy Act (1966). Forced repatriation back to the land was another result, together with the more regularly used forms of "denying services to squatter areas, enforcing expensive building codes on them, and periodically demolishing structures that contravened these established high-standard . . . building codes" (Muwonge, 1980:595). A third result evolved through the provisions of the Tripartite agreements of 1964 and 1970, which sought to create employment by government fiat. The trade unions attempted to support this latter effort by calling a moratorium on strikes and demands for wage increases for one year while private employers and the government increased their respective labor force by ten percent.

The base of the problem was seen as a case of defective agricultural methods in the rural areas resulting primarily from the ignorance of peasants and their poor habits of husbandry. Some of the suggested remedies included soil conservation schemes, destocking, land tenure measures, and controlled introduction of some commercial crops where ecological circumstances were favorable. But, without the ability to evaluate these measures within the context of the total economic policy structure and within the inherited institutional structure, such measures proved less than effective in the thrust for national growth and development. The government's attitude, moreover, did not help much since many of its "agricultural programs were revitalized with the sole objective of keeping people out of the city" (Muwonge, 1980:595).

The squatter settlements not only remained but expanded around the cities, giving importance to the need for information on migration because of its direct relationship to governmental planning efforts. Any sudden influx of people in a rapidly growing population center induces stronger pressures on housing, educational, and health facilities for which local authorities were able originally to make only specified levels of allowances, since there was no way to forecast the annual increases of rural-to-urban residents.

Throughout Kenya between 1948 and 1962, the urban population rose "from 285,445 to 670,000, a growth rate of 135 per cent or an average compound rate of growth of 6.3 per cent every year over the intercensal period of fourteen years" (Ominde, 1968:183). During the most recent intercensal period, the decade between 1969 and 1979, the urban population of Kenya increased at an average annual rate of 7.9 percent. Nairobi almost doubled its population in the decade between 1947 and 1957, while the number of urban centers, including townships with more than 2,000 inhabitants, virtually doubled from 47 to 90 between 1969 and 1979 (World Bank, 1982a:2).

Kenyans moved to towns between 1948 and 1962 at an extraordinary 174% rate, with Nairobi and Mombasa receiving the bulk of the rural-urban migration. Nakuru, Eldoret, Kitale, and Naivasha, however, received their share. Most of the growth was experienced among the

TABLE 1 Population of Kenya, 1962–79

Year	Total Population	Urban Population	Urban Percentage	Number of Urban Centers
1979	15,322,000	2,307,000	15.0	90
1969	10,943,000	1,080,000	9.9	47
1962	8,636,000	748,000	8.7	34
	Intercensal Growth Rates			
1969–79	3.4%	7.9%		
1962–69	3.3%	5.4%		

SOURCE: Population Census, Kenya, 1962, 1969, 1979 (provisional).

TABLE 2 Population in Nairobi

Year	Population Growth in Nairobi	Population of Nairobi by Major Racial Groups		
		Africans	Asians	Europeans
1962	350,000	59.54%	31.40%	8.05%
1969	510,000	83.04	13.19	3.77
1979	828,000	—	—	—

SOURCE: Nairobi City Council Planning Department, 1979.

African population, who registered between 1962 and 1969 a net population increase of 23.5%.

During the 1970s the pattern of urban growth shifted significantly from the major cities to the secondary towns, whose share of the total urban population grew from 7% to 31%. Nairobi and Mombasa underwent a decrease in population share from 70% to 51% over the same period (World Bank, 1982a:2). This decline in the capital city's relative population in Kenya is quite unlike the case of most other African countries. The 1979 census data fail to provide sufficient information to establish why this pattern has occurred in Kenya. A historical review of the planning process of Kenya's independent government, however, demonstrates that Kenyanization meant the institutionalization of a planning method characterized by the government planners' refusal to follow the inherited regional planning theory and approach of Britain. This fact is illustrated by a recent study by the World Bank, reporting that urban growth in Kenya between 1969 and 1979 appears to have been determined by the strong rural-urban linkages of the economy, which have focused migration more into the secondary towns. It is also likely that the relatively neutral policies which Kenya has followed toward rural-urban income distribution . . . have been important in preventing a shift in migration toward the largest cities (World Bank, 1982b:6).

The basic problems nevertheless remain. The relative political stability of Kenya as demonstrated through its image of commercial and industrial growth serves to accentuate the problems of urban growth. According to recent surveys, Nairobi is caught in an array of push-pull factors greater than its own centripetal forces. The high growth rates of population "in the rural areas, the very slow progress of the program to create alternative growth poles in the upcountry areas, and the real land pressure existing in many of the high potential districts, are contributing to Nairobi's swelling population" (Muwonge, 1982:60). Migrants have created and settled in squatter settlements on the fringes of municipal boundaries, often subdivided only by agricultural lands. The boundaries of such municipalities have been expanded recently to include various existing rural settlement areas. Most Kenyan towns, therefore, had large expansions in their boundaries during the 1970s, with corresponding inflation of their apparent growth rates.

Demographic studies do not forecast a significant slow-down for Kenya's overall population growth rate in the near future. Hence, "the outlook for urban areas will depend critically on the ability of the agricultural sector to absorb a large increase in population, which will require major investments to expand arable land and difficult political decisions concerning land redistribution" (World Bank, 1982b:7). Both the urban and rural areas will have to absorb significantly increased population growth by the year 2000. Nairobi's population alone is expected to triple to 2.3 million, even with a reduced estimated urban population share of 27% over the same period. Secondary townships will require special governmental assistance to prepare them to meet the challenges of population and economic growth and national development.

KENYAN DEMOGRAPHY AND ECONOMIC GROWTH

After receiving its independence in 1963, the Government of the Republic of Kenya, under Jomo Kenyatta, was undergirded by a "rapid growth of domestic products, strong fiscal performance, low rates of inflation and manageable, external accounts" (World Bank, 1982c:vii). The economic stability of the East African Community in a large sense was tied to Kenya. While external economic and political pressures remained severe, the basic cooperative arrangements between the nations of the Community served to reduce their individual vulnerability. Kenya's economic growth in those early days, 1964–72, averaged 6.5%, with policymakers, among others, anticipating a continual increase in the nation's gross national product (GNP). This high expectancy level for Kenyan success permeated the society in spite of the inherited structural, institutional problems associated with various critical public and private sectors (education, agriculture, industry, etc.) of the nation.

By 1972, less than a decade after its independence, Kenya's average rate of growth, according to recent World Bank reports, was 4.1% per annum. This reduced growth rate held sway over the nation throughout the decade. Added to the nation's growth problems was the 1974 world economic crisis, fueled by high-priced oil imports, on which Kenya continues to be dependent. Moreover, "the collapse of the East African Community, the major market for Kenyan manufactured goods, international recession and high international interest rates have resulted in a steady tightening of the foreign exchange constraint on growth, while dramatic swings in the prices of Kenya's key exports, coffee and tea, have compounded already difficult problems of economic management" (World Bank, 1982c:vii).

Rural development generally was accepted as a key to national growth and development in Kenya. The farming sector, according to Luigi Laurenti and John Gerhart in their report to the Ford Foundation in 1973, provided upwards of 30 percent of the nation's GNP, supported 90 percent of the population, provided 50 percent of the wage employment, and accounted for 60 percent of the country's export earnings.

> One might go further and argue that rural development is important, not just for national development, but for the development of the urban sector itself. [For] . . . agriculture earns foreign exchange vital to the urban sector; it provides food surpluses to feed the increasing urban population; increased rural incomes provide a growing market for manufactured products; the rural sector can provide more employment at a low cost per job (Laurenti and Gerhart, 1973:13–14).

The Third National Development Plan (1972–80) called for an intensification of governmental activity with specific emphasis on rural development programs (Government of Kenya, 1975:35). This plan resulted in a clear linkage between Kenya's rural and urban development goals.

Kenya has followed through on its 1975 plan to introduce new macroeconomic policies. Until recently, the nation had in operation a highly balanced rural development program with appropriate supportive roads and transport links, markets, and related services. The government basically pursued a neutral policy approach to agriculture itself. While it intervened with policy initiatives on occasions during the mid-1970s, and although such initiatives usually handicapped agricultural sectoral growth, Kenya generally instituted only minimal policy regulations. Moreover, the government did not provide socioeconomic subsidies in the urban areas, which in other countries served as magnets for rural dwellers to migrate into urban centers. As a result, the 20 percent of Kenya's land which is arable is fully utilized and produces at a meaningful or rational economic level, but cannot be expected to expand much beyond its existing capacity. The only available methods for increased land output and farm incomes, therefore, are more sophisticated and high-priced intensification programs, smallholder innovation, and agricultural concentration (World Bank, 1982c:xi). In short, the expansion of capital formation in the Kenyan rural environment is rapidly becoming less possible. Urbanization appears to be the more attractive and appropriate mechanism for achieving the required national growth. Rural-to-urban migration must be planned and encouraged in light of these realities.

The population growth of Kenya is estimated to be one of the highest in the world at its present 4.2 percent per annum. A large segment of this expanding population could be used more effectively in the urban areas than in the present rural-urban distribution. The rapidly growing urban areas present the greatest opportunity for the expansion of capital formation through market products.

For this reason, urbanization must be recognized as a major national concern and should be employed in the national plan to increase incomes and alleviate poverty. Computers and related high technology apparatus, heavy machinery, information-management equipment, pharmaceuticals, and medical devices are examples of marketable products appropriate for Kenyan urban entrepreneurs. The list of such products is expanding at a rapid rate, and their utilization in business ventures will require increased urban manpower. Such products provide both the capability for individual employment and continuing potential for economic expansion. Such expansion in the marketplace would serve to generate larger and more diverse sources of revenues for the Kenyan government. This funding is required in light of the government's inability to increase urban investments at a rate equal to rapidly expanding urban population growth (World Bank, 1982b:14). Urban institutions will be forced to seek their own sources of support.

One potential source is the small-scale urban informal sector. This economic sector is a part of Kenya's semi-autonomous local structures, derived from both their traditional local experience and their colonial legacy. Working closely with such structures and reducing governmental regulatory actions in such areas as local revenues, budgetary responsibility, and central-local relationships, the Kenyan government could make a fundamental contribution to its urban policy objectives. For, as it is now, the central government's involvement has almost always caused

> the country to rely heavily on large, sophisticated foreign-owned or -managed firms, using capital-intensive technology and foreign-acquired or expatriate skills, necessitating protected markets and the loss of foreign exchange. The informal sector, on the other hand, operating on a small scale with inexpensive and labor-intensive technology and with skills acquired outside the formal school system, can manage with a minimum of foreign exchange and without the tariffs, quotas and trade licenses that undermine competition and raise prices (Werlin, 1974:206).

The benefits to the national economy through less expensive and labor-intensive technology, reduced prices, and independency of foreign exchange and expensive expatriate managers are self-evident in the current international economic environment.

The employment of a new approach could provide increased capital, for example, for the servicing of urban land. At present, when a choice is made between quality and quantity in urban land use and housing construction, the choice is weighted in favor of quantity. Public housing projects are extremely expensive and slow. Private housing construction, on the other hand, fails to meet high governmental standards, but provides high volume to meet basic needs. The government should shift its priority to supplement the private sector's efforts by "emphasizing the provision of basic services and minimum planning controls" (World Bank 1982b:82). Such action on the part of the central government would demonstrate its capacity to provide the necessary supports and incentives for urbanization. Urban dwellers then could focus their attention more creatively on those competitive arrangements which increase capital formation to the mutual advantage of the urban and rural areas.

Kenya has been quite willing to tolerate a "diversified institutional structure, with an enlarged role for both the traditional/local community and the private commercial sector." Nevertheless, while the "smallholder agricultural sector has grown more rapidly than in Tanzania or Lesotho," Kenya's distribution of incomes and benefits has not been any more equitable (Lele, 1973:33). Much of this has to do with the fact that Kenya is perceived as a rural country, and poverty is more readily observed in the rural areas. The government's ability to distribute supportive resources, however, is reduced somewhat by the sheer character of the rural population: more than 70 percent are smallholders, with the remaining 30 percent divided beween the landless wage workers on large farms, pastoralists, and migrants to semi-arid regions (World Bank 1982c:x). The mechanism for more equitable distribution of national wealth within the rural-based Kenyan society does not exist through present internal structures.

The traditional credit-exchange/loan system among family and ethnic group members might serve as an economic model for policymakers to encourage self-employment rather than wage-earning as a goal among both urban and rural residents. The system may serve further to distribute incomes more equitably. In Ukamba, for example, the ability of the Akamba to adapt to and involve themselves in commercial enterprise is explained in their socioeconomic ideology of *umanthi*. Credit arrangements traditionally were established and honored with exceptionally low ratios of nonrepayment. The family or ethnic unit held the power as well as the managerial structures and skills necessary to assure this result. This relationship and the structures for such credit exchanges, loans, and guaranteed repayments still are inherent parts of the society. Such customary systems are not unique to the Akamba of Kenya.

Indeed, most of Kenya's ethnic communities have an ideological frame of reference, historic in nature and rational in its economic function, which governs their individual desires to acquire a posture of self-reliance within their wider communities and social organizations. Remittances or transfers between rural communities or between rural and urban communities—although now in decline[3]—as well as Kenyans' ability to provide sufficient agricultural foodstuffs for themselves before colonialism, are examples of the continued attempt to maintain an economic support base. In short, cooperative institutional frameworks exist in Kenya through which shared management responsibilities can be achieved between government and local authorities.

Present-day policy decisions are often at odds with the structural framework of the country. The government's ability to transform largely colonial-created structures into a more Kenya-centered system is primary to its capacity to meet its macroeconomic plans, whether identified in long-term or short-term developmental schedules. Ample evidence attests that reductions in Kenya's agricultural growth, for example, are directly related to problems of institutional support.

Long-term efforts must be made to improve productivity in the rural sector of the society, even though the growth potential here is small. At the same time, the issue of urbanization must be raised to a level of national priority, for it is clear that urbanization is the only hope for the expansion of capital formation in Kenya (World Bank, 1982b:91). These two efforts are crucial to more rapid growth and the reduction of poverty in the country. The results will depend upon the government's capacity to exploit available national resources to their optimum. A recent World Bank report concludes that "growth of agricultural production has been prohibited by government intervention in the pricing and marketing system, by difficulties in dealing with politically sensitive and complex land issues, and by problems in planning and execution of projects and programs designed to raise agricultural output" (1982b:6).

One objection against the involvement of local rural organizations in policy implementation is the amount of time required to convince local authorities to support policy decisions. The government could address this factor by providing additional technical and agricultural educational institutions to service the local areas. Such an effort would assist in reducing mistrust and, at the same time, in increasing the pool of trained human resources to meet manpower shortages in labor, administrative, entrepreneurial, and technical personnel.

Manpower shortages are not the only obstacles to Kenyan growth. Problems with housing, health care and educational facilities, overcrowding, and employment opportunities place serious financial strains on the national budget while playing havoc with national development plans. Moreover,

> The rapid growth of population is probably the single most important obstacle to raising living standards in Kenya over the longer term. It is intimately linked to the problems of land scarcity, adequacy of food supply, opportunities for productive employment and the ability of the society to satisfy elementary basic needs. The growth of the country's population has been accelerating as rising living standards have reduced mortality, while increasing fertility (World Bank, 1982c:xi).

Unfortunately, the costs of confronting the array of problems facing Kenya are borne almost exclusively by the government.

Currently, there are more than 200 parastatal agencies in Kenya. Most are involved in activities ranging from purely advisory to regulatory functions, while the others are involved directly in production, marketing, and financial functions. The government bears the burden of financing much of the parastatal sector with an ever-increasing net outflow of budgetary funds. The loose, rather undefined relations between government and the parastatal sector raises the question of why these "parasites"—as most of them are—remain in existence in a country needing all of its resources. Parastatal agencies compete with potentially productive private sector organizations for the same limited government funds. Their strategic locations within the governmental structure often gives them advantage over their more productive counterparts in the private sector. The machinery established to examine proposed investments in parastatal agencies and to monitor their record of performance is totally inadequate. In summary, Kenya's developmental problems can be traced to two broad areas of concern: fundamental structural problems, and inappropriate policy decisions. There has been a tendency to develop broadly defined policies to expect them to meet the specific national and local needs of the country. Governmental leaders, finally, must recognize that persisting colonial-created structural arrangements were designed to support an economic growth plan external to Kenya. These inherited structures generally have burned themselves out, are no longer relevant, and are in need of fundamental change.

CONCLUSION AND POLICY IMPLICATIONS

The high density of populations migrating into urban and wealthy rural centers in Kenya will force notable changes in governmental methods. The national government will need to develop procedures and policies which allow the local authorities to *share* in the governance of the nation with specific expectations and financial supports. The rapid urban population growth which characterizes Kenya, like many other African nations, will force changes in the planning and evaluating of programs and should result in the creation of "new" local and national institutions.

The rural-urban migrational impact on Kenya will continue to force changes in the government's institutional methods of educating its youthful population. To achieve this goal, it is vital that the

> inherited educational system, including the schools at all levels and the entire mass communication network, . . . be reorganized to ensure that it plays an appropriate role in helping to build the

necessary sets of understanding and attitudes among the masses of the population as well as those administering the state machinery to enable them to participate in formulating and implementing the program to rebuild institutions at national and local levels to allocate resources to attain meaningful development (Seidman, 1974:116).

Planned and clearly defined governmental support for rural to urban migration should raise the vitally important issue of urbanization to a level of national priority and serve as a catalyst for the expansion of capital formation. The capacity for the rural area to meet this goal is becoming more contracted.

Special governmental consideration must be given to the abolition of most, if not all, of the parastatal agencies. Those remaining should be forced to prove their value in terms of specific contributions to the nation's capital gains or growth of the GNP.

National growth centers, with clearly articulated plans and goals for low-cost housing and related educational and urban services, should be created to encourage migrants to assist in reducing the major problems associated with trained manpower shortages. Multinational enterprises or foreign corporations conducting business in Kenya should be involved actively in the early planning associated with the development of such centers. They should be made to understand their expected role as "partners-in-development" rather than as visitors motivated by short-term profits. The goal is to have these outside corporations, as well as those few domestic African entrepreneurs who have accumulated a little capital in their export-enclave activities, contribute more significantly to the long-term restructuring of the national economy.

National policies, moreover, must be designed at long last to remove, as much as possible, dependency on both expatriate "experts" and foreign aid and indebtedness. Such policy objectives should be aimed at moving the nation into a more interdependent relationship with (1) other African nations, (2) other Third World nations, and (3) the wider international community.[4]

The challenge to African and Kenyan leaders is to set their own national priorities, in light of constraints and pressures, with emphasis on the realities of their national constituencies. This developmental approach could succeed in increasing national productivity and in raising the standard of living for Africa generally and, in particular, for Kenya. External support and assistance, then, could be made more productive in the long term and could aid in the achievement of African economic independence and international cooperation.

NOTES

1. *Parastatal agencies* is the term used herein to refer to all firms or industrial companies in which the government has some budgetary involvement, either in the form of equity participation, long-term loans, or recurrent grants. In short, they may be fully owned by the government or have either majority or minority government ownership.

2. The notable works include Todaro, 1969; Stiglitz, 1969; Harris and Todaro, 1970; Shultz, 1971; Schwartz, 1973; Levy and Wadycki, 1974; and Beals, Levy, and Moses, 1976.

3. See especially Knowles and Anker, 1981:205–26.

4. See especially *The Lagos Plan of Action* (officially titled *Plan of Action for the Implementation of the Monrovia Strategy for the Economic Development of Africa*, OAU, 1980) and the *Berg Report* (officially titled *Accelerated Development in Sub-Saharan Africa*, World Bank, 1981). Robert S. Browne, senior research fellow, African Studies and Research Program, Howard University, sees these two documentary prescriptions for African development in direct opposition—"on a collision course"—to each other as a result of the viewpoint and approaches proposed to solve the specific sets of problems identified in the documents. Browne's analysis is available under the title, *The Lagos Plan of Action vs. The Berg Report: Current Issues in African Economic Development* (co-authored by Robert J. Cummings), ASRP Monograph Series, 1984:4.

REFERENCES

Acharya, S. 1981. "Development Perspective and Priorities in Sub-Saharan Africa." *Finance and Development* March:16–19.

Beals, R.E., M.B. Levy, and L.N. Moses. 1976. "Rationality and Migration in Ghana." *The Review of Economics and Statistics* 49:480–86.

Caldwell, J.C. 1968. "Determinants of Rural-Urban Migration in Ghana." *Population Studies* 22, no. 3:361–77.

Clausen, Lars. 1972. "Industrialized Man—The Zambian Case of Radical Social Change." In Heide and Udo Ernst Simonis (eds.), *Socioeconomic Development in Dual Economies: The Example of Zambia.* IFO—Institut fur Wirtschaftsforchung Munchen Afrikastudienstelle.

Cummings, R.J. 1975. "Aspects of Human Porterage with Special Reference to the Akamba of Kenya: Towards an Economic History, 1820–1920." Ph.D. diss., UCLA.

Elkan, Walter. 1960. *Migrants and Proletarians: Urban Labour in the Economic Development of Uganda.* London: Oxford University Press.

———. 1967. "Circular Migration and the Growth of Towns in East Africa." *International Labour Review* 96, no. 6:581–89.

Ghai, D.P. 1970. "Employment Performance, Prospects and Policies in Kenya." *East Africa Journal* 7, no. 11:4–11.

Government of Kenya. 1975. *Development Plan, 1974–1978.* Vol. 1. Nairobi: Government Printers.

Gugler, J. 1969. "On the Theory of Rural-Urban Migration: The Case of Sub-Saharan Africa." In J.A. Jackson (ed.), *Migration: Sociological Studies, No. 2.* Cambridge: University Press, 134–55.

Gulhati, Ravi. 1980. *Eastern and Southern Africa: Past Trends and Future Prospects.* World Bank Paper no. 413.

Gulliver, P.H. 1957. "Nyakusa Labour Migration." *Rhodes-Livingstone Journal* 21.

Haddon, A.C. 1927. *The Wanderings of Peoples.* Cambridge: University Press.

Harris, J., and M.P. Tudaro. 1970. "Migration, Unemployment and Development: A Two-Sector Analysis." *American Economic Review* 60, no. 1.

Henley, J. 1972. "Over Commitment: Some Reflections on the Structuring of Kenyan Labour Force." 8th Annual Conference, Nairobi, East African Universities Social Sciences Council, paper no. 26.

Jackson, J.A. 1969. *Migration: Sociological Studies, No. 2.* Cambridge: University Press.

Kay, G. 1964. "Sources and Uses of Cash in Some Ushi Villages, Fort Roseberry District, Northern Rhodesia." *Rhodes-Livingstone Journal* 35:14–28.

Knowles, J.C., and R. Anker. 1981. "An Analysis of Income Transfer in a Developing Country: The Case of Kenya." *Journal of Developing Economics* 2:205–26.

Laurenti, L., and J. Gerhart. 1973. *Urbanization in Kenya: Rural Development and Urban Growth.* International Urbanization Survey Report to the Ford Foundation. New York: Ford Foundation.

Lee, Everett. 1966. "A Theory of Migration." *Demography* 3, no. 1:47.

Lele, Uma. 1979. "A Revisit to Rural Development in Eastern Africa." *Finance and Development* December:31–35.

Levy, M.B., and W.J. Wadycki. 1974a. "What is the Opportunity Cost of Moving? Reconsideration of the Effect of Distance on Migration." *Economic Development and Cultural Change* 22, no. 4.

———. 1974b. "Education and the Decision to Migrate: An Econometric Analysis of Migration in Venezuela." *Econometrica* 42, no. 2.

Lugard, F.D. 1972. *The Dual Mandate in British Tropical Africa.* Revised. London: Cass.

Migot-Adholla, S.E. 1973. "Migration and Rural Differentiation." Working Paper no. 92. Nairobi: I.D.S.

Mitchell, J.C. 1959. "The Causes of Labour Migration." *Inter-American Labour Institute Bulletin* 1.

Muwonge, J.W. 1980. "Urban Policy and Patterns of Low-Income Settlement in Nairobi, Kenya." *Population and Development Review* 6, no. 4:595–613.

———. 1982. "Intra-Urban Mobility and Low Income Housing: The Case of Nairobi, Kenya." In Morrison and Gutkind (eds.), *Housing and the Urban Poor in Africa*, no. 37 (Syracuse), chap. 5.

Ominde, S.H. 1968. *Land and Population Movements in Kenya.* Evanston, Ill.: Northwestern University Press.

Peterson, William. 1961. *Population.* New York: Macmillan.

Rempel, H. 1971. "Labour Migration into Urban Centers and Urban Unemployment in Kenya." Ph.D. diss., University of Wisconsin.

Schultz, T.P. 1971. "Rural-Urban Migration in Colombia." *Review of Economics and Statistics* 53, no. 2.

Schwartz, A. 1973. "Interpreting the Effect of Distance on Migration." *The Journal of Political Economy* 81:1153–69.

Seidman, Ann. 1974. "Key Variables to Incorporate in a Model for Development: The African Case." *African Studies Review* 17, no. 1 (April).

Soedjatmoko, W. 1971. "Comparative Factors of Development." *Development Digest* 9:141–48.

Stiglitz, J.E. 1969. "Rural-Urban Migration, Surplus Labour, and the Relationship Between Urban and Rural Wages." *Eastern Africa Economic Review* 1, no. 2.

Todaro, M.P. 1969. "A Model of Labour Migration and Urban Unemployment in Less Developed Countries." *American Economic Review* 59, no. 1.

Udo, R.K. 1964. "The Migrant Tenant Farmer of Eastern Nigeria." *Africa* 34, no. 4 (London):326–28.

Van der Horst, Sheila. 1957. "A Note on Native Labour Turnover and the Structure of the Labour Force in the Cape Peninsula." *South Africa Journal of Economics* 25, no. 4:275–89.

Van Zwanenberg, R.M.A. 1972. "The Economic Response of Kenya Africans to European Settlement, 1903–1939." In *Hadith—4*. Nairobi: Kenya Literature Bureau, 207–32.

Werlin, H.H. 1974. "The Informal Sector: The Implications of the ILO's Study of Kenya." *African Studies Review* 17, no. 1 (April).

World Bank. 1982a. *Kenya—Economic Development and Urbanization Policy, Vol. I: Executive Summary.* Washington, D.C.

World Bank. 1982b. *Kenya—Economic Development and Urbanization Policy, Vol. II: Main Report.* Washington, D.C.

World Bank. 1982c. *Growth and Structural Change in Kenya: A Basic Economic Report.* Washington, D.C.

9

TOWARD NEW ANALYSES OF MIGRATION AND DEVELOPMENT: CONCLUDING REMARKS

BEVERLY LINDSAY

A clear pattern emerges in the preceding eight chapters as the reader is steered across the vast continent of Africa south of the Sahara, across cultures with varied traditions and colonial experiences, and across academic disciplines of differing perspectives. The pattern consists more of questions than of answers, but the answers are not altogether absent.

One element in the pattern stands out: the complex interrelationship between migration and development. Another common theme is the paucity of evidence supporting any one explanatory theory or even one mode for conceptualizing the interaction between development and migration. The message for scholars and students is that Africa offers a broad scope for social research. The message for policymakers is that an eclectic, pragmatic, and holistic approach is in order for Subsaharan Africa—an approach based on current African realities.

Two complicating motifs underlie this book's theme of young sovereign nations coping with voluntary population movements while attempting to develop modern economic, political, and social institutions. The first complication is the legacy of colonialism, which not only undermined many indigenous institutions but also prejudiced many African political leaders against traditional approaches. Given the legacy and remnants of colonialism in the form of neocolonialism, it is quite difficult to discern clearly the positive features of traditional approaches in a contemporary era. Traditional approaches are often removed from current problems. The other complication is the refugee problem: the largely involuntary migration of five to seven million Africans fleeing political oppression, war, or famine. (A second United Nations-sponsored International Conference on Assistance to Refugees in Africa met in Geneva in July 1984 to address the problem of poor countries that give asylum to displaced persons; the recommendations have yet to be disseminated widely.) The sudden influx of thousands of refugees can halt even the best-designed policies and programs for national development.

THE CURRENT ISSUE OF REFUGEES

Indeed, the current Sahelian drought—affecting more than 35 million people—is having a devastating impact on African national development. Although the resulting famine has been most severe in Ethiopia and has received the greatest media attention there, the drought has hit twenty-seven African countries. Three of these—Sudan, Kenya, and Somalia— not only have felt the impact of the drought but also have received thousands of starving refugees from neighboring Ethiopia.

Within Ethiopia, efforts have been focused on temporary famine relief rather than long-term solutions. Over half a million tons of food were donated to Ethiopia from fall 1984 to June 1985, according to journalistic estimates. The United States has donated more food to Ethiopia than any other nation in the world. But recent U.S. assistance has not concentrated on developmental projects: improved agronomy with peasant participation; road-building and other improvements in the infrastructure; and construction of permanent grain-bagging machines at Ethiopian ports. This aid policy has been followed because American law prohibits the U.S. government from giving other than "humanitarian" aid to nations that have nationalized American property without making "good faith" efforts to pay for it (cf. *Washington Post*, December 1, 1984, p. A-1). The Ethiopian government contends that efforts are being made to compensate Americans. The Soviet Union also has not concentrated on economic or developmental aid. The Soviets provided more military than developmental aid to Ethiopia from the early drought period of the 1970s to the mid-1980s.

Reports in the press and on television indicate that, even when aid is provided, the Ethiopian government often seems preoccupied with military maneuvers against rebel forces in the North. Army trucks are often used for military purposes rather than humanitarian efforts as requested by the United Nations. When the trucks are used for food delivery, they reportedly are sometimes attacked by rebel forces. These current actions stem from the 1974 overthrow of the monarchy by the military, who are staunch advocates of socialism.

Ethiopia and its neighboring countries confront the challenge of attempting to design policies and programs for national development in the face of problems caused by or accentuated by refugees. This challenge is exceedingly difficult in a climate stricken by drought, when external economic aid may be shortlived or unavailable as a result of different political ideologies, and with an Ethiopian government engaged in domestic warfare. Currently the need in Sahelian Africa is for short-term and long-term agricultural and economic solutions as exemplified by the efforts of African civil servants and farmers working with foreign experts.

A RE-EXAMINATION OF CONCEPTUAL VIEWS

Some of the conclusions about voluntary migration reached by the eight contributors to this volume are not surprising. Among these findings are the existence of both push and pull factors in migration, of both institutional and personal causes for population movements, and of both healthy and unhealthy interactions between migrants and stay-at-homes. People move because they are pushed by unsatisfactory conditions at their places of origin and are pulled by expected improvements at their destinations. The Yoruba started going into trade a century ago when the market for their traditional craftwork and crops began to decline, nurtured their outstanding commercial talents, and set up shop throughout West Africa wherever opportunity beckoned. Identifying push and pull factors in this entrepreneurial ethnic group would be a challenging undertaking, as a reading of Niara Sudarkasa's chapter 3 makes clear. The push factor is stronger in some villages in rural Mali than it is in others, according to chapter 4 by John Van D. Lewis, who develops a hypothesis to explain this differential phenomenon. His hypothesis gives more weight to institutional factors than to personal ones in the encouragement and discouragement of migration. Yet, among Zambian women, personal factors loom large in impelling movement to the city—though institutional factors are not inconsequential—according to Bennetta Jules-Rosette in chapter 5. Finally, migrants can contribute to social health, wealth, and wisdom—either directly or by remittances sent home—or can exacerbate crime, disease, vagrancy, and ignorance. That point is clear in all chapters. In short, the relative importance, as well as the interplay, of factors related to African migration and national development needs much further investigation, particularly if sound country policies and programs are to be created and implemented.

Another unsurprising conclusion is the consensus among contributors that a macro view of the impact of migration on African development may obscure matters that are evident in a micro view. In Kenya, for example, a strong annual increase in gross national product during that nation's first eight years of independence masked a weak national and local infrastructure. This weakness was exposed, as Robert J. Cummings shows in chapter 8, by the 1974 world oil crisis and by Kenya's persisting population explosion. In Senegal, a relatively high national investment in higher education obscures the underrepresentation of the rural majority. Both the composition of the university student body and the nature of the curriculum, as Robert C. Johnson shows in chapter 7, cause a brain drain from rural or agricultural to urban areas. In Lesotho, a nationwide tally of hospitals and clinics might indicate an adequate health care system. Yet, as Nellie B. Kanno reports in chapter 6, the Lesotho government recognizes the need for decentralization if the system is to serve the health needs of all demographic sectors. Many aspects of migration and national development in Subsaharan Africa require continuing research in terms of microeconomics, micropolitics, and microsociology.

Most surprising of the findings among all contributors—surprising at least to the non-Africanist—is the importance of indigenous institutions in discouraging ill-considered migration and in easing the shock of relocation. These institutions include traditional groupings of ancient origin such as the patrilineages and age-sets of Mali, long-established relationships like the trading networks of the Yoruba, and such relatively new organizations as the male beer-drinking circles and the female cooperative and apprenticeship circles of Lusaka. The importance of these purely African institutions can be seen not only in their positive effects where they flourish but also in the social gaps they leave when they break down. Physical and mental health have suffered in Lesotho where traditional family and community support groups have disappeared, and economic prosperity has been damaged in Kenya by a decline in familial and ethnic credit sources. Economic anthropology faces many research challenges in Subsaharan Africa.

A surprise to the ideologically inclined is the relatively weak explanatory power of any single grand theory of development—neocolonialism, dependency, interdependency, or independency—in the face of the reality of Subsaharan Africa's human dynamics. The reality is that most national and international policies cannot always be created in light of a sole grand theory. Unexpected economic, political, and social conditions necessitate contingency plans by wise leaders.

As Elliott P. Skinner points out in chapter 2, some African labor migration definitely contributes to economic and cultural dependency, exacerbating underdevelopment—and some does not. Both he and

Cummings hold that foreign and multinational corporations can be "partners in progress" with African and other Third World countries—in principle and perhaps in practice. On the one hand, Sudarkasa recounts how the Yoruba for generations have traded in goods imported from throughout Africa and the outside world, without total loss of their identity. On the other hand, Lewis describes how some of the Sahelian people become rootless wage workers in order to buy new-fangled foreign gadgets. Neocolonialism, independency, interdependency, and dependency appear, to some extent, to be matters of attitude and definition, particularly for researchers and scholars. How to transfer these myriad views into workable policies and programs is the central issue for African policymakers— a fundamental concern addressed throughout this volume.

African policymakers face three crucial questions, according to this book's contributors, in grappling with the problem of national development while under the pressure of voluntary and involuntary migration. First, to what extent should their nations' policies be more holistic, balancing social and political objectives against purely economic goals? Second, to what extent should their nations' policies stress decentralization, with greater attention to local infrastructures as contrasted with centralized national agencies? Third, to what extent should their nations' policies be based on a new perception of both the nature and the relative importance of dependency, interdependency, and independency—that is, a new view of what may often be the results of the colonial legacy?

NEW POLICIES AND PLANS

All the contributors, whether writing about Anglophone or Francophone Africa, support the position of Doudou Diene of UNESCO that economic, social, and political factors necessarily interact in the development process. Although such interaction seems obvious to the trained observer, it may be overlooked by some policymakers. The result can be policies that are "out of sync." For instance, a seemingly adequate allocation of national resources to meet medical costs may fail to deliver adequate health care to some social groups, including migrants, as Kanno elucidates in her chapter on Lesotho. Generous overall support of higher education may neglect the needs of politically weak rural areas—as Johnson shows in his chapter on Senegal—even when increased agricultural output is needed by the whole nation. When skilled merchants such as the Yoruba encounter political discrimination or even expulsion, a valuable economic resource is sacrificed by the host nation, as Sudarkasa demonstrates in her chapter on West Africa. In short, effective policymaking for national development must be holistic.

A corollary point is that infrastructures require as much attention from policymakers as the national "superstructures." Inadequate infrastructures for health care delivery and educational administration, respectively, in Lesotho and Senegal, help explain the programs' social deficiencies. The government of Ghana failed to shape the nation's infrastructure to integrate the Yorubas' commercial expertise into the Ghanaian economy. Policymakers in Mali should identify the more stable and productive agricultural villages, as Lewis argues, and then try to foster "the institutional basis of their stability and productivity." In Zambia, according to Jules-Rosette, rural women who migrate to the metropolis might play a more constructive role in national development if policymakers encouraged "informal training or apprenticeship programs and the growth and licensing of small-scale home enterprises." In Kenya, the need for a drastically reformed national infrastructure is urgent, Cummings contends in his chapter, both to increase agricultural production by a shrinking rural population and to increase industrial employment for an exploding urban population. Cummings urges policymakers to turn away from neocolonial "parastatal agencies" and to emphasize a combination of traditional cooperative enterprises and new private enterprises. Both, he argues, should be supported by national growth centers "with clearly articulated plans and goals." The necessity for clarity in the articulation of development objectives—clarity both to policymakers and to the general citizenry—is stressed by all the contributors to this volume.

African policymakers need to formulate new conceptions of dependency, interdependency, and independency. To begin with, African leaders should abandon the bias of "Third World ideologues," as Skinner calls them, against all foreign expertise. Foreign experts, including representatives of some multinational corporations, will often accept roles as "partners in development" if they are asked to do so tactfully but *forcefully*. A policy of "give and take or exchange" with the more developed nations, according to Doudou Diene, is feasible as well as desirable. As this type of policy is developed and implemented, heavy dependency on the First World will be less likely. Consequently, the politically and socially stultifying effects of dependency will be lessened and developing nations can address their acute problems, especially since economic conditions in developed nations will not permit "aid" in the sense of pure altruistic giving.

Skinner observes that foreign experts, because of their freedom from African parochial loyalties and prejudices, "may be the harbingers of that

Pan-African unity without which African states cannot really develop." Although "unity" may be too visionary a goal, history proves that no nation can reach a high stage of development by "going it alone." Some degree of regional, if not continental, economic cooperation is as essential for Subsaharan Africa as it is for North America or Western Europe.

A prudent policy for the African nations, Cummings argues, might be to shape their interdependency in concentric circles, moving outward from Africa to the other Third World countries to the former colonial powers. Though hotly debated and opposed by the West, this idea was central to the formation of cartels—for example, OPEC—among Third World nations. To what extent might this practice or similar ones be attempted successfully to enhance national development in Africa? The July 1984 unveiling of the Eastern and Southern African Preferential Trade Area (PTA) Treaty is a most recent attempt among fourteen African nations to control their economic development. Similar trade agreements were formed in 1983, with the establishment of the ten-member Central African Economic Community. And in 1975, the sixteen-nation West African states formed the Economic Commission for West African States.

Through the Organization of African Unity (OAU) and the Economic Commission for Africa (ECA), African nations have attempted to devise continental economic development strategies. In July 1979 the African heads of state issued the "Monrovia Declaration," which called for African nations to rally around a program of mutual support and development, self-reliance, and economic integration. The OAU and ECA prepared an extensive document which suggested steps to undertake toward the achievement of the broad objectives identified in the Monrovia Declaration. This document was adopted by the heads of state and government of the OAU in Lagos in April 1980. The document has come to be known as the *Lagos Plan of Action for the Economic Development of Africa 1980–2000*—or simply the *Lagos Plan of Action* [LPA] (Browne and Cummings, p. 12). This plan is to build upon the following: (1) collective self-reliance via a partial delinkage of Africa from the global trading system and enlarged emphasis on intra-African trading rather than on exports; (2) interactive agricultural and industrial development within a network of strong subregional frameworks; (3) multilateral and bilateral aid to assist in building the infrastructure and improving agricultural efficiency; and (4) private investment (including foreign) to participate in development of mining and heavy industrial sectors but with African self-interest definitely paramount. The African heads of state continue to recognize the necessity of collective self-reliance plus cooperation with the more industrialized countries to the extent that conditions permit.

A recent study by Richard G. Braungart and Margaret M. Braungart supports Cummings' recommendation. The Braungarts' analysis of the behavior of 28,000 of the foreign subsidiaries of the world's largest enterprises in 133 countries led them to conclude: "Direct corporate investment does not flow from the 'capital abundant' nations to 'capital scarce' countries. To the contrary, resources are channeled into nations that are already highly developed. . . . We also find that within the newly developed areas of the world, US and non-US corporations are more likely to establish subsidiaries in the relatively wealthier rather than poorer nation-states." (Braungart and Braungart, 1980:181–83).

This conclusion simply illustrates that poorer nations clearly need to go further in pooling their own resources; it is not the *definitive* view of all Western multinational corporate endeavors. History shows, however, that no amount of international cooperation can serve as a substitute for national initiative. Independency and interdependency must go hand-in-hand. This conclusion underscores the significance of one finding made by all the contributors to this book: the existence of a large, untapped reservoir of human resources which can contribute to national development throughout Subsaharan Africa. From the Yoruba traders to the "small scale urban informal sector" of Kenya, from the women potters of Lusaka to the village health workers of Lesotho, from the university students of Senegal to the cooperative farmers of Mali, the people of Subsaharan Africa have the capacity for a much higher level of self-sufficiency. The question of the optimum level of interdependency which can promote national development must be viewed within the context of domestic and international trends. Migration is one major trend that has often impeded—but can actually enhance—national development.

REFERENCES

Braungart, Richard G., and Margaret M. Braungart. 1980. "Multinational Corporate Expansion and Nation-State Development: A Global Perspective." Vol. 3, *Research in Social Movements, Conflicts and Change.* Greenwich, Conn.: JAI Press, 169–86.

Browne, Robert S., and Robert J. Cummings. 1984. *The Lagos Plan of Action vs. The Berg Report: Contemporary Issues in African Economic Development.* Washington, D.C.: Howard University, The African Studies and Research Program—Monographs in African Studies.

INDEX